Making Your First
Feature Film

Making Your First Feature Film

Lessons I Learned the Hard Way

Dominick Bagnato

McFarland & Company, Inc., Publishers
Jefferson, North Carolina

LIBRARY OF CONGRESS CATALOGUING-IN-PUBLICATION DATA

Names: Bagnato, Dominick, 1984– author.
Title: Making your first feature film : lessons I learned the hard way / Dominick Bagnato.
Description: Jefferson, North Carolina : McFarland & Company, Inc., Publishers, 2017 | Includes bibliographical references and index.
Identifiers: LCCN 2017033354 | ISBN 9781476670348 (softcover : acid free paper) ∞
Subjects: LCSH: Motion pictures—Production and direction—Handbooks, manuals, etc.
Classification: LCC PN1995.9.P7 B275 2017 | DDC 791.4302/32—dc23
LC record available at https://lccn.loc.gov/2017033354

BRITISH LIBRARY CATALOGUING DATA ARE AVAILABLE

ISBN (print) 978-1-4766-7034-8 (softcover
ISBN (ebook) 978-1-4766-2949-0

© 2017 Dominick Bagnato. All rights reserved

No part of this book may be reproduced or transmitted in any form or by any means, electronic or mechanical, including photocopying or recording, or by any information storage and retrieval system, without permission in writing from the publisher.

Front cover image from *A Convenient Truth*, 2015, Leonard Wingmon (Kevin Hauver) and Coleman Burleson (Alan Berman); film clapper © 2017 pablofdezr/iStock

Printed in the United States of America

McFarland & Company, Inc., Publishers
Box 611, Jefferson, North Carolina 28640
www.mcfarlandpub.com

Making Your First Feature Film

Lessons I Learned the Hard Way

DOMINICK BAGNATO

McFarland & Company, Inc., Publishers
Jefferson, North Carolina

LIBRARY OF CONGRESS CATALOGUING-IN-PUBLICATION DATA

Names: Bagnato, Dominick, 1984– author.
Title: Making your first feature film : lessons I learned the hard way / Dominick Bagnato.
Description: Jefferson, North Carolina : McFarland & Company, Inc., Publishers, 2017 | Includes bibliographical references and index.
Identifiers: LCCN 2017033354 | ISBN 9781476670348 (softcover : acid free paper) ∞
Subjects: LCSH: Motion pictures—Production and direction—Handbooks, manuals, etc.
Classification: LCC PN1995.9.P7 B275 2017 | DDC 791.4302/32—dc23
LC record available at https://lccn.loc.gov/2017033354

BRITISH LIBRARY CATALOGUING DATA ARE AVAILABLE

ISBN (print) 978-1-4766-7034-8 (softcover
ISBN (ebook) 978-1-4766-2949-0

© 2017 Dominick Bagnato. All rights reserved

No part of this book may be reproduced or transmitted in any form or by any means, electronic or mechanical, including photocopying or recording, or by any information storage and retrieval system, without permission in writing from the publisher.

Front cover image from *A Convenient Truth*, 2015, Leonard Wingmon (Kevin Hauver) and Coleman Burleson (Alan Berman); film clapper © 2017 pablofdezr/iStock

Printed in the United States of America

McFarland & Company, Inc., Publishers
Box 611, Jefferson, North Carolina 28640
www.mcfarlandpub.com

To my parents, who always encouraged me
to pursue my passions and taught me to work hard,
which, incidentally, are the same thing

Acknowledgments

With a book tied so closely to the creation of a film, there's a temptation to replicate the entire end credit roll to thank everyone who made the film possible. After all, without the film, there would be no book, and the film wouldn't exist without the help of those scores of people. To avoid such duplication, and with full understanding that I'll be leaving many deserving people out, I want to acknowledge a very small selection of people who've specifically helped with this writing.

I do want to take a moment to thank the producers of *A Convenient Truth* (2015), Charlie Pinto, Beth Renfro, and Patrick Steward, who dedicated more hours of their lives toward completing the film than any of us can count—and without whom I would have never gained the experience that allowed me to write this book. And, of course, my eternal gratitude is owed to Alan Berman, who brought the main character of the film to life and stuck with the production through its crazy timeline.

I'd also like to thank sociologist Richard Sennett for showing me on a daily basis that writing is a job as real as any other (and on some days more real). He never rests on his accolades and gets more writing done each day before noon than many people who call themselves writers do in a week. It's inspiring to be a small part of that.

I'm grateful to my entire crazy Italian family, and especially my parents, Pietro and Josephine, my sister Ariana, who is already a better writer than I'll ever be, and my brothers. Chris and Dan, thanks for always making me laugh and being there to knock me down a peg when I'm taking myself too seriously. And extra thanks go out to my older brother, Frank, whose idea it was to compile all of these thoughts into a book in the first place.

Finally, I want to thank my wife, Kim, who has been in my life since I was making my senior thesis film at New York University but has stuck around anyway. I've never met anyone else with the ability to make nearly every task seem effortless whom I didn't hate for it. Your grace inspires.

Table of Contents

Acknowledgments	vi
Preface	1

PART ONE: PRE-PRODUCTION

Deciding to Make an Independent Film	4
Set a Date for Your Shoot	5
Build Your Film Crew	6
Three Indie Film Casting Considerations	8
Casting	9
Script Breakdown	14
Scheduling/Stripboarding	16
Budgeting	18
Pre-Production Wrap-Up	20

PART TWO: PRODUCTION

A Convenient Truth—Scene 1	22
Stock Footage Can Be Your Friend—Scene 2	24
Film Locations Equal Production Value—Scene 3	26
Using Green Screen—Scene 4	27
Acting While Directing—Scene 5	29
Give Your Actor a Beat—Scene 6	30
Man-on-the-Street Interviews—Scene 7	32
Actors Who Write—Scenes 8 and 9	33
A Good Film Editor Will Save Your Ass—Scene 10	35
Talking Head Interviews—Scene 11	37
Directing Flexibly—Scenes 12 and 13	39
Improv—Scene 14	41
Camera Movement—Scene 15	43
Pre-Reveal in Film—Scene 16	44
The Reveal—Scenes 17–20	46

The Reaction—Scenes 21 and 22	49
Script Departure—Scenes 23–27	52
Use Your Actor's Face—Scene 28	56
Character Introduction—Scene 29	57
Direct First, Produce Second—Scene 30	60
Inserts and Reaction Shots—Scene 31	61
Free and Easy Pre-Visualization—Scene 32	63
Pre-laps and L-Cuts—Scene 33	66
Picking Your Shot (and Why Windmills Are Unpatriotic)—Scene 34	68
Four Considerations for a Joke in Your Film—Scene 35	70
Locations: Just Ask, and When to Bend Your Own Rules—Scene 36	71
Framing and Visual Match Transitions—Scenes 37 and 38	73
Conflict in Comedy—Scene 39	76
Structure in Your Film—Scene 40	78
Evergreen Satire—Scene 41	80
Static vs. Non-Static Frames—Scene 42	82
Directing Is Listening—Scenes 43 and 44	85
Jump Cut (for My Love)—Scene 45	87
"Cheating" Multiple Locations—Scene 46	89
Transition Scenes and Your Film's Spine—Scene 47	91
Burleson Labs Advertisement #1—Scene 48	93
Free Color Correction—Scene 49	95
Building Sequences—Scenes 50–53	97
Creative Character Introduction—Scenes 54–56	100
Shoot the Script and Then Check Your Gut—Scene 57	103
Long Takes—Scene 58	105
How to Know When You're Done Editing—Scenes 59–61	108
Creating a Stylistic Look—Scene 62	112
Film Arcs—Scenes 63 and 64	114
Tempo and Sequences—Scenes 65–67	116
Serendipity in Filmmaking—Scene 68	119
Rule of Threes—Scene 69	121
Acting Is Reacting—Scenes 70 and 71	123
Four Lessons from a Montage—Scene 72	125
Resourceful Filmmaking—Scenes 73 and 74	127
Offensive Satire—Scene 75	129
A Scene in Three Shots—Scene 76	130

Planning a Scene—Scene 77	132
Get an Impossible Shot … with Two Shots—Scene 78	135
Language Sequence—Scenes 79–88	138
Mining Film Locations—Scene 89	144
Slapstick Comedy—Scene 90	147
Pacing: The One-Hour Mark—Scenes 91–93	149
Offensive Satire, Revisited—Scenes 94–96	152
Five Ways We Fixed a Dull Scene—Scene 97	155
Editing Choices—Scene 98	167
Staging the Casual—Scenes 99 and 100	169
Context Changes Everything—Scene 101	172
Your Time Is Limited—Scene 102	174
Saying No to My Entire Film Crew—Scene 103	175
Changes from Script to Screen—Scene 104	178
Additional Production Writing—Scene 105	180
Scheduling Can Breed Creativity—Scene 106	182
Seven Images, Seven Lessons—Scene 107	184
Serendipity in Editing—Scene 108	188
Beginning of the End—Scene 109	191
Final Scene: Make It Count—Scene 110	193

PART THREE: POST POST-PRODUCTION

So You've Made a Feature Film	198
Independent Distribution	201
Eleven Kickstarter Campaign Lessons	203
The Four-Wall Experience	206
Digital Distribution of Your Independent Film	209
Plan for Self-Distribution from Day One	217
What's Next?	218
A Note About Post-Film Recordkeeping	220
Podcasts to Keep You Going	221
Don't Quit (or Apologize for) Your Day Job	223
References	225
Index	227

Preface

The purpose of this book is no more and no less than to document the lessons I learned while making my first feature film, *A Convenient Truth* (2015), in hopes that those lessons might be helpful to you as you set out to make your first feature.

I make no assertions that I made a good film or even that you'd like it if you watched it. What I do know is that I completed a feature film and that there are a lot of people out there who would like to do the same. If you're reading this, you're probably one of them. I also know that I wished a resource like this existed when I was figuring out how to will my film into existence.

I've tried to keep this book light on theory and philosophy and to focus it on the practical. After all, the practical, the logistical, those are the true realms of independent filmmaking. So, these pages include not only what filmmakers should get done to make their films a reality, but also *how* they can go about doing so. With that in mind, I've kept these lessons as brief as possible. You don't need extra words; you need the point. You're an independent filmmaker; you've got other things you should be doing right now.

The best way I knew to approach these lessons was to work out from the narrow experience of making my own first feature film with the belief that these details will be broadly useful. If you read this book closely, you will learn a few lessons that I had to learn the hard way, and if I can prevent you from making even one mistake that you would have otherwise, the time you spent reading will have been a worthwhile investment.

Part One
Pre-Production

Deciding to Make an Independent Film

"Begin at the beginning," they say—something so simple that it almost never needs to be said again. But, in deciding where to tell the story of the making of an independent film, this is an interesting question. Do I begin with the script? The idea for the script? Going to film school? Discovering a passion for film? You see the rabbit hole here, and no one wants to hear the story of my conception. (Hopefully, I never will.) With all this in mind, I want to begin with a specific moment in time that I consider to be the first important moment for any independent filmmaker: the decision to make a film.

I cannot stress enough that this is a decision. There is nothing passive about it. Lots of people think about making movies, but no one thinks about it for a while and then wakes up one day with someone asking them where the camera goes for the next scene. So:

1. Do not think you will make a movie unless you have decided to make a movie. (It's circular, but it makes sense.)
2. Do not take the decision to make a movie lightly. It boggles the mind to know people who agonize over their breakfast orders but think they can fall into making a movie.

This needs to be a difficult decision because you are deciding what is going to take up all of your spare time (and some of the time when you're supposed to be doing other things—writing other scripts, honing a craft, being a good parent, etc.) for very likely the next three years or so. Think about that. Actually consider it. Three years. Time is the most important currency. By the time you've completed your film, you'll have to weigh what you've accomplished against both the financial debt that you'll probably be in and against all of the things that you could have otherwise done with that time. This isn't to say that you shouldn't make a film, but rather that you should—and you should love the material so much that you don't balk at the idea of starting—even with the knowledge of what it will entail. (Hopefully my tortured musings will help you gain some of that knowledge along the way).

When I Decided I Was Going Make My First Feature Film

My moment of decision to make *A Convenient Truth* (2015) came well after the script was written. In February 2009, I got a call from a buddy of mine from film school. Let's call him Charlie (because that's his name). Charlie had just read a draft of one of my screenplays called "A Modest Proposal for the California State Energy Crisis or: A Convenient Truth," which I'd written at some point in 2008. It was a cold winter night when he called, and I was practicing being a hermit in my Brooklyn apartment, as I was apt to do. I had just completed the first draft of the fourth feature screenplay that I had written since graduating from NYU's film school and was about to start the fifth. I think the film only exists because he called at that exact, opportune moment. I had submitted the screenplay that he read to two screenplay competitions, and it had gotten positive recognition from both—at least more positive than I expected. Though that was true, Charlie pointed out an important thing to me: we had gone to school to make films, not write scripts. I have nothing against screenwriting, and it is my favorite part of the whole process of making a film, but he had a point.

Charlie knew that I didn't believe in purposely writing to a low budget because it limits the imagination, and he convinced me that I had already written a script that was inherently so small that we could make it the way we would want for very little money. That is, I hadn't written the script small with the intention of being able to film it. I had written the script exactly how I wanted, and it happened to be small enough to make. The movie is a mockumentary, so the style dictates that it be made on video instead of film (which was a much bigger consideration only a few years ago). It also lends itself toward interviews and smaller scenes that would not be difficult to film. The locations were mostly interiors. Perhaps most importantly, the script was partially a direct reaction to Al Gore's Oscar-winning documentary, *An Inconvenient Truth* (2006). Charlie pointed out that the further removed we got from that film, the more we'd lose some of what made our script good. He was right. Right about all of it, and I knew it.

Right then and there, I had a decision. I could thank Charlie for his kind words about the script, hang up, and go back to outlining my next screenplay, or we could decide we were going to make our first feature film. A quick calculation told us that if we wanted to begin principal photography in the summer, and we estimated a need for six months of pre-production, we would need to begin prep ... a couple of weeks ago.

When I hung up the phone, we were in pre-production.

SET A DATE FOR YOUR SHOOT

After Charlie and I had decided we were going to make our first feature film, I could barely sleep. I imagine that he hung up, lit a cigar, and went back to being cool. I was vibrating with excitement and nerves. I remember being almost out of breath as I paced my apartment, as if my mind was outracing my lungs. I knew what it meant: one way or another, this was going to change my life.

Charlie and I met a few days later, and we did the most important thing that an independent producer and director can do when beginning to plan a movie: we set a start date. Was this somewhat arbitrary at the time? Was it possible that we'd never be ready? Of course. Did we approach it that way? Absolutely not.

On August 10, 2009, we would begin principal photography on *A Convenient Truth*. It is important to know this date from the beginning for all of the obvious logistical reasons, but it is even more important psychologically. That date was on our calendars for six months. It was imbued with meaning. It also meant that we were specific when we talked about the film with others. You'd be surprised how differently a conversation goes when you say, "We're filming for three six-day weeks beginning August 10th," as opposed to, "We're shooting a film at the end of the summer." (Yeah, you and everyone else.)

If you're making an indie, you're probably not going to have a lot of money. That's okay—even expected—but you have to be aware of this and make up for it with the highest level of professionalism that you can manage.

If you've decided to make a film, the next question should be: when will we make this film? Set a date and have an answer. If you try to do all of the pre-production work in a vacuum, with the intention of setting a date when the time gets closer, you will never make the film. Even when you do set a date right away, the nature of filmmaking is such that 70 percent of the pre-production will be done as things come up in the month directly preceding your shoot. Don't make that month any harder on yourself than it needs to be.

Side Note: A running general theme for filmmaking is that things will come up that are beyond your control that you could not possibly have planned for. Do yourself a favor and be sure to plan for everything that is possible to foresee.

BUILD YOUR FILM CREW

You cannot make a (good) movie alone. Sure, there are exceptions to this rule. There will always be the loner genius who makes amazing stop-motion films in his basement with a Bolex and a penlight. But since you're reading this book, I'm going to assume you're not one of those. Additionally, I realize again how much times have changed just since I graduated film school in 2006. Today the loner geniuses have probably never heard of a Bolex and are making their contemporaries jealous with an iPhone and the LED reading light from their Kindle. (Meta moment: that reference will already be outdated by the time this book goes to print.)

For everyone else, you will now need to build a team for your film. Strike that. You now get to pick a bunch of collaborators who will help you will your film into existence and improve it. That is the mindset that you should embrace. The people who will work with you on your independent film are doing it for one of three reasons:

1. They are your friends and want to help.
2. They like the material and want to be a part of the project.
3. They are learning their craft and will take whatever jobs they can get.

Each of the above is a helpful motivation type for you. If you consider that the alternative is being surrounded by a crew that is more professional but only there for a paycheck, you may as well acknowledge the situation and use it to your advantage. Making a film should be fun, and an intimate crew is one way to make that happen.

So, with all that in mind, you should determine who you would like to be the heads of the major departments on your film set. You will find that most of your crew comes together through your extended network, but there are also online resources like mandy.com (or even Craig's List if you get really desperate) to help you find interested people.

You'll have to do some searching to find the sites that are relevant and active today. Each project will have different needs from the start of pre-production, but you will usually want to work with:

1. Director
2. Producer
3. Director of Photography
4. Art Director
5. Sound Recordist
6. Writer

Chances are, one or two of the above positions will be filled by hyphenates, but I don't recommend taking on more than one role for your first film. I wrote, directed, produced, and edited my first sync short film (*Awkwardly*, 16mm Color Negative, 8 min.) in my junior year of film school, and I vowed that I'd never produce my own film again. Why do we think we can do two jobs when we are still learning how to do one?

When I Was Building My Team for A Convenient Truth...

Charlie and I already represented roles 1, 2, and 6. We immediately contacted someone we'd worked with in the past, on my senior thesis film (*Initial Conditions*, 24p DVCPro50, 27 min.), to shoot it. Adam Orellana was a great DP to work with, and I imagine we treated him well on the student film shoot because he was happy to be asked to work with us again on this film. This underscores a point I made earlier about independent film and professionalism. Adam is a few years older than I am and was already well into making his living shooting professional projects when we contacted him. We were probably able to offer him roughly what he earns in a single day for two weeks of filming! But he re-joined the team anyway.

A few days later, I ran into another friend, Patrick Steward, from film school who is extremely talented, and we began discussing what we were up to. When I told him we were about to make our first feature, he was interested, and soon after he came on as a second producer for the film. This is part of the magic of being in New York City. It's also the single largest advantage of going to film school.

And, just as we'd been taught in film school, we proceeded to hold weekly production meetings with the core team. The meetings should have a standard day of the week, time, and location. If you try to set up ad hoc meetings, you will waste a lot of time trying to coordinate schedules, and the process will be both less effective and efficient. This is an important note. Once you've built your team, and you all have responsibilities, it is important to have a regular meeting (with a meeting agenda and everything) for everyone to check in on the progress. This weekly meeting is a great motivator. No one wants to show up to next week's meeting without anything new to report. Also, within the meeting, you can set specific goals and deadlines that everyone will be aware of. Without this, weeks can pass without anything major getting done because the shoot date still seems so far away, and there is nothing creating an urgency or accountability. The weekly production meeting should also be an open environment, so that if a crewmember is stuck on a particular problem, the others can lend their experience and knowledge to help guide him or her in the right direction.

The shoot date will be here sooner than you think. And both you and your team need to know that.

THREE INDIE FILM CASTING CONSIDERATIONS

There is no shortage of quotes about the importance of casting in relation to making a film. I won't waste time recounting them here, but it is safe to say that I agree with most of them. Instead, I will make three obvious, yet under-considered, points—as they related to my casting process for *A Convenient Truth*.

1. Consider the ramifications of your casting in terms of distribution.

The reason that movie stars have the power that they do in the industry is because the majority of audiences choose the film that they will see next based on their desire to see the lead actor. Whether you like it or not, people (especially in the U.S.) much more rarely go to a film because they love the director than because they want to see a particular person on the screen.

Distributors know this fact, too. So, this is another moment to remember that you are not making a film in a vacuum. You're making a film that you hope will one day be seen by others. Distributors are one way for you to accomplish your goal of reaching wider audiences, and you'll have a much easier time at festivals, with sales agents, and with distributors directly if you have a name or recognizable face that will help you sell your film.

Make a wish list of actors that you'd love to play your roles. If the material is right, you'd be surprised how available some actors will be. There is a SAG deferment contract for every level of budget, so that shouldn't be a deterrent for you. Attaching a name actor to your film can make your budget larger, but it will also increase your desirability among potential investors.

The background on *A Convenient Truth* is that I wanted the film to play like a straight documentary for as long as possible. With that in mind, I made a creative decision ("creative decision" is code for a choice that you know is going to bite you in the ass later but you do it anyway) to cast only actors who wouldn't be recognized by the audience. My thinking was that as soon as the audience thought of Coleman Burleson as a character the illusion would be broken. I wanted audience members to feel like they were watching a documentary. This meant no recognizable actors. It also meant no marketable stars.

For the sake of the film, I still stick by this decision—though it was certainly a decision that echoed loudly when we embarked on a bid for distribution.

2. What is the general attitude/availability of the actors?

One of the other reasons that I am happy with the casting decisions that I made is that they worked for our crazy schedule. Since *A Convenient Truth* was to be shot in the nature of a documentary, we needed actors who would be available with relatively short notice, over a long period of time, and would come to shoots enthusiastically. The lead actor, Alan Berman, stuck with us over three years of filming here and there. This is a huge risk. The instant that you've committed an actor to film or video in a role, there is no going back. (Filmmaking Nightmare: You've shot half of your film and your lead actor drops out. This renders all of your current footage useless.) We had to trust that we'd be able to film Alan for five days in one month and then turn around a year later and film again without his enthusiasm waning.

If you have a particularly difficult or long shoot to contend with, it will be important to weigh the attitude of your actors. Like with your crew, you need people who will have fun with the filmmaking process and are there for the right reasons.

3. Can the actor improvise?

Though *A Convenient Truth* is a scripted mockumentary, I always knew that improvisation was going to be an important part of the process. It is important to consider this when you approach your casting process, and you may even want to mention it in the casting call. You'll soon learn that acting and improvising are two very different skill sets. They are not mutually exclusive, but you can't count on getting one just because you're getting the other either. With this in mind, we looked through acting submissions with an eye for potential comedic timing or improv training. Anything that hinted at a comfort with comedy was a plus.

CASTING

We put out casting calls in the most traditional way that I know—again a remnant of casting student shorts in film school—by putting a low or no pay ad in the hardcopy newspaper version of *Backstage*. Within a week, we had more headshots than we could easily handle. We filled binders for each character (alphabetically, by actor's last name).

Backstage has since transitioned into an online system, too, but I haven't yet had to deal with it. The supplemental systems that we used were www.mandy.com and Craig's List. I've never gotten a successful hit off of Craig's List, but it was worth a free shot. Mandy.com, on the other hand, can be a useful resource. The advantage of an online system is that you can create a brand new e-mail address for the film and organize submissions within your inbox. This makes headshots easy to sort and share with your team. It also has the tremendous ability to integrate links into the casting process. Headshots are very often misleading, but a link to prior work or an acting reel can be effective tools for both the actor and the filmmaker.

Side Note: A separate casting channel that was useful to us, and can be useful to all indie filmmakers, is collaboration with local casting agencies. In many cases, a low-budget film won't have the money to hire a proper casting agent, but there are other levels of service that casting agencies can provide for all budget levels. Specifically, for our supplemental casting, we paid a local casting agent in the Philadelphia area a reasonable fee for an e-mail blast to her extensive network of actors and the use of some of her space to hold local auditions.

Back to our main auditions for *A Convenient Truth*, one actress submitted her headshot and resume to us with a link to a web series that she created with some friends. The

'A CONVENIENT TRUTH' | Living Daylights Pictures, LLC | -Multiple Locations- | Nonunion Film
Details | Locations | Contact | Questions |

Project/Job Description:

'A CONVENIENT TRUTH'

Living Daylights Pictures, LLC is casting *A Convenient Truth*, an HD mockumentary feature about a California assemblyman who proposes his plan to cure the energy crisis, unemployment, illegal immigration, obesity, our dependence on foreign oil, and more by strapping the undocumented workers of California to electricity-generating bicycles. Charlie Pinto, prod.; Dominick Bagnato, dir. Shoots Aug. 9-29 in NYC and NJ.

Seeking—**Coleman Burleson**: early-to-late 40s, distinguished assemblyman, LEAD; **Leonard Wingmon**: late 40s-early 50s, Coleman's lawyer and personal fan boy, supporting role; **Kitty Burleson**: late 30s-early 40s, Coleman's supportive, WASPy wife, supporting role; **Eleanor Burleson**: late teens, Coleman's sweet, perhaps overly enthusiastic daughter; **Cardamom Burleson**: 8-12, Coleman's daughter, naive and completely supportive, his inspiration; **Men** and **Women**: 20+, to play various "documentary subjects" who have been positively affected by Burleson's plan in action, several supporting roles available; **Mexican-Americans**: 15+, to play several supporting roles as well as cyclists in Burleson's energy plant.

Casting notice for *A Convenient Truth*.

web series was a mockumentary that was heavily dependent on improvisation—exactly what we were looking for! The link was enough to get the actress an audition, and she was ultimately cast in one of the roles. In cases where you don't have an actor sharing a link with you proving he or she is perfect for the role, it is important to give the actor a fair chance to prove it as part of the auditioning process. There are a few keys to ensuring that the auditioning process is as effective as possible.

Preparing to Hold Auditions

Once you've narrowed down the list of people you'd like to bring in for auditions, there are a few steps you should take. The most important thing to do is to secure a space for the amount of time that you'll need. It is best to secure at least a couple of weeknights and one weekend day, to allow for the most flexibility in working with the actors' schedules. The space doesn't have to be fancy but should have one room for the actual auditions and another that can act as a green room, or holding room, for the others who are coming in to audition. It is best for the space to be in public or semi-public building. Do not try to hold auditions in your apartment. A separate audition space sends the signal that you are operating at a professional level and also protects you from potential crazy people that you call in knowing where to harass you in the future.

That said, this space doesn't need to cost you money, either. In New York, there are many small rehearsal rooms that can be found, but there are also thousands of underused conference rooms in buildings that can serve your purposes. You'd be surprised how many people you know who would be willing to stay late in a closed office to allow you to use their space. (This can apply to filming, too.) By starting with your contacts who work in nice spaces and working backward, you should have a good chance of finding someone who can help you without breaking any rules or costing anyone anything.

While we were casting *A Convenient Truth*, I used a conference room at an NYU department to hold our auditions. If you have an affiliation with any school, you should look to them as a space resource. Since we'd secured the space for the nights that we needed, I now took the next, organized step toward making the auditions happen. That is, I contacted the actors that I wanted to bring in to audition. However, I treat this as a small moment to prove that I have a respect for the actors' time. Rather than simply calling or e-mailing all of the actors with the available audition windows, I make up a very simple worksheet that covers all of the available time slots in 15-minute increments. Then, whether I'm calling or e-mailing the actors about coming in to audition, we find a specific appointment time that works well for both of us. The purpose of this is two-fold:

1. Prevent the unnecessary wasting of actors' time by having them wait in a large room with a bunch of their competitors.
2. Achieve a lower no-show rate by confirming a specific date and time for each actor.

This is a straightforward process that is helpful to everyone involved, but many directors don't take the time to do this one simple step. As with directing in general, beginning with the auditioning process, it is the director's job to make the actor feel comfortable and appreciated. This approach informs how everything should be done at the actual auditions.

Holding Auditions

When it came time to hold auditions, Charlie and Patrick (producers) and I took part on the production side. We wanted to have enough people to be able to converse about our opinions, but not so many people that the actor would feel uncomfortable lining up before a firing squad. For similar reasons, we considered whether or not we should record the auditions. We ultimately erred on the side of safety and did record them, but I can honestly say that I've never made a casting decision based on going back and looking at the audition footage. For the most part, we used it to re-watch auditions that were we already excited about in the room. Most of the footage never got watched at all.

It was also important for us to have a floater person who could run in and out of the room to greet actors as they arrived. It is a good idea to give the actors a contact number, in case they have any trouble finding the location. Again, ease and transparency are good here. There is no need to shroud the audition process in mystery to make things seem important. It is already important, because you're deciding who will be in the film that you are going to make.

When an actor arrived, she would be directed to a larger holding room (in our case a large conference room adjacent to the smaller room that we were using to hold the auditions). This room held sides, or excerpts, of the script with character names written large at the top and with all of the appropriate dialogue highlighted. If you've done your prep correctly, the actor will know what part she is reading for and be able to familiarize herself with the script while she waits.

This takes us to a place where my practice diverges from the norm for auditions. Many auditions will be based primarily on completely cold reads of the sides or cold reads with only brief time to prep. I don't agree with this protocol. Again, from a logical, respectful, and (frankly) fair perspective, it does not make sense to make a judgment about an actor without giving her time to prepare. We are not looking for the best cold reader; we're looking for an actor. If acting is a skill set that is heavily reliant on preparation, it just makes sense to allow an actor to show you what she's got after having time to prepare.

So, all of my auditions actually begin with a monologue. Though monologues are not inherently cinematic, it gives the actor a chance to come into the audition room and show us what she can do when she has the proper time to become familiar with the material and make real decisions. Since we were filming a comedy, we told actors that we preferred comedic monologues, but that was overruled by a desire for them to bring whichever monologue with which they were most confident. Especially since our comedy has a lot of straight, dry humor, the dramatic monologues were sometimes even more effective.

Following the monologue, when the actor is (hopefully) feeling good about what she has just presented, we went into the sides. It is best to have an actual actor in the room to read opposite the auditioner, if possible. We didn't have this luxury, so Charlie and Patrick took turns reading with the actors. What's most important is that the director is not reading the scene with the auditioner. Reading with an actor makes it extremely difficult to gain the perspective necessary for later decisions.

Following the reading of the sides, we would take a moment to ask the actor if she had any questions about the scene or character. If she did, we were sure to make a mental note to check if the answers that we gave informed the second version of the reading. This leads to one more important note. We use the audition process to not only see if the actor can play the role, but also to see if she can take direction.

In almost all cases, I would have the actor read the sides a second time with an adjustment. Depending on how tedious the process was getting for our team, I would sometimes give wild adjustments that had nothing to do with how the character would actually play the scene. However, the point is not to see how an alt-universe version of the character would play the scene. It is to see how the performance changes from one reading to the next. In this case, an actor could give you a great performance and then the same great performance the second time around—ignoring the adjustment. This tells you that you have a potential good fit for the role on your hands, but you might also have a non-responsive actor, which will be very difficult to deal with whenever you find yourself in the middle of shooting a scene where her first instincts aren't right on the money.

Finally, given the highly improvisational nature of our mockumentary, it was very important for me to assess each actor's ability to improvise. So, we finished each audition session with a short improvised scene. It was quickly apparent who relished this and who froze up. Again, neither was an immediate hire or deal breaker, but it was important for us to make casting decisions with this piece of information informing them.

After about a week of deliberation, we were ready for callbacks...

Callbacks

Even for our small independent feature, we found (as we always have in the past in casting our short films) that New York is an embarrassment of riches when it comes to tremendous, hungry acting talent. We had at least two options in mind for almost every one of the primary and secondary leads that we were casting, and it was now time to narrow that down.

The first thing that we did when we knew who we wanted to call back was to write each of the actors to thank them for coming in for the audition, request a callback, and provide them with the full screenplay.

We did this as soon as possible, to both show our excitement about potentially working with the actor and to give her the longest amount of time possible to read the script. This means that we can realistically expect each actor to have a good sense of her character when she shows up for the callback audition.

I'll never forget the date of our callbacks: June 25, 2009. The reason I'll never forget is that it was the day that Michael Jackson died. The news broke as the actors were filtering in for the callback session, and it was all anyone could talk about. We were all taken by surprise, and the vibe was decidedly contemplative. It was strange to have actors who were effectively competing with each other bonding over their Michael Jackson stories and associations. Still, we plowed ahead.

Since we had multiple actors for the roles, our main decision-making tool was to put the actors into scenes with each other in varied combinations. We were able to see versions of the scenes unfold in front of us for the first time. It is a surreal and magical moment for a director, especially one who has written the script, and I took a moment to relish the thing coming alive. You should too.

After the scenes were done in all sorts of configurations (actors running in and out of the room fluidly), we moved onto improv scenes in the same way. Now that the actors had an idea of their characters' relationships with the others, I could make up scenes on the spot and watch how they would unfold. This once again tested improv skills and the ability to react in character.

Again, this is not because I enjoy being a puppet master. In this specific case, I knew that some of our filming would entail me (as the in-film interviewer) asking the characters questions on camera. It isn't enough for the actor to be able to be spontaneously funny; she has to be able to be funny as her character. Unless you value having hours of unusable outtakes more than the content of your film, you'd do well to keep this distinction in mind.

The callback improvs were a real moment of collaboration for me. I got to test out entire scenes that I'd been kicking around without ever having to fully write them: a situation, a couple of hidden character goals, and go. Let's see the scene. In fact, this is the only time that the actors are free to bring what they've assumed about the character to the role—before I've tainted their view of the character with my input. In a couple of instances, character traits or ideas that actors brought to the roles were actually incorporated into who that character became. Essentially, we created the characters together with the purest of beginnings.

Casting Decisions

After you've made the list of pros and cons, conferred with your peers, contemplated every possible cast permutation, it's time to forget all that and cast the people who your gut says you need to work with.

Especially when dealing with low-budget projects, I realized that I was casting a person as much as an actor. Larger productions have big money to attract talent and contracts to hold them in place. On an indie film, it is important to cast someone who is going to show up because they want to do the work. Now that I'd met with the actors at both the auditions and the callback and had a chance to chat briefly on the phone a few times, I was able to get a sense of the level of seriousness for each actor. Almost as important as "Can he act?" are questions like, "What is his schedule like?" "How committed is she to her acting career?" In the case of *A Convenient Truth*, we were shooting the film over a protracted period of time—more like a true documentary time scale than a traditional narrative—so we needed someone who could both knock the role out of the park and who we were confident would stick around for the long haul. We were incredibly lucky to find Alan Berman to play Coleman Burleson, who not only ticked both of these boxes but also was increasingly instrumental in the film's completion as time went on.

As soon as we'd made our choices, we called everyone who we wanted to join the cast. This is one of the fun moments! Recognize it. Revel in the joy of it. Let the actors know not only that they have the role but that they are really good and that you can't wait to work with them. I see this call as the shift in the relationship. I am now calling as the actor's director, and I need to begin making her feel comfortable and valued immediately, to create an optimal space for a vulnerable performance.

As a courtesy, you should also contact all of the actors who you called back who did not get a role. It's important to do this, but it's also good to hold off for a few days until after you've gotten full commitments from your first choices. You don't ever want to be in the position of offering a role to someone who knows she was your second choice.

That said, all of the actors who came in to audition gave you some of their time, and you should treat them with the respect that that deserves.

It's also worth mentioning that this level of transparency and openness has served me well on short films in the past. On one occasion I was shooting a short film with a group of five guys, but we had one more qualified actor than we had roles to fill. I explained to the Actor #6 that we thought he was a great actor, but we simply didn't have room. Weeks later, one of our original actors bailed out, and I was able to contact Actor #6 for the empty role. Had Actor #6 simply never heard from me after his audition, I don't know how likely he would have been to fill the role, and there would have been an awkwardness that we had to overcome before working together. On several other occasions, I've also been able to keep actors in mind and call them at later dates to ask them to fill smaller roles, which they've happily accepted.

Moral of the story: Be a good person. Or, more palatably: Don't be a douche.

SCRIPT BREAKDOWN

It's now time to attack your script. Up until now, the screenplay has been your baby. It's excited you enough to dedicate a portion of your life to writing it. It's convinced you to dedicate even more time to transforming it into a movie. And its words have garnered enough interest from others to get them to join you on your mission.

But it's now time to begin using it as the blueprint for a film that it was always meant to be. Those pages are still your babies, you're just going old school and putting your kids to work on the farm. The script is now nothing more than a tool for you—a document that helps you figure to how to make the finished product that you desire. This might seem reductive, but, after all, you didn't write a novel.

Scene #: 69		Sheet #:	70
	Breakdown Sheet	Int/Ext:	INT
Script Page: 45		Day/Night:	
Page Count: 7/8		Est. Time:	

Scene Description: Meet Thomas.
Settings: CORPOLANT HOUSE
Location: ▮▮▮▮▮ Old Bridge, NJ 07747
Sequence: Script Day:

Cast Members	Background Actors	Props
6. CAMERAMAN 8. THOMAS 36. MRS. CORPOLANT (O.S.) 50. SAM 52. SOUND GUY	Crew Member #1 Crew Member #2	Cereal Bowl Snickers Bar Spoon
	Stunts	**Vehicles**
Special Effects	**Wardrobe** Tight shirt for Thomas	**Makeup/Hair**

A partial breakdown sheet from *A Convenient Truth*.

This is the point where your spec script becomes a shooting script. Each scene gets a number, and you begin thinking about scenes in terms of the important elements for filming them. In an organized way, you will now do a script breakdown that includes every scene in your story. There are ways to do this directly by importing your script file into Entertainment Partner's Movie Magic Scheduling, but I recommend doing it manually on paper first and then inputting your data into the program. There are things that you will only see if you are physically circling, highlighting, color-coding, etc., on a page in front of you.

These breakdown pages dissect your script into workable production elements. Sure, you could try to remember that you need a candy bar for the actor to eat in the next scene, but on a feature length film everything needs to be broken down on a sheet or major issues will arise on a daily basis. Remember, a filmmaker should be delegating, which means sharing as much as possible with your crew and relying on transparent systems of communication to assist you.

The breakdown sheets include: Scene #, Script Page, Page Count, Interior or Exterior, Day or Night, Scene Description, Script Setting, Actual Location, Cast Members, Background Actors (Extras), Props, Stunts, Vehicles, Special Effects, Wardrobe, Makeup/Hair, Set Dressing, Greenery, Special Equipment, Notes, Music, and Sound.

By the end of the session you should have a binder full of breakdown sheets for your entire screenplay. Every scene should be represented with all of the key information that anyone would need to begin prepping to shoot the scene.

Side Note: You've probably just read this quickly and sort of banked it in your mind as something you could do. Don't. Think of it as something you need to do. Trust me. It's worth spending one tedious afternoon for all of the issues it will prevent. If you're still kind of nodding along but don't really plan on breaking the script down—ask someone else to do it. Tell her you need fresh eyes to make sure nothing is missed, and then at least buy her a drink when she hands you that binder full of magically completed sheets.

These breakdown sheets are the basis for the next most important pre-production step: the schedule.

SCHEDULING/STRIPBOARDING

Now that you've broken down each scene in your script, you have all of the elements necessary to complete the next major stepping-stone for pre-production: the shooting schedule.

The standard tool for creating a shooting schedule is called a stripboard. Though this is now usually done in a computer, the original practice was to write down the crucial information for each scene on a thin strip of paper that could easily be moved around and manipulated on a board in order to find the best ways to group and organize the scenes that need to be shot.

Entertainment Partners Movie Magic Scheduling program allows you to generate a stripboard from your breakdown sheet data and then play around with the strips on your screen.

It wasn't until the first time that I scheduled a movie that I came to truly appreciate the script form. Again, the screenplay is a document meant to help you create a film, and proof of that is in its very format. Looking at the scene heading for any given scene, it contains the three most important bits of information for scheduling:

INT. DOM'S APARTMENT—NIGHT

The first element of the scene heading, "INT.," stands for interior. It is critical to know if a scene is an interior or exterior (EXT.) scene. INT. scenes can flexibly be shot without consideration of daylight but will usually also require more elaborate lighting setups. EXT. scenes can (usually) only be shot during the part of the day when the scene is actually taking place.

The middle element, which is the story location of the scene, tells you where the scene takes place. Whenever possible, all scenes in one story location should start grouped together within the shooting schedule. The aim is to "shoot out" each location and never have to return. (In general, scheduling has a lot of moving parts and some variables could make some of these generalities untrue, but I'm stating the basics here.)

In addition to grouping scenes that take place in the same location, you should also start to think about the schedule with your available locations in mind. For example,

EQUIPMENT PICKUP					
Sheet #: 69 3/8 pgs	Scenes: 68	EXT	SUBURBAN TOWN Approach the Corpolant House.	Day	6, 36, 50, 52
Sheet #: 70 7/8 pgs	Scenes: 69	INT	CORPOLANT HOUSE Meet Thomas.		6, 8, 36, 50, 52
Sheet #: 76 3/8 pgs	Scenes: 75	INT	CORPOLANT HOUSE Thomas gives thanks.	Day	8
Sheet #: 52 1 pgs	Scenes: 51	INT	KITCHEN Tess assesses the situation.	Day	55
End Day # 1 Monday, August 8, 2011 -- Total Pages: 2 5/8					
Sheet #: 51 5/8 pgs	Scenes: 50	INT	HORACE'S BEDROOM Horace gets a wakeup call.	Morning	1, 12
Sheet #: 55 5/8 pgs	Scenes: 54	INT	HORACE'S BEDROOM Horace's explanation.	Day	12
Sheet #: 31 1 4/8 pgs	Scenes: 30	EXT	GAS STATION Meet the Minutemen.	Day	1, 6, 10, 27
Sheet #: 32 1 pgs	Scenes: 31, 32	INT	ARTIE'S DEN Minutemen interviews.	Day	10, 27
End Day # 2 Tuesday, August 9, 2011 -- Total Pages: 3 6/8					

An example stripboard for two shooting days from *A Convenient Truth*.

with *A Convenient Truth*, I knew that we were able to use my brother's house for one of the shooting locations. This meant that any general room in the house could potentially be filmed there (kitchen, bedroom, etc.), but I also knew that he had a dated wood-paneled basement, which would be perfect for a den in which a scene with the Arizona Minutemen was set. As you can imagine, one of our shooting days involved grabbing three distinct scenes in three very different looking locations without any company moves. (You're making an indie movie—AVOID COMPANY MOVES!) If you have to move your entire cast, crew, and equipment in the middle of the day, prepare to lose an hour to the ether—that's an extra hour, beyond the "generous" move time you've actually planned to lose.

The last element of the scene heading is the time of day. For the purposes of production, scenes take place at either DAY or NIGHT. This is where you curse at the writer in you that put "DUSK," "CONTINUOUS," "LATER," etc., into all of those scene headings. Either at the breakdown stage or the scheduling stage, you'll want to transform all of the irregular time elements to NIGHT or DAY. For that matter, do yourself a favor and change them to DAY. (This is an exaggeration. Yes, artistically, some parts of your movie might need to take place at night.) Parenthetical aside, cross your fingers that most of the night scenes take place indoors. Lighting a night scene that takes place outside is incredibly hard to do well on a low budget.

Side Note: If you have to shoot night exteriors, wet down the street before filming. The water will reflect the light and bring up the ambient light level in helpful ways.

Additionally, since your shooting days need a minimum of twelve hours in between them, transitioning between day shoots and night shoots gets really tricky.

Once you've taken the main three elements (INT. or EXT. / Location / Time of Day) into account, it's important to plan the shooting days for the convenience of your actors' schedules. This is good for two reasons:

1. It shows respect for your actors—so they aren't wasting time shooting for a day and then having to come back three days later for one more.
2. In terms of budgeting, actors will often be paid by the week, so you want to minimize the amount of weeks that you are paying each. If an actor only works two days in a given week, she is still paid the weekly rate.

There are a ridiculous number of variables to creating a scheduling stripboard, but it's important to not allow that to overwhelm you and prevent you from creating one. Just as when I'm writing a script, it is helpful for me to think of this as a first draft. Knowing that the document can, and will, change in the future allows me to put perfectionism aside and put in the time necessary to be productive.

Although I stand by the "ridiculous number of variables," I also realize that a general rule of thumb might be helpful for those who are scheduling for the first time. For an indie film, my rule would be to plan to shoot about five script pages per day. The script is broken down into eighths (⅛) of a page, and that level of gradation can be really helpful. The reality is that you'll be able to shoot more than five pages on dialogue-heavy days and far less for complex action sequences. Most days will be planned based on locations and the number of camera and lighting setups within those locations, but you might not have that level of knowledge at the initial planning stages—especially if you're not the director.

Experience will give you a feel for what can be done quickly (two actors sitting at a table talking with conventional coverage) and what will take a lot of time (many actors, extras, action sequences, an uncontrolled setting, special effects, etc.), but the five pages per day rule of thumb should both keep you from being too easy on yourself—letting the numbers of days expand unnecessarily—and that manic moment when you believe you can shoot those 14 pages in one day.

The main reason that the schedule is so important is that it is impossible to create a budget without a shooting schedule. The number of days that you shoot is the single largest factor affecting how much your shoot will cost. Now that you've scheduled your shoot, you're ready to start budgeting.

BUDGETING

What "version" of the movie you are going to make often comes down to the film budgeting. At the writing stage, I tend to think that it is better to allow the imagination to run wild and come up with the best way to tell the story. However, when faced with creating a budget for a film that you are actually going to produce, you will quickly be shaking your head at that nighttime car chase scene you wrote that takes place in the 1940s. There is no way to do certain things cheaply. For even more things, there is no way to do them cheaply and well.

As I mentioned, I decided to make *A Convenient Truth* because I believed I could make the movie close to the way I envisioned it as I wrote it on a low budget. It is important to take an honest look at your material and be realistic about what you can do and what you can't. The breakdown sheets should be very helpful in doing this.

Scale

Though it seems crass, a sense of the film's budget it actually part of the shorthand that will be used to convey what the film will be like to others in the early stages. For the sake of communication, numbers will make sure everyone is on the same page. That is, it is important to discuss the scale of your film, and numbers are a quick-and-dirty way to do so. If you tell me that you're making a hard-boiled detective story and go into all the twists and turns of the enthralling mystery, I'm definitely going to want to know if you're imagining something like *The Maltese Falcon* (1941) or *Brick* (2005). The first is a classic studio noir with huge stars. The second was made for about $500,000. Both are excellent films, but you see why it is important to be clear about what you're pitching. Further, my assumption is that anyone reading this is actually planning on making a first film at an even smaller scale than *Brick*—as I did.

The reason I bring this up is because budget is a far too complicated topic to cover in depth within the framework this book. However, one thing that I learned over the course of trying to raise funds for my film is to be wary of wasting a lot of time with potential investors. The first budget that we made up for *A Convenient Truth* came in at around $600,000. Since I didn't have anywhere near that amount of money lying around, this meant that the version of the film that I wanted to make required backing from outside investors.

Don't Ask for Permission

I don't want to let this point pass without special notice: The indie film that I was making still required someone else's "permission" to get made.

With all of the compromises that come with low-budget filmmaking, one of the major advantages is supposed to be that you don't need anyone's permission. You want to make a film and no one can stop you. This is a great position to be in, and you should relish it. Do it. Go out and make your film.

With *A Convenient Truth*, we ultimately went out and made a $150,000 version of the movie over a long period of time, but not before wasting a lot of time trying to raise money for the $600,000 version. Not only did this expand the timeline, but it also robbed us of the independent spirit that could have been so energizing to us along the way. Instead, because we failed to decide to make the more manageable version of the film from the start, every compromise to the smaller version of the film became a defeat, rather than an artistic decision that we made for the film's direction.

I'm not advocating that every indie filmmaker go out and make the smallest version of his or her film possible because not all films have a viable scaled down version. You shouldn't compromise if you ultimately won't be happy with the results. However, had we decided to go ahead and film the $100,000–$200,000 version of the film from the start, we would have completed the film more quickly and had a completely different perspective along the way.

Finally, keeping the budget as low as possible is just always good practice. Even if you are using someone else's money, you should never spend more than you need. Ultimately, the lower the budget, the less you have to make back in the case of a sale or self-distribution.

Pre-Production Wrap-Up

There are still dozens of pre-production topics that I've yet to cover here. These include making a film prospectus, creating a business plan, fundraising, location scouting, rehearsal, etc.

But, for now, I'm going to wrap-up the pre-production section of this book with one anecdote and then proceed with the more specific film production section.

Listen to Your Team

If you're about to jump into the actual photography of your film—congratulations! If you've made it this far, you only did so with the help of a team. In the indie world, that's very likely a team that has already done you a bunch of favors for little or no money. They've gotten you here, and the first way that you can repay them is to listen to them.

My example of listening to my team during the pre-production of *A Convenient Truth* involves another filmmaker's nightmare. About one week before principal photography was set to begin, I got a call from the producers, Charlie and Patrick. Because of the nature of our mockumentary, we had many isolated characters and locations. We were planning on getting the bulk of our movie shot over an upcoming two-week period, and the locations were mostly in New Jersey and New York, with a later section happening in Pennsylvania.

This call changed all that. Charlie and Patrick told me that we simply didn't have enough money to properly follow through with all of the shooting days right now. We were going to have to postpone the Pennsylvania part of the shoot. This meant canceling all of the actors who were supposed to shoot in those locations (after months of preparation) and only having one week worth of the film in the can after all of our pre-production work.

At this point in the story, you'd expect there to be some magic benefactor who swoops in and gives us the money that we need to proceed with the entire shoot as planned. But this is indie film. That didn't happen. Instead, I agonized over the terrible news and denied its reality. I couldn't have the film fall apart, but I knew that the money just wasn't there. So, ultimately: I listened to my team. Charlie and Patrick didn't want to make that call any more than I wanted to hear it, but they were doing one thing that good producers do—presenting the reality of the situation.

Sure it was a huge blow when it happened, but it was ultimately the right call for the film. Because we treated the actors professionally throughout the process, we were able to be honest with them and every single one of them came back in the ensuing months—when we had the funds to shoot the scenes properly. Even though I had access to our budgets, and I knew how much things were going to cost, would I have made the same decision on my own? Definitely not. I needed the perspective that my team had. The only credit I can take for the decision is that I listened to them.

Part Two
Production

For the production section of this book, I am going to go through each scene of my recently completed first feature film, *A Convenient Truth*.

Each section contains at least one still image from a scene of the film—in the order in which they appear in the film—and at least one lesson that I learned in the making of that specific scene.

The hope is that each of these lessons will be specific enough to be engaging and universal enough to help other filmmakers venturing out for the first time.

A Convenient Truth—Scene 1

This section is the first in a series that will chronicle the lessons I learned making my first feature film, *A Convenient Truth*, scene by scene.

The screenplay for *A Convenient Truth* opens with solemn, dramatic voiceover narration. It looks like this:

```
FADE IN:
EXT. CALIFORNIA COUNTRYSIDE–DAY
Various classic landscapes dissolve into one another accompanied by some SOUL-
    CRUSHING STRINGS.
A forest of majestic Redwoods.
Old Faithful in Calistoga.
Miles of beautiful vineyards.
Forestiere Underground Gardens in Fresno.
A sunset over the Pacific.
                               COLEMAN BURLESON (V.O.)
                               These are just a few of the seemingly
                               endless views that our great state of
                               California has to offer.
Six ducklings strive to keep up with their mother.
```

Though the film is a comedy, it is also a mockumentary, and the concept was to make everything before the main character's controversial proposal is revealed feel like a serious documentary. On the page, this worked fine. However, in the practice of watching the cut, we realized that we needed to tease the viewer to keep them interested in what the reveal would actually be. The solution was an old friend of the filmmaker:

The cold open.

The film now begins with a cold open where we meet our main character immediately. He speaks directly to the camera saying:

Coleman Burleson (Alan Berman) talks to the cameraman in the cold open of *A Convenient Truth*.

> "How did I get this idea? I don't know how many great thinkers can answer that question. I truly believe this is an idea that found me. I'm just the vessel with which it's going to be proposed and implemented across this great sphere of ours. It's truly an idea whose time has come."—Coleman Burleson

This serves the aforementioned purpose of teasing the audience. Ideally, viewers are immediately wondering what the "idea" that he references is. They are actively engaged in the film. It also gives them a reason to care about the information they are getting before they find out what the idea is. We've solved the pre-reveal problem by letting the audience know that there is a reveal to wait for—essentially, letting them know that they should pay attention to the setup of the joke because there will be a punch line.

Separately, the cold open means that the viewers get to see the main character before they listen to his voiceover. They know who is talking when the voiceover begins, and they have already begun forming opinions about him based on his mannerisms and delivery. They also immediately know that they are watching a documentary (or at least something in the documentary style) because the main character is responding to a question and directly addressing someone beside the camera.

Since we didn't know we'd need the cold open until well into the editing process, this could have easily led to a pickup shoot to film such a scene. Luckily, we didn't have to resort to that because:

Cut one scene in half and you have two.

That's right. Our cold open—scene 1—is actually half of scene 12 in the screenplay. We had already cut scene 12 in half because it was too long and a bit repetitive where it lands in the film. However, rather than simply discarding the other half, we realized that it would work perfectly up front—for exactly the reasons that I've stated here. It also acts as a nice visual bookend to the pre-reveal section of the film. The audience has already seen the setting at the very beginning of the film, so returning to the same frame recalls the opening and gives them a sense that we're almost ready to find out what the "idea" that he mentioned is.

In Brief:

1. If something isn't working at the beginning of your movie, don't be afraid to consider a cold open that shakes everything up.
2. Keep good track of the scenes that you cut down. You never know when that scrap on the cutting room floor might come in handy.
    a. (Be glad that you're not editing with film, and a bin, and a literal cutting room floor. It is brutal.)

STOCK FOOTAGE CAN BE YOUR FRIEND—SCENE 2

As mentioned in the last section, the original opening for *A Convenient Truth* involved majestic landscapes, aerial shots, and other expensive things. The first inclination for an indie producer is going to be to cut this huge opening for budgetary reasons. It's just not feasible to shoot them on a small budget. However, the reason these shots are written into the script is to open the film in a visually impressive way and to cover the opening speech that the main character is giving. You don't want to open the film with a long lecture scene, but you don't have the money to rent a helicopter and fly around California grabbing beautiful nature shots to cover it either. This is when stock footage can be your friend.

Stock footage of the Golden Gate Bridge to establish the California setting of the film.

This is especially true of documentaries (or in our case mockumentaries) because the form allows for it. Music videos can also benefit from the prudent use of stock footage. The use of stock footage in standard narratives rarely works well—or at least I haven't seen any.

So we began the very long process of searching for stock footage that could work for us. Most sites will even allow you to download low resolution "comps" of the footage to put into your editing timeline for testing. Once you've found the clips you definitely want, you can purchase the full resolution versions of only those clips.

Getty Images is probably the most comprehensive database of stock footage that exists, but you'll quickly see that using their catalogue is cost prohibitive—with each short clip costing between $750 and $4,000. So to save you some of the legwork, I'm mentioning all of the sites that we used to source some of the clips in A Convenient Truth.

What I'm calling "Scene 2" is actually an opening montage of mostly stock footage clips that cover the main character's lecture, which reads as voiceover narration. Without further ado, the sources for our stock footage are:

Pond5

My favorite resource for stock footage for three reasons. First, it has the most "random" selection of videos—in a good way. Second, the footage is uploaded by filmmakers, and they get a percentage of what you pay for it. Third, since filmmakers set the prices, it's the only site where you can find clips that you might actually want starting at $5.

ShutterStock

We used four clips from Shutterstock for a total of $220, which is quite a bargain. We also spent $34 to be able to download and use up to five still images in the film. The site is well-organized, easily navigable, and makes it easy to store photos as you search.

Video Blocks

Take advantage of their seven-day free trial, which allows you to download and keep up to 20 clips a day for a week. After that, they have decent pricing on clips but also offer a subscription model, which allows you to download everything you want for a year for $99! If you're doing a lot of work that includes stock footage, this is a no-brainer.

Bottle Video

This site has a lot of stock footage for free and can be really useful. However, it will only be free for low-quality SD clips. There are fees for HD clips, but I don't have any experience with that, since the clips I wanted were only available in SD. Definitely worth taking a look.

eFootage.com

A good source for older/archival footage. We only used one clip from this source, but their rates are very reasonable—with HD clips ranging from $49 to $299. You can get SD clips starting at $29.

Footage Firm

This site is now only accepting paid orders through Video Blocks, but it is still a good spot for some free footage. They used to sell DVDs full of grouped footage (40 clips at a time) for very small amounts, so I'd still check back to see if they are offering anything like that.

WhiteHouse.gov

We sourced one clip from whitehouse.gov, which has a photos and video section. Clips posted there are in the public domain.

Prelinger Archives

Side Note: We didn't use this source for *A Convenient Truth*, but I've since read about it as a good source of older stock footage in the public domain, so definitely take a look if you need that type of material.

FILM LOCATIONS EQUAL PRODUCTION VALUE—SCENE 3

Scene 3 is the first time that we see our main character, Coleman Burleson, giving the lecture that will be the spine of the entire film. Much like Al Gore in *An Inconvenient Truth* (2006), we return to Coleman's presentation throughout the entire film, so it's important for those setups to look good. Our first instinct was to search for lecture locations at NYU because of my affiliation with the university, but this was still going to be limited and expensive.

This is where your networks come in. Tell people you're making a movie. They will want to help you. They'll offer you things you don't need. You'll be handsomer than ever. In this case, one of our producers got his former high school to let use their theater—for free! This is huge.

We were able to film for three days in a 1,400-seat theater with a Broadway caliber stage—for nothing more than a handshake and proof of insurance. Since we were filming in the summer, the school was empty and happy to help us out. Once we had the location, we were able to take stock of what was available to us, and the nurse's station, a classroom, and the weight room also made the final film.

Additionally, thanks to the stage's lighting grid and a great DP, we were actually able to cheat that one stage for four different locations in the film by creating very different lighting setups. This gives the illusion that Coleman is giving his speech in several different locations without ever having to change shooting locations.

The simple act of asking people about stages that might be available saved us thousands of dollars in location rental fees and raised the production value of the film tremendously. The scenes can now include wide shots, which let the audience feel that Coleman is legitimate and talking to large crowds. If we had paid for smaller locations that we could afford, the result would actually have been a higher budget and a cheaper looking movie.

Coleman Burleson (Alan Berman) giving his lecture on stage.

Mini Lesson: Zooming Within the Frame

To transition from the "Scene 2" montage of scenic landscapes into Coleman's speech, we wanted a dynamic shot that would bring the audience into the heart of the film. We didn't have that shot. (Good job, Mr. Director.)

The solution was to begin the shot zoomed into the frame within Avid—focusing on Coleman's presentation—and then zoom out to get to the ultimate frame that you see at the top of this section. We essentially created the shot in the editing software.

Two Caveats

1. Never zoom into the frame. You don't have the pixel information to properly blow something up, so you don't want to draw attention to the degraded image. (Think of a low-resolution jpeg really large on your computer monitor.)
2. Only consider this for documentaries or mockumentaries. Don't use zoom (practical or digital) in a narrative film. There is no faster way to make your movie feel like a wedding video from the 1980s.

Using Green Screen—Scene 4

If you're the writer/director of an independent film, be ready for those moments when the director version of you wants to ask the writer version of you what the hell he was thinking. It didn't cross my mind when I was writing the screenplay for *A Convenient Truth* that it might not be a good idea for me—a New York–based filmmaker—to write a movie that is inextricably set in California. Similarly, I didn't think twice about writing a scene that takes place in the U.S. House of Representatives. That should be an easy location, right? In spite of my aversion to digital effects, there was one solution: green screen.

Green screen used to be for high-budget studio movies, but computer-generated effects are becoming more and more feasible for independent filmmakers to employ. I'm still a big proponent of getting as much done in and in front of the camera as possible, but scene 4 is an example where this just wasn't possible. With that in mind:

Five Tips for Using Green Screen in Your Indie

1. Light the green screen as evenly as possible. Color only exists within light, so a shadowy area of green is not the same to your effects software as an area of that same screen that has more light falling onto it.
2. Make a precise list of the shots that you absolutely need to get for the scene.
3. Find the background images or video clips that you will composite into the image before shooting anything.
4. Position your actor a good distance away from the green screen to allow for depth—preferably matching a similar distance to the background that you'll be compositing.
5. Don't forget about your actor. It can be challenging for an actor to essentially work in a vacuum, so it's the director's job to make sure she has everything she needs. Ultimately, you're directing the performance.

Coleman Burleson (Alan Berman) speaking to the House of Representatives through the magic of green screen.

There are any number of technical articles by experts that can explain how to best use green screen, but the five items mentioned above are what I've come away feeling are the most important from a directing perspective.

ACTING WHILE DIRECTING—SCENE 5

If everyone who knows me were asked to pick 1,000 words to describe me, not one person would pick "performer." Acting is one of my nightmares, and I've managed to avoid it at all costs for the majority of my life. (I'm the guy who is uncomfortable if there might be audience participation at a play.) I have great respect for the craft of acting and the people who are able to make themselves vulnerable enough to do it well. I'm also self-aware enough to know that I'm not one of those people. So, when scene 5 of *A Convenient Truth* came around, and I'd written myself into a corner, I was more than a little squirmy. Since the crew making the film is also playing the crew within the film, a scene with the film's director meant a scene with me in front of the camera. Yikes.

In this scene, Coleman Burleson (Alan Berman) and Leonard Wingmon (Kevin Hauver) want to talk with the director to ease their minds about the documentary that they are about to undertake. To keep the illusion that we were making a documentary, we made the decision early on that the crew would all play themselves. That way, if we accidentally dipped into any of the shots, they wouldn't necessarily be ruined, and we could use this to our advantage in certain places.

To make things more complicated, I wanted to get this entire scene in one shot because it was supposed to be a "captured moment," so I didn't want to have traditional

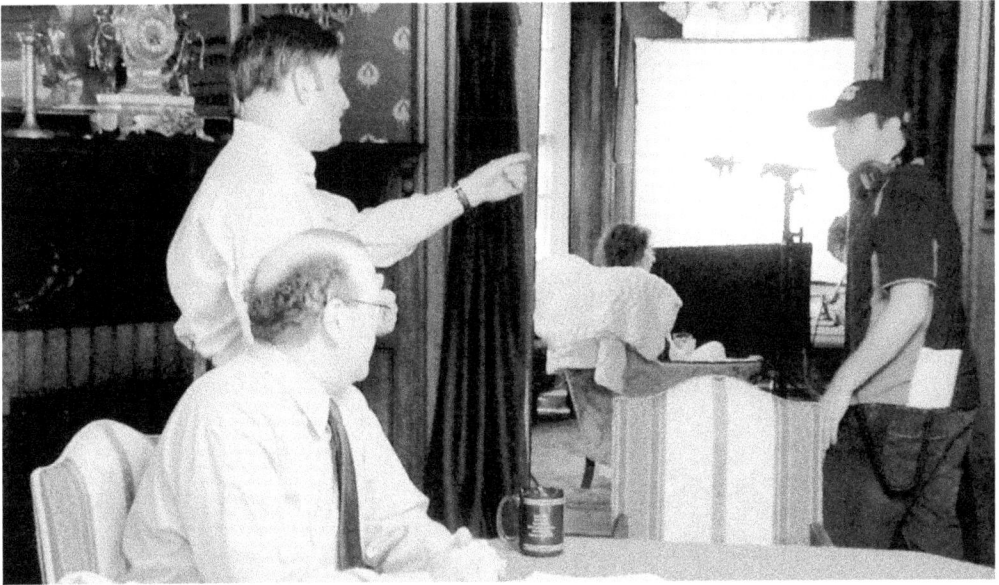

Coleman Burleson (Alan Berman), Leonard Wingmon (Kevin Hauver), and Director Dominick Bagnato talk through the making of the in-film documentary. Kitty Burleson (Elise Rovinsky) awaits her interview in the background.

coverage. Though I was nervous, the schedule of independent film keeps things moving, so I called action, and the scene began.

Coleman and Leonard are chatting amongst themselves when I come up to tell them that they can shut off their microphones if they don't want us to be able to hear them at any time. This is a simple enough way to get into the scene, but then they grab me to talk about their concern for some of the documentary subjects. The plan was to let the scene play out loosely, and after the first take I learned a very important lesson:

You can be acting. And you can be directing. But you can't be doing both simultaneously.

As the first take progressed, I realized a couple of things. First, I wanted to change Leonard's position within the frame. Second, this scene was going on way too long. I wanted to make sure we got through all of the beats once before calling cut, but I made a critical error. I was thinking about all of this instead of reacting to what was going on in the scene. At one point, I was even signaling to Kevin with my eyes that we should start wrapping up the scene!

This is where working with talented individuals is always helpful. Immediately after the first take, Kevin came up to me very politely to say, "You know, you can't be doing that. You can't be directing the scene while you're in it because it means we can't be in it." Of course, he was completely correct. Not only was I not "in" the scene, but I was actively taking my actors out of it by having them play against someone whose mind was already on the next take.

This is what I mean by not being able to act and direct at the same time. Obviously, there are tons of people who have done both successfully within one film, but this means that they are taking off their directing hat as soon as they are in front of the camera. It's impossible to be reacting to the emotions on someone's face and contemplating his eye light at the same time.

My advice would be to empower someone else to worry about the technical parts of the scene for the scenes that you are acting in. If you don't trust someone enough to do that, at least fully invest yourself in the scene as you're shooting it. You can always go back and watch the take on video once it's complete.

After adjusting my mindset and doing six or seven takes, we were able to get the take that we used in the film.

Mini-Lesson: Visual Transitions

You can see a light and microphone setup in the background of the frame in this section. The next scene is our introduction to Kitty Burleson (Elise Rovinsky), and we were shooting her scenes in a connected physical space. Our great DP, Adam Orellana, had the idea to show this setup in the background. It makes the frame more interesting and adds to the "real" feel of the continuous space.

GIVE YOUR ACTOR A BEAT—SCENE 6

The performances in *A Convenient Truth* are the element of which I'm most proud. Scene 6, our introduction to Kitty Burleson (Coleman's wife, played by the incredibly talented Elise Rovinsky), is one example of why this is true. I'd already gotten myself 80 percent there through great casting, but I almost failed to get myself the rest of the way by rushing the filming of this scene. Which brings me to a simple but important lesson:

Remember to give your actor a beat!

When we were filming scene 6, we had one weekend to film a ridiculous number of scenes, and this scene was one of the easier ones—a single actress sitting down in an interview setup with a locked-off camera. I distinctly recall that we were filming this scene before lunch one day, and I was very aware of our schedule—too aware.

We would roll camera, and I'd immediately call action. Then, as the take was playing out, I'd already be thinking about what I'd want to do differently for the next one. Or, I'd know that we got what we needed. Either way, I'd call cut as soon as the lines were captured. Never do this. In a way, I was punishing Elise for handling the scene so effortlessly.

We'd get what we needed and reboot or move on. To her credit, after a few takes, she asked if she could have a beat or two at the end of the scene. These moments gave her time to let the character breathe and react to what she had just said. Her instincts were totally correct and, to a certain extent, these beats were even written into the script, but all of this went out the window when I let my worry about "making the day" be prioritized over my desire to make the best film possible.

After I realized this, we began giving the scene a few more moments at the beginning and end, and the resulting takes were by far the best. We were essentially letting an actor act. (It is literally the simplest advice possible but also easy to forget in the middle of a challenging production schedule.)

Trust me, it's best to make sure you are allowing your actor to give you the best she possibly can. As the director, it's not your job to worry about starting lunch 15 minutes late. You're responsible for collaborating with your actors and making the best possible film.

Kitty Burleson (Elise Rovinsky) begins her interview.

Three Mini-Lessons

1. Take advantage of your locations. When we were scouting locations, we hooked up with two great guys (Mark Sharp and Bruce Truman) who have a historic Victorian in North Plainfield, New Jersey. They were willing to let us use their amazing house to shoot in because of a mutual friend. Once we saw the place, I immediately began thinking of things we could shoot there. Within that house, we shot scene 5, this scene, a scene in Coleman's office later in the film, and an additional attic scene that was ultimately cut from the film. For indie film, more scenes in one location are imperative because company moves will break your schedule.
2. Attentive framing can elevate simple scenes. As I mentioned, this was one of the simpler scene setups, but that doesn't mean it's unimportant. In fact, since this is the setup for Kitty's interview within the film, we return to this frame for two other scenes—so we don't want it to be boring. Our DP, Adam Orellana, found this frame, and it is one of my favorite in the entire movie.
3. Letting the camera roll a bit before calling action is a great way to capture some silent moments of coverage that can save you in the editing room.

MAN-ON-THE-STREET INTERVIEWS—SCENE 7

Scene 7 is the first completely unscripted scene in the film. We ventured out into the real world for "man-on-the-street" interviews.

Side Note: If your first thought is that the phrase "man-on-the-street" is politically incorrect because of its gender bias—please don't watch this movie.

Because *A Convenient Truth* is a mockumentary, we were able to employ certain production staples of real documentaries. In this case, Coleman Burleson and a small crew (me, DP, sound recordist, and a production assistant with a bounce board to fill in some light) went outside to find out what real people thought about global warming. (You should also have a floating PA or two around with clipboards and release forms to chase down the people that you grab to interview.)

We conducted the interviews in complete earnest. Coleman never broke character, and we were never making fun of our interviewees. The goal was for the truth of our current reality to create the comedy, and we accomplished this with great success.

This is an important note for satire and for the feature film length. If we wanted to make a short, farcical film, we could have easily gone over-the-top with the street interviews and made everyone involved look like a fool. As tempting as this might be, the director has to keep the entire film in mind and service the overall structure. Especially for interviews like this that occur before Coleman's proposal is revealed, one false moment could have jeopardized the entire setup of the film.

The man-on-the-street interviews were some of the most popular segments with our test audiences and have gotten good reactions since the film's release. This is no accident. The interviews that made it into the film are extremely curated. We interviewed dozens of people and culled through hours of footage to grab the few moments that made

Coleman Burleson (Alan Berman) conducts spontaneous man-on-the-street interviews.

it into the film. Like with anything else in film, the more you have to choose from, the easier it will be to make a strong film.

We were able to let the interviews tell us where they should be placed within the film. They allowed transition moments for us in the cut when certain scenes weren't playing nice with each other, and they also allowed for certain juxtapositions to create moments that didn't exist before. Placing a quick man-on-the-street interview before an existing, scripted scene can be a way to force the audience to view the following scene in a specific light—either in support or opposition of the preceding statement.

Interviews Force a Director to React

If you're making a documentary or mockumentary, even if you don't use any of the footage, interviews can be a helpful exercise. Going out onto the street is a great way to inject some fresh ideas into the film and can re-energize the editing process because, like improv, you're genuinely reacting to something that's not in your control. Especially if you also wrote the script, by the time you're in the editing bay, anything that is new to you will bring tears of joy to your eyes.

ACTORS WHO WRITE—SCENES 8 AND 9

Film is a visual medium, so working with beautiful actors is an obvious choice. What should be equally obvious (but often isn't), is that it's just as valuable to work with intelligent actors who write.

Top: Eleanor Burleson (Gilli Messer) talks about her father's big proposal. *Bottom:* Cardamom Burleson (Jillian Leigh) weighs in about the film's subject.

Scenes 8 and 9 are our introductions to Coleman Burleson's two daughters, Eleanor (Gilli Messer) and Cardamom (Jillian Leigh). Each of these actors is also a writer and maker in her own right, and *A Convenient Truth* is a markedly better film for it.

Within the recent months alone, Gilli Messer has starred in a short film, *Santa Slayer*, which is her first produced written work. Additionally, her short script, *The Tutor*, was a semi-finalist in the 2014 BlueCat Screenplay competition, which is one of the most important competitions of its kind. (For some perspective, this means her script was selected as one of the top 30 out of more than 1,600 short scripts.)

Jillian Leigh authored the play *Pie*, which was accepted into the First Annual Festival of Female Writers in New York City and performed in late May 2014 in Manhattan. More recently, her play *Hooked* was well-received in Los Angeles.

Though scenes 8 and 9 were scripted, the writing intelligence of each of these actors really shines through in their subsequent scenes. Interviewing these actors as their characters was essentially the same as workshopping a character with a fellow writer—except even better because no one has more of a commitment to a character than the actor portraying that person.

I imagine that another writer/director (perhaps with the paradoxical combination of larger ego and more insecurity than I) would be intimidated by working with such talented and intelligent actors, but that makes no sense. If I managed to find great actors who are also better writers than me—yay for me!

The best way to learn a craft is to surround yourself with others who are better at that craft than you. Accepting that you can learn a lot about writing from your actors is a huge opportunity to learn as a writer and make your film better in the process.

Mini-Lesson: Frame Composition for Neighboring Scenes

You can see from the two frames in this section that Eleanor is looking to the left of the camera for her interview, while Cardamom is looking to the right. Since these scenes were planned to be back-to-back from the script stage, this is a good way to make the transition from one scene to the next a little more dynamic. It wouldn't be the end of the world if they were both filling the same side of the frame and looking in the same direction, but the variation is nice to have.

A Good Film Editor Will Save Your Ass—Scene 10

I made my first mistake for scene 10 when I wrote the script, which looked like this:

INT. BANQUET HALL—DAY
DOZENS OF PEOPLE populate the large room in their best formal wear. A banner reads Burleson Campaign Fundraiser.
A cluster of suits form a pocket around Coleman. Kitty and Leonard stand on either side of him. Everyone has a drink in hand. Kitty holds two.
                    COLEMAN BURLESON
        It's like when people brag about
        their jobs in that minimalist way.

Between the slug line and the very first line of scene description, I've already created two nightmares for the indie producer:

1. I wrote the scene in a banquet hall. This isn't insurmountable but will cost some real money if done right. The space itself is expensive. The art direction needs to make it look sufficiently fancy, and the costumes all have to be formal wear.

2. "DOZENS OF PEOPLE" is always going to be a tricky and expensive thing to pull off. Getting lots of people to give up their day to stand around in their Sunday best is easier said than done. Even if you can find the interested people for free, you'll have to feed them at the very least—which often becomes one of the largest expenses in an indie film budget.

The realities of production transformed our banquet scene into the dinner party scene that is pictured here. It includes three of our main characters and one additional day player. We created a much more manageable scene without sacrificing much, and all of the issues that the writer (me) created were solved. This is when the director (also me) creates new problems.

I wanted to shoot this entire scene in a long take. That is, I wanted the scene to feel captured by one documentary cameraman who was floating around the room but not interacting with the subjects.

One Camera Means No Cuts

Whereas a traditional scene is filmed from several different angles, or coverage, having the scene play out in a long take means zero coverage. We still shot multiple takes of the scene, but the intention was to choose one and use it all—as opposed to editing together the best parts of these different takes.

If done perfectly, you will have made the film editor's job as easy as it possibly can be. Plop one take onto the timeline, and the scene is done. More likely, not getting ample coverage will make your editor want to berate you for being an inept director. As one might expect, when we went through all of the takes of scene 10 in the edit suite, we were not fortunate enough to have one that we wanted to use in its entirety.

Leonard Wingmon (Kevin Hauver), Kitty Burleson (Elise Rovinsky), and Coleman Burleson (Alan Berman) toast the film's proposal.

Luckily, Charlie Pinto is a patient man and, more importantly, an experienced editor. Since our cameraman was floating around and changing the framing while each take was playing out, Charlie was able to go into the individual takes and essentially find the bits that were distinct enough to look like separate coverage. The resulting scene has an establishing shot, two-shots, and even close-ups all through the magic of creative editing.

Charlie was able to find a scene that really did not exist before he sat down with it.

The clearest example of this comes in the final cut of the scene, when the characters toast Coleman's proposal, calling it a "cure-all." This moment is accentuated by a cut that focuses on the four glasses of wine and spirits clinking together. Charlie essentially added a joke to the film by juxtaposing the visual of drinking with the aural reference to a cure-all. He claims this was there all along, but if it was it was subconscious, and he brought it to the surface.

Mini-Lesson: Let the Actors Say It Naturally

Part of the reason that scene 10 wasn't working in our initial takes was that the wording for Coleman's character was too—well—wordy. The point of the scene was getting confused, and it was difficult for Coleman to get his meaning across. After some discussion with Alan Berman about the core of what we wanted to impart, we talked through how Coleman could say that, and changed the words accordingly. The result was a happy actor and a clearer scene.

TALKING HEAD INTERVIEWS—SCENE 11

Scene 11 of *A Convenient Truth* is a standard talking head interview. That is, the scene is a character sitting down and talking to the camera—or to someone directly beside the camera, to be more accurate. There are some documentaries that choose to have interviewees look directly into the lens (and that is a valid stylistic choice), but that is more rare than having the interviewee speak to someone just beside the camera. (It's more natural for an actor or interview subject to speak to a person.)

In this scene, Leonard Wingmon (Kevin Hauver) gets his introduction to the audience. He recounts how he met Coleman Burleson and begins to describe his excitement for their work. This scene was only half a page on paper, but in production it turned out to be 55 seconds long. This is a long talking head scene. And it felt long. Once we identified a potential problem area, we adjusted accordingly:

Five considerations for a better talking head.

1. Cover your talking heads. The most basic way to help out your talking head scene is to show your audience something else. Maybe not anything else, but almost. After the audience has had a few moments to see someone speaking, they are ready to see something new. If there are any reasonable visuals related to what the person is discussing, you should look to cut to those visuals as the

Leonard Wingmon (Kevin Hauver) gets his official interview introduction.

speaker continues. In our case, we used very short clips of deleted scenes that show Coleman at work. We were especially happy to show scenes of Coleman and Leonard interacting, since this is the most pertinent to what we're hearing about. Covering the scene in the middle portion means we only see Leonard for 13 seconds before cutting away. Then, we come back to him for 29 seconds to end the scene. Those 12 seconds of coverage in the middle of the scene make a huge difference for the pacing and feel of the scene.

2. Mise-en-scène essentially refers to everything that you put into the frame. Talking head interviews often settle for less-than-interesting settings, but you should consider how the frame can supplement the audience's understanding. The setting might reinforce what the talking head is saying. Or there might be a great opportunity to subvert the audience's expectations.

3. Trust your audience. As you see in the still, Leonard gives his talking head interview with a taxidermied pheasant casually sitting beside him. This usually gets a chuckle, or at least a confused laugh—and that is enough. It gives us something to react to other than a guy sitting and talking to the camera. We trusted the audience enough to throw this in and, importantly, never refer directly to it. Trying to make it a full joke would be forced and an insult to the intelligence of the audience. The pheasant also leads us to…

4. Let your location work for you. Professor Dalton Conley was nice enough to let us use his office as a location for free. The pheasant was there when we arrived, so we used it.

5. Set up later scenes. A checkerboard also sits in the lower left of the frame. This is directly referred to later in the film as a throwaway line that gets us into another scene. The fact that we've already seen the board makes this work a bit more eas-

ily. Similarly, we later have another scene in a different part of Leonard's office. We used a different pheasant for that frame, and the audience immediately connects the two shots as part of the same space—even though one limitation of shooting in a real office made it impossible for us to get an establishing shot that explicitly tied to the two spaces together.

DIRECTING FLEXIBLY—SCENES 12 AND 13

Directing a film, like any good form of leadership, requires a certain vision. As the director, lots of people had questions for me every day, and I always had to have an answer. This isn't about making up answers on the spot for the sake of having something to say. It's about earning the confidence of your cast and crew.

I remember one of my professors at NYU saying that this was the real reason a film director needs a trailer. If the art director came up to him asking what color the curtains should be and he didn't have an answer, he'd say, "Yes, of course. I'll tell you as soon as I get back."

He'd then pretend that he was on his way to attend to some other fire, escape to his trailer, contemplate how the color of the curtains could serve the story, and return with an answer. The key is to always return with an answer—a real answer. As a director, if you don't know (or care), then no one can.

All of this is to say that a director must have a very clear idea of what needs to

Eleanor Burleson (Gilli Messer) performs a man-on-the-street interview.

happen at every moment—for every element of the film. With that given, the real trick is to simultaneously remain flexible enough to adapt to the realities of the day.

Scene 12 above exemplifies the necessity of flexibility in two ways:

1. Gilli Messer, who played Eleanor Burleson, flew out to the east coast to shoot her scripted scenes for a few days. The schedule allowed for her scenes to be shot on one day, but she was in the area for a few more. Knowing that we wanted to have her in the film as much as possible, we squeezed the schedule to allow her to venture out onto the street to perform her own man-on-the-street interviews. The result is more continuity in the film and more variation in the street interviews—so that they're not all conducted by Coleman. (On the one hand, it was crazy to mess with the meticulously plotted schedule of an indie film. On the other, being flexible enough to push for something outside of the schedule was a great move.)

2. For this specific scene, you'll notice that there are yellow subtitles for the responses—even though the responses are in English. At the test screenings, this scene wasn't getting the reaction that I knew it deserved. Rather than cutting the scene, we realized that the problem was that we knew the film too well. We'd seen this scene dozens of times in the edit, and we knew that the response was funny in context. The issue was that an audience couldn't understand all of that as it was happening. We added subtitles to allow the audience to register the words on-the-fly, and the scene now works much better.

You'll notice that scene 13 looks remarkably like scene 7. That's because it's the same interview. Our initial concept for the man-on-the-street interviews was only to grab very quick sound bites. The script had very specific moments where we could add some brief interviews without messing with the overall structure of the film.

Coleman Burleson (Alan Berman) continues his man-on-the-street interview.

However, these two interviewees were extremely entertaining, and it's important to remember that entertainment is the end goal. So, we adapted and broke their interview up into three distinct scenes. This allowed us to use the best parts and actually provided a direct segue into the reveal of the film—a segue that wouldn't exist if we weren't flexible enough to diverge from the formula we established before filming.

Improv—Scene 14

"If I had to explain my father's proposal to somebody who didn't have any idea—or had never heard about it—I would say that he is, in such a way, using the resources that California, and the world, already has in an effort to—make new things. My dad's recycling ... in a sense."—Cardamom Burleson

Scene 14 of *A Convenient Truth* is completely improvised. The dialogue at the start of the scene is part of an interview that I conducted with Cardamom Burleson (Jillian Leigh) after we'd filmed the three scripted scenes for the character.

Obviously, this won't work for every film, but there is a reason that the mockumentary style and improv are so often linked. They complement each other really well because the relatively simple visual setups allow for the actor to talk without worrying about hitting marks or complicated camera moves getting in the way.

With the advent of digital technology, films can also use multiple cameras to capture two or three angles of the same scene simultaneously. This ensures that any spontaneous moment will be covered from more than one angle for the editor. However, given our

Cardamom Burleson (Jillian Leigh) teases her father's proposal.

low budget and more traditional approach, we only ever used one camera at a time—proof that it can be done.

So, directing this scene included a bit more preparation than others. After we shot the scripted scenes, I launched into a list of about 30 questions that I'd come up with in advance of the shoot. Jillian had no knowledge of these questions before we were rolling, so she was truly responding in the moment. This entire scene is an example of what can happen if the improv has been properly prepped:

Three ingredients for good film improv.

1. Casting is paramount. Jillian has a talent for improv. This skill is different from traditional acting. Some actors have one or the other, some have both. It's fine that not all actors can improvise, but you better know if yours can.
2. She read the entire script and had a sense of the appropriate tone for her responses.
3. She knew her character really well. This is extremely important because otherwise you could waste a lot of time filming improv and getting hilarious responses that won't make the cut. Funny improv without a sense of character is a great recipe for some good times as you sit beside your editor. But those good times will quickly be quashed when you realize that the two of you will be the only ones who will ever see the hilarious but unusable scenes.

With these ingredients in place, this specific scene has three additional reasons why it works. We captured a couple of hours of great responses within one night of shooting, and this scene (like all of the scenes that made the cut) also fulfills the Goldilocks principle. In this case it is just right because:

1. Cardamom's response piques interest in the audience. We think that she might tell us more about her father's proposal—which we know the film is about but hasn't yet been explained.
2. Cardamom's delivery has the perfect amount of hesitance, which shows us that her character is a bit guarded and/or ambivalent about what she is saying.
3. Though not actually revealing what her father's proposal is, Cardamom does give us more information than we previously had to keep the narrative moving and keep us guessing. "My dad's recycling … in a sense." In what sense? We want to know!

Mini-Lesson: Repeat the Question

It's also worth noting that Cardamom begins her statement with a reiteration of the question. This isn't strictly necessary, but it prevents the audience from having to listen to too much off-camera questioning, which can get tiresome.

When possible, it's great to get the actor used to this practice. You can always cut the question part of the answer out, but you'll never regret having it.

Camera Movement—Scene 15

"What's my motivation?" Just as every director should be able to answer this question for an actor (who will hopefully be asking in a less trite way), the director should also imagine the camera asking the same question. Each camera movement (or lack of movement) should be seriously considered and informed by the story. There should be a clear motivation behind whatever state you've chosen for the camera at each moment.

Working within the mockumentary style, our film has a lot more static shots than most and can't justify many beautifully orchestrated camera moves. How would a real crew know what was going to happen in advance? They wouldn't, so neither can we. In scene 15 of *A Convenient Truth*, the camera is handheld and quickly following along with Leonard Wingmon (Kevin Hauver). This is intentional. Within the scene, Leonard is talking about how exciting it is to work at Burleson Labs. He's speaking to the camera while hurrying around the office—busied by all of the excitement he is discussing. It's a no-brainer to have the camera match his frenetic energy and bob around with him.

This camera movement is also motivated by the scene's relation to its surrounding scenes. Originally, this scene was a continuation of Leonard's monologue in his introductory scene—scene 11, which is a talking head interview. Scene 15 is therefore a walk-and-talk in order to continue the talking head interview in a more dynamic way.

You'll notice that we put a cameraman into the wider frame. This allows us to get coverage by showing the audience that there is another source for the close-up footage. We establish that there are multiple cameras covering the scene, and the audience is immediately waiting for the cut to the closer camera. It's almost a reward when the cut

The cameraman (Adam Orellana) follows Leonard Wingmon (Kevin Hauver) through a busy office at Burleson Laboratories.

comes. It's a small detail, but tiny ways of keeping your audience engaged are always helpful.

The scene—and the camera movement—has an organic rhythm, which are all in concert. The camera follows this character because it has to. The scene ends as he has finished his thought and is about to move on to the next room.

There are clear reasons why we made these choices. Does that mean they are objectively the only correct choices? No. For example, one could easily imagine a scene in which Leonard is talking about how exciting it is to work at Burleson Labs while sitting in the middle of a mostly vacant, dark room. His words could echo in the surrounding silence. And the camera could be completely stationary, gazing at a tiny man who is telling us exactly the opposite of what the visual is showing us.

This juxtaposition would lead to an entirely different reading of the scene, and it would be equally valid. But, importantly, it would be motivated. This would be a conscious choice about how to visually tell the story.

A lack of intentionality or consideration to your camera movement is one of the worst things that you can do as a director because it also takes away from the effects that similar camera movement will have elsewhere in the film. You want to pick your moments wisely because your climactic chase scene isn't going to feel all that special if the camera hasn't stopped floating around for the past hour. Similarly, the audience is not going to feel the weight behind the stillness of your dramatic long take if the camera has sat passively on the tripod for everything preceding it.

Pre-Reveal in Film—Scene 16

Any film that relies on a reveal really relies on a pre-reveal. This should go without saying, but it's important to truly digest this at the script stage because it's likely too late by the time the camera is rolling.

Imagine walking around telling people only the punch line to a joke. Imagine a magician pulling a rabbit from his hat before showing you the hat was empty. The power in any reveal comes from the anticipation created—the release of your anxiety or payoff on your expectation.

Too often, when something falls flat, it's easy to blame the ending. Indeed, from the audience's perspective, the end (of a sequence or an entire film) is the flaw. But in reality, the ending or reveal never had a chance because of previous structural problems.

Scene 16 is the end of the extensive pre-reveal sequence that opens *A Convenient Truth*. We'll soon see that the reveal of Coleman's proposal is the end of Act I for our film. (In this case, the end of Act I is the moment in the film when the audience has enough information to know what the film is about and mentally prepare to watch it unfold.) That said, scene 16 is one of the last moments that we get to tease the audience a bit more.

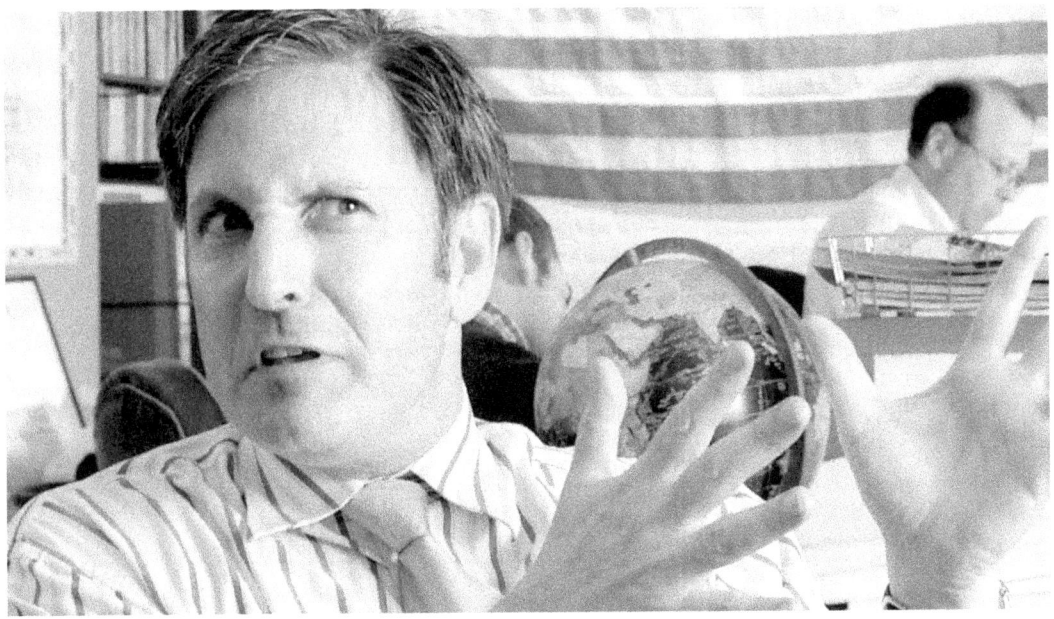

Coleman Burleson (Alan Berman) hypes up his proposal a bit more.

Foreplay

As mentioned in scene 1, scene 16 is the other half of the cold open for our film. Psychologically, the audience feels the importance of a return to that opening frame. During the cold open we knew nothing. Fifteen scenes later, we've met several characters,

Coleman Burleson (Alan Berman) puts a button on his mini-monologue to camera.

gotten pieces of the puzzle, and heard several allusions to this "proposal" that everyone keeps referring to.

The visual return to the cold open gives the audience a slight relief. We are no longer jumping around from scene to scene, character to character. We've settled, briefly, back onto the main character, who is sitting in the same place in which we originally met him. He's talking to us in a way that is comforting in its recognizability. We've seen this before, and that means that we might now be about to see something new—to finally get the information we've been waiting for. This visual cycle is a very powerful tool.

The hope is that by the time we return to Coleman's interview here in scene 16 the audience is practically screaming on the inside: "So what is this proposal you keep talking about already?!"

THE REVEAL—SCENES 17–20

The reveal of *A Convenient Truth* is more easily discussed as a sequence than as separate scenes. The first scene in the sequence, scene 17, is a continuation of the man-on-the-street interviews that we've already seen in scene 7 and scene 13.

None of this interview was scripted, but these interviewees gave us the perfect segue into our reveal:

"Well, look at the state the country is in, and all over the world.
People all over the world is not satisfied. It's not only here. It's all over the world. People

Coleman Burleson (Alan Berman) begins the process of revealing his proposal.

Coleman Burleson (Alan Berman) introduces the animation that will reveal his proposal.

are not satisfied. And what does that tell you? Something is screwed up." (FADE OUT).

After a long fade, we come back to our main character giving his lecture. If something is screwed up, what's the answer?

And that's exactly how we begin our next scene. "What are we gonna do about it?" Coleman asks with a smirk on his face. Because he's about to tell you. And he's so proud of himself for it.

"So then…" not "and then…"

This is a good place to point out that your scenes should follow each other in a natural "so then" format that forms sequences. This can help you figure out your structure and minimize blocks that can occur from being overwhelmed with infinite choices. That is, I could follow "and then" with literally anything that I can think of. However, "so then" reminds me that the scene should follow directly from the previous one:

The man on the street proffers that something is screwed up, so then Coleman acknowledges that something is indeed screwed up and launches into how he is going to do something about it.

So then he finally plays an animation that reveals his proposal to the crowd.

So, naturally, the crowd reacts with shock and awe. Cameras flash in quick succession as the audience is desperate to capture proof that Coleman has actually just proposed what he has.

So we end this reveal sequence with a distinct sense of relief. We now know what Coleman is proposing. Even though this is the main thrust of the scene, we also don't lose sight of where we're going.

Top: An animation reveals the film's proposal. *Bottom:* Coleman Burleson (Alan Berman) relishes his reveal moment on stage.

So then how are people going to react to this plan?

You guessed it. Beginning with scene 21, the film will deal with the reaction to Coleman's controversial proposal.

Mini-Lesson: Flawed Reveal

You might notice that the still from the animation does not match the still behind Coleman in the frame on the previous page. This fact plagued me for months. We shot the reveal scene during our first round of photography—before we had an animator do a proper animation for the reveal. (We originally made a really crappy animation ourselves that we used, but I decided it was more important for the film to go for an impressive reveal than it was to go for the cheap laugh of a terrible animation.)

Changing my mind, however, meant that the shots didn't match. If we had thousands of extra dollars, we could have paid an FX person to replace the shot in the background, but that is actually a very difficult thing to do with Coleman moving in the foreground, the camera moving, and flashes constantly changing the lighting of the shot. This being indie film, we didn't have any extra money to throw around.

So how do we avoid confusing the audience? After all, we're cutting back to the scene from the animation, but the animation on the auditorium screen doesn't match. The solution was to have the narration of the animation overlap with Coleman's speech. As we come out of the animation and back to Coleman, the narrator and Coleman simultaneously say, "And that's how electricity is made." Aurally tying the two disparate scenes together makes everything clear for the audience, and I haven't yet gotten even one confused comment.

THE REACTION—SCENES 21 AND 22

Okay, so you've spent the first ten minutes of your film building up anticipation about your main character's secret—in this case, Coleman's proposal. So then the secret is finally revealed (hopefully in a satisfying way.) What's next? What follows logically? The reaction to this big reveal.

A Convenient Truth bases its humor on a ridiculous proposal being presented in a completely solemn form. We want the audience to have a visceral reaction to Coleman's proposal. The laughter that the reveal elicits is an uneasy laughter, and that reaction gets us through the moment. However, after that initial shock subsides—in order for the film to have legs and be a satire rather than a farce—we need to present characters reacting to the absurd proposal in ways that the audience can empathize with and in believable situations.

In a horror film, we complain about the character stupidly choosing to run up the stairs rather than out the front door because we are putting ourselves in that character's shoes, and we would not act so stupidly. Similarly, if we are appalled by Coleman's proposal, we want to see characters who are equally outraged. We want to feel like we share a world in common, and in our world there would be tremendous backlash to such a proposal.

If we ignored this backlash it would be at our own peril. We'd have a farcical film that takes place in an un-relatable world. The beauty of a satire is that it exists in a completely relatable world and heightens our awareness of certain real things. We don't have

Coleman Burleson (Alan Berman) and Senator William Harris (Michael Anderson) engage in a local debate to react to the film's proposal.

to shy away from the fact that this proposal is ridiculous and the uproar it would create. In fact, these are precisely the things that we will lean on to create our comedy.

With all that said, scene 21 is a local debate scene between Coleman and his direct opponent, Senator Harris (Michael Anderson).

Senator Harris is the immediate surrogate for the audience. We've all found out Coleman's plan, and Senator Harris pops onto the screen seconds later. The moderator literally asks him for his response to Coleman's proposal. The audience gets to watch a character speak out against the proposal. All of the things that they want to shout at the screen are expressed in the next 30 seconds. We've again let the audience know that they are in good hands by relieving the tension surrounding the reaction to the proposal. Just as Coleman is about to give his rebuttal ... we cut away.

It's not time for that now.

Good ol' Leonard to the rescue. Once we acknowledged that this proposal has been met with some opposition in scene 21, scene 22 is where Leonard continues this train of thought but puts a positive spin on it. (Hey, that's just like real politicians...)

INT. STUDY—DAY
Leonard rocks back and forth in his desk chair.

                            LEONARD
         It was Einstein who cleverly quipped
              "Great spirits have always
           encountered violent opposition
               from mediocre minds."
Beat.

                        LEONARD (CONT'D)
     Sure people reacted poorly initially. Most people think
      this is a terrible idea when they first hear it. But that's
       the thing about revolutionary ideas. If everyone thought
this way, it wouldn't be visionary. It would just be ... the way it is.

Leonard Wingmon (Kevin Hauver) issues a disclaimer about the film's proposal.

Now we know not only that this proposal is controversial in this world. We also know that the main characters acknowledge that fact. Further, Leonard asks us to think about all of the great people in history who were initially laughed off for having different ideas.

Know the Audience's Reaction

You never want your audience to be ahead of you. Always imagine how the audience will react to what you're presenting them with. You can then either use that to know where to take them afterward or play directly on their expected reactions to go the other way. Either way, don't forget that you're in the game of making people feel things, so you should probably consider what those things might be ahead of time.

Mini-Lesson: Repeat Framing

Scene 22 is the first of what I imagined at the script stage as "Leonard's Disclaimers." The conceit was that every time something over-the-top or ridiculous happened, we'd have Leonard pop onto the screen to assure us that everything was going to be okay.

Knowing this ahead of time, I was able to push this further by repeating the exact framing for all three of these scenes. We set the camera, made sure nothing changed, and filmed these three scenes in a row. By the third time Leonard pops on screen, audiences are already primed to laugh—regardless of what he says. In a couple of screenings, savvy audiences have even recognized the pattern by the second "disclaimer" and laughed accordingly.

Mini-Mini-Lesson: Use Your Relationships

Michael Anderson was one of the leads in my short film, *Initial Conditions*. He's a great actor, so I asked him if he'd play the role of Senator Harris for one day of shooting, and he accepted—to my great delight.

Script Departure—Scenes 23–27

This is not a golf scene. It was written as a golf scene. And so begins a lesson on script departure. In short, it's going to happen. Especially when a director is also the writer of the script, it can be easy to see every departure from the script as a failure—a compromise from the original vision.

My advice is to quickly get over this. In indie film (all film really, but more so in indie), there are going to be all sorts of necessary changes that arise. Your vision will change when that vision comes face-to-face with the realities of production. That said, it's important to try your hardest to figure out how to make those compromises work for your story—even become advantages.

I don't remember the source, but I recall a related story about one of the funniest comedies of all time, *Monty Python and the Holy Grail* (1975). The script opens with a knight "riding" onto the scene. When it came to production, horses were very expensive. Knowing that Foley artists often use coconuts to re-create the sounds of horse hooves in post-production, someone had the genius idea to incorporate this into the comedy. The

Coleman Burleson (Alan Berman) defends his proposal while attempting to play tennis.

film now opens with one of our main characters "galloping" onto the scene quickly followed by another man banging coconuts together. The result is an extremely low-budget gag that immediately sets the tone for the entire movie and injects comedy into the film. After all, if they had more money, that would now just be a scene of a guy on a horse...

Back to *A Convenient Truth*: When we were prepping to shoot this scene, golf course locations were proving unwelcoming, expensive, or both. We wanted to shoot the scene, but it was clear that some sort of script departure was going to be necessary. In this case, the solution was relatively simple: re-write the scene as a tennis scene. I knew that there were a few tennis courts that we could shoot on for free, and tennis is also a more visually dynamic sport, so we made a few changes and adapted the scene.

The dialogue of scene 23 mostly continues the themes of scene 21—the reaction to Coleman's proposal. Coleman discusses the backlash with Leonard as they play tennis. We get to play with the visual of Coleman being a terrible tennis player while also getting the necessary exposition. However, the action of shooting a tennis scene presented its own issues. Asking actors to deliver lines while running around a tennis court and playing the game isn't easy. It's also very difficult to cover and match the play with one camera.

As it often does, the solution came in editing. What was written as one continuous golf scene in the script became a tennis sequence with interluding scenes illuminating exactly what Coleman and Leonard were discussing.

Why is this so important?

It means we can cut wherever the hell we want.

Scenes 24 and 25 are both examples of more great improv from Cardamom (Jillian Leigh) and Eleanor (Gilli Messer). We had an abundance of these short, funny sound bites that we were always looking to find a place for in the film. Cutting them into the tennis sequence allowed us to do just that and also only cut in the tennis footage that we really wanted.

Cardamom Burleson (Jillian Leigh) speaks out against her father's detractors.

Eleanor Burleson (Gilli Messer) takes a diplomatic approach to defending the proposal.

Let me clarify this a bit more. Imagine Coleman says something great, and it looks great. Then, imagine there are some flubs or dead time as he goes to recover a tennis ball. After that, he delivers another line perfectly, and we want to use it.

If we don't have a device to cut away, we are forced to make the audience watch that middle bit in order to let them see the beginning and end that we like. This can't be done. Your audience will resent you for the lull—and they should.

Leonard Wingmon (Kevin Hauver) and Coleman Burleson (Alan Berman) sit down for a joint interview.

By cutting the short scenes above into the sequence, we can come back exactly when Coleman is about to deliver that perfect line. Again, this is a script departure that made the film better.

Script Departure and Structure

The dangerous thing about departing from your script is that you're abandoning your plan. The plan that was well-vetted. The plan that everyone was on board with. So you better make sure you're improving the movie.

Even departures from your script need to have a logic and structure to them. In the case of the tennis sequence, if we only cut in once, it would seem random or like we were trying to hide something. Cutting in twice makes it feel a bit nicer, but that old rule of threes really is special. Cutting in three times just feels right. So, we cut in for the third time with scene 26.

Scene 26, which we came to refer to as the "red chair interview" (you can't stop our creativity), is an example of a script departure that isn't improv. That is, this is a scene that was not in the original script but an additional scene that I wrote in between scheduled photography. This is one advantage to taking such a long time to make your film—you can literally rewrite it as you go to respond to your needs.

So Coleman and Leonard give more supporting evidence for the terrible backlash that they've had to face since the proposal was made public. Again, these scenes are all directly related to one another—not thrown in simply for comedy, which would kill the momentum of the film.

The sequence finally cuts back to our tennis scene. Coleman and Leonard wrap up both their game and the "thought" of the sequence—that "thought" being about the negative reaction to his proposal.

Coleman Burleson (Alan Berman) and Leonard Wingmon (Kevin Hauver) conclude their tennis match.

The scene ends—again looking forward to the next scene—with a comment about the first worker that they hired to work at Burleson Labs...

USE YOUR ACTOR'S FACE—SCENE 28

"We didn't need dialogue. We had faces!"—Norma Desmond (Sunset Blvd., 1950)

The very last frame of scene 28 is a close-up of Juan "Pepe" Blanco's (Guy Wellman) face, which we've held on for a really long time. I mean a really long time. Coleman asks Juan a direct question, but no answer is immediately forthcoming. We don't know how Juan feels about what he's just been asked—or even if he understands it. But we wonder what his response will be and that "wonder" is an audience actively engaged with the film.

In this case, no verbal response that Juan could give would be better than his face. In fact, his silence is a nice balance to the rambling that Coleman offers to the scene. The scene ends in a really nice beat, and I distinctly remember waiting for what seemed like ages before calling cut when we shot this take. I wanted to linger on Juan's face. And linger we did—to (hopefully) comedic effect.

This touches upon something that everyone knows but is hard to quantify or define in any universal way. Namely, comedy is timing. If we had cut away too soon, the joke would have been lost. If we'd lingered any longer, it might have felt stale and fallen flat. Obviously, we had to make a judgment call in the edit about the perfect amount of time

Juan "Pepe" Blanco (Guy Wellman) is introduced to the audience.

to settle on Juan's face. (Sometimes you'll want to find that perfect point, purposely hold it too long, and wait for the comedy to come back around again. This can work in some circumstances, but you might need test audiences to help you decide if that's actually happened, or if you've just fallen in love with the material.)

The point is, Juan's face was saying everything that needed to be said. His face, paired with carefully selected timing, gets a completely visual laugh.

Timing Within the Film Structure Counts Too

Along with the above example of timing within a single shot, it's also worth noting the importance of this scene's timing within the overall structure of the film.

The previous scene, scene 27, ends with Coleman talking about how his gardener, Juan "Pepe" Blanco, was the first employee that they recruited to work at Burleson Labs. So, naturally, scene 28 is our introduction to Juan "Pepe" Blanco, right?

You'd think so, and you'd be right, but this wasn't always as obvious as it should be.

Scene 28 was originally scene 40 in the screenplay. To give you a sense of this, it now comes at 18:41 into the movie, whereas in the script it wasn't supposed to come until about the 30th minute—as part of the section on illegal immigration.

Since Juan is originally an illegal immigrant in the film, it made perfect sense for us to meet him in the illegal immigration section. However, a director has to follow the most logical progression for the sake of the film as a whole. The film was calling out for us to meet the gardener Coleman referred to.

And You Must Listen to Your Film

Sure it would have fit if we met Juan 11 minutes later in the illegal immigration section, but it might also have gotten buried there—in a section that is already filled with other characters. Additionally, we might not have been able to expect the audience to make the connection between the gardener that Coleman alluded to earlier in the film and the person we were meeting at that moment.

This was one of those epiphany moments that you hear about in the edit when Charlie and I almost couldn't believe that the scene wasn't always where it is now. Again, we listened to what the film was telling us, and we weren't too afraid to risk necessary script departure.

CHARACTER INTRODUCTION—SCENE 29

Scene 28 of *A Convenient Truth* has Coleman asking his gardener, Juan "Pepe" Blanco (Guy Wellman), to become a worker at Burleson Laboratories. Juan ends the scene with a decidedly confused non-answer to Coleman's question. Naturally, Coleman enthusiastically takes Juan's silence as a tacit acceptance. So, scene 29 follows with Juan's real character introduction.

This is one of those moments that we wanted to make big. After all, in this movie about recruiting Mexican-Americans to ride bicycles that generate electricity, we're meeting the first one to ever sign on. The audience needs to take notice. There are a ton of ways to go with this, and the most obvious would be to set up fish-out-of-water interactions for Juan at the lab. However, I thought it would be more interesting to consistently question why every scene would be in the film. That is, if Coleman were going to make a film about his proposal, would he include any explicitly negative aspects of it?

Instead, I decided to frame our introduction to Juan as a piece of propaganda for Coleman's proposal. The comedy comes from the contradiction of what we are seeing and the way in which it's being presented. Easily said, but how do we do that?

Tools for Visual Character Introduction

Going with the propaganda idea, I quickly knew that we wanted to go over-the-top with this character introduction. I decided to write one of the most mundane situations that I could think of (a guy getting ready for work) and present it in the most spectacular way possible. The tools we used to accomplish this are:

- MONTAGE—Few things stand out as much as a montage—especially in a mockumentary film. Most of the first 28 scenes have been visually rough, guerrilla-style, and feel on-the-fly. So let's stick a fully-orchestrated slick montage in the middle of that. You can be sure the audience will take notice.
- SLOW MOTION—Another tool that should be used sparingly and is used poorly 80 percent of the time is slow motion. One thing slow motion can do, however, is make something instantly cheesy, which is fine if it's purposeful. We shot the entire sequence at 60 frames-per-second, so that we could play it back at roughly

Juan "Pepe" Blanco (Guy Wellman) prepares for work at Burleson Laboratories.

30 frames-per-second and get a slow-motion effect. We also pushed that in editing, but it's still good to capture more frames than usual while filming a scene that will be in slow motion to ensure that you have the information you need.
- MUSIC—Putting a happy, polished pop song behind visuals that are telling another story is not something that I invented, but that doesn't mean I can't use it.
- LIGHTING—In order to further distinguish this character introduction from the other scenes in the film (and each shot from the others within the montage), we used several stylized lighting setups to make each shot special.
- COMPOSITION—Similar to what we accomplished with varied lighting, we made sure to change the composition of the frames from shot to shot to build variation into the sequence.
- INTERJECTION—Another common tool for character introduction is to put the character in a specific situation and have him add a small comment that immediately tells the audience who that character is. In this case, in the middle of the sleek montage, we allow Juan a "record-screech" type moment where the music stops as he's putting on a helmet. He mentions that he doesn't need the helmet for the work. "The bike no … move," he states plainly, and we instantly know what he thinks about what we're seeing.
- CONTEXT—As with other character introductions throughout the film, the context that we meet them in gives us a great deal of information. Naturally, we staged Juan's "suiting up" montage in a garden shed. He dresses amongst the tools and random debris of a shed—again contradictory to the triumphant presentation of the scene. Interestingly, an actual shed would have been far too small to shoot in, so we dressed a small production shed on the premises of the sound-

Juan "Pepe" Blanco (Guy Wellman) emerges from the shed, ready for work.

stage to look the part. We then captured a single shot of Juan emerging from an actual shed to tie it all together. The final shot of our character introduction is in slow motion, set to a pop song, in the golden light of the fading sun, and includes a snap zoom that pushes in on Juan's face. People remember this character introduction.

DIRECT FIRST, PRODUCE SECOND—SCENE 30

The nature of independent film is that everyone is wearing multiple hats—doing jobs they have no business doing. The kid who was driving the van and running apple boxes on day one is pulling focus by the end of the shoot. This is also true at the highest level, with hyphenates (writer-director-producer-editor-composer-babysitter-etc.) becoming the norm. The most dangerous of these is the director-producer. Even when not formally taking a producing credit, an indie director is going to be confronted with producer-ly worries on a daily basis. With larger budgets, the producers can protect the director from the minutia of budget concerns, but that just won't be possible on an indie. With that as a given, it is paramount to remember to direct first and produce second.

The still from scene 30 of *A Convenient Truth* in this section is a reminder of a time on set when I almost let the worries of a producer overtake the duties of a director. As I mentioned in "Mini-Lesson: Repeat Framing" in the section about scene 22, there are several scenes in the film that are "Leonard's Disclaimers." The framing is identical for

Leonard Wingmon (Kevin Hauver) issues another disclaimer to set the record straight.

comedic purposes. Naturally, these scenes were shot in direct succession. Once the camera was set, it couldn't be moved without destroying the effect.

We had a tight shooting schedule that day (as will be true on every day of an indie shoot), and we were banking on grabbing these scenes quickly—since there was no need for coverage. It was grab it and go—or it should have been.

We shot all three scenes straight through and got a great performance from Leonard (Kevin Hauver). That should have been the end of the story, especially with time ticking away. But I wasn't totally in love with the framing that I had initially chosen. It was too tight and didn't give the audience the context that they would need to instantly recognize the frame as Leonard's office. It was essentially a medium close-up, which didn't give much more visual information than Leonard's face. We could have been simply seeing Leonard again, rather than knowing that we were seeing Leonard in the same exact space in the same exact way again.

The easiest thing to do—the thing that would make a producer happy—would be to acknowledge that the scenes that we needed were in the can and consider them "good enough."

Directing is not about things being "good enough."

As soon as I realized/admitted that I wasn't happy with the framing, we reset and shot all three scenes over again. Was this terrible for our schedule? Yes. Was it asking a lot of an actor to deliver another great performance when he had just done his job perfectly? Yes. Was it the wrong decision to set us back and redo scenes that we'd already shot? No.

A director can't take all of the credit for a film, but he will take all of the blame—as it should be. If I wasn't confident standing behind a decision within the film, then it was on me to correct it. And I couldn't let the producer side of me forget that.

After we reset and re-shot the scenes, it was clear that the new frame was much better than the original. Sure, we were a little behind schedule for the day, but there would be opportunities to make up that time. The goal should always be to "make your day," but it needs to be to make a good movie first. In the end, no one is going to be angry that you're holding things up if you're making the movie better.

Again, the writer-director-producer hyphenate can often be under pressure to be a good boy or to please people but never at the expense of being a good director.

INSERTS AND REACTION SHOTS—SCENE 31

Make a shot list. Even if you're not going to follow it, make it. That shot list will obviously include all of the coverage for the scenes that you're going to shoot that day, but it should also include inserts and reaction shots. These are usually way down at the end of the list and are the first to go when you realize that your shot list was ridiculously ambitious. You have twice as many setups as you should? Well let's scratch out the insert shots, since they're not integral to the telling of the story. Except…

Coleman Burleson (Alan Berman) describes the effect that his proposal can have on energy use.

Inserts are integral to your ability to edit.

Similar to when I talked about departing from the script by integrating short clips into the tennis sequence, insert shots free you up to cut when you want on a scene level. You might need to hide a flub or just need a good way to transition the focus to something else, and sometimes insert shots are exactly the way to do it.

Ever watched a film and wondered why there was that random cut to the clock? Or why we needed a close-up of feet shuffling under the table while our conversation continues above? Sometimes these are creative choices (though usually much better shots than the examples I just mentioned). Often, however, they're tools for getting around the edit. When done well, inserts are meaningful—or at least benign—ways to smoothly continue the scene. At the very least, they should be less jarring than whatever other option you might cut to.

Cutting scene 31 of *A Convenient Truth* was heavily reliant on reaction shots of the audience. Sure, we had adequate coverage of Coleman continuing his speech—a wide, medium, and close-up of the entire scene—but too much cutting around in this scene would have been unnecessary and drawn attention to itself.

Additionally, it turned out that I liked the performance in one particular take a lot. But that can be its own problem.

You don't want to go too long without a cut. (Actually sometimes you do, but long takes are a separate discussion.) You also can't cut from one shot to itself. (Actually you can, but jump cutting is discussed in another section.)

Reaction shots of the crowd were the solution. Adam Orellana, our great DP, would turn the camera and float around the audience of extras in between takes—grabbing everything that he could. We were then able to strategically place these shots wherever we wanted for pacing and performance. This meant that we could cut wherever we wanted. It also meant that we could use different parts of the same take that we liked easily.

To clarify, imagine you have a wide shot with ten perfect seconds. Then you have a pause that you don't like. Or you have a line that you don't think is necessary. Directly after that comes the ending to the scene that you know you want to use. As long as you have inserts or reaction shots that you can viably cut to, you have no problem. If you had neglected to get those shots, however, you would have to include that pause or unnecessary line. Or, you'd be forced to cut to some other angle with a performance that you like less before you can get back to the ending that you want to use.

So, make sure that you have a handful of inserts and reaction shots on your list when you arrive on set. Then, based on your location, set decoration, and props, add a few more inserts to the list. Then chat with your DP, and add a couple more. And actually shoot them.

You will never curse yourself for having too many inserts.

Failing to get a good number of inserts, however, will create one of those moments when your editor (justifiably) hates you. You'll know in that moment that you have no business directing a film. You'll question why you subjected yourself to the terrible process of making a film in the first place. And after you're done rocking back and forth in the fetal position, you're still going to have to figure out how to edit that damn scene.

So just shoot the insert shots.

Free and Easy Pre-Visualization—Scene 32

It's no secret that my favorite film of all time is *Willy Wonka and the Chocolate Factory* (1971). What does that film have to do with my film, *A Convenient Truth*? Almost nothing. Except that no film is made in a vacuum. As filmmakers today, we have the advantage of decades of film references to help shape and share our vision of a scene. We also have pre-visualization tools that can similarly make what you see in your head more clear as you plan and discuss with your team in pre-production.

When I realized that I'd written a scene that involved pushing through great doors to reveal a location that we've only heard alluded to in a film, I immediately thought of the scene in which golden ticket winners in *Willy Wonka and the Chocolate Factory* enter the Chocolate Room for the first time.

The Burleson Laboratories Cycling Room was my Chocolate Room. Granted, Coleman doesn't burst out into "Pure Imagination," but there is a lot to be learned from this reference scene. The two items that I took away were:

1. Pacing—The scene takes its time with each shot, building up the suspense and anticipation for what we're about to see. It also lingers once we do get to see the Chocolate Room. We get to spend time marveling at the visuals, and we appreciate it.

2. Reactions—I also learned not to underestimate the importance of the characters' reaction shots within the sequence. Sure, the images offer a great spectacle on their own, but part of the magic comes from watching the characters experience

Coleman Burleson (Alan Berman) gets ready to take the film crew into his Cycling Room.

the room. (Side Note: *Willy Wonka* director Mel Stuart kept all of the actors away from this set until they were filming because he wanted to capture their pure reactions on the first take.) In my sequence therefore, I was not going to forget to show characters reacting to what they/we were seeing—a moment which gets a laugh every time.

Once I had a reference in place, the next step became a pre-visualization of the shots. This isn't necessary for every scene, but it is a great thing to do for more complicated set pieces.

In our case, this was complicated because we had to build the doors to the Cycling Room and place them into an office building that served as the rest of Burleson Laboratories. Then, we had to place a blue screen behind the doors because the actual Cycling Room was miles and miles away on a soundstage in Philadelphia. We would have to composite these two distinct locations in post-production to make them feel like one continuous space. Further, the shot that we were compositing (the one in the Cycling Room) contained a green screen within itself.

If you can draw, then old-fashioned storyboards will do the job. If you can't but you're great at animation programs, you can use those to build your worlds and share them with others in preparation for the shoot. Unfortunately, I can't do either of those things. If you can't either, a great pre-visualization solution is:

Google Sketchup

I first came across this free program as a very simplified architecture tool for people who didn't have or know how to use AutoCAD for design, but I quickly found that it can also be used as a very simplified pre-visualization tool for people who don't have or know Maya.

Sketchup can be particularly helpful if you've already done your location scouting

Free and Easy Pre-Visualization—Scene 32 65

and you know what physical space you'll be shooting in. If you take down the dimensions of the space, Sketchup will allow you to re-create that room in the computer with simple drawing that anyone can learn in an afternoon. You can also draw from a huge database of models to place within your space, which is helpful in order to place actors in the space and get a sense of scale. Once you have the space created, you can place a camera within it, move around, and get a real idea of what you'll be dealing with. You might even save some time blocking the scene.

I used Google Sketchup to create the imaginary space of the lab in order to play around with shots.

You can get a sense of the final results from eight shots that I've selected to show from the actual entrance into the Cycling Room.

Eight shots from the sequence of entrance to the Cycling Room.

Finally, I can't move on from discussing this scene without one more lesson that I learned:

Keep shooting until you get it.

You're reading that slate correctly. This is take 18 of this shot. One reason why planning and pre-visualization is so important is because it allows you to be sure of what you absolutely need to get to make the scene work. Since I knew that this walking push through the doors was the way we wanted to open the scene, we did as many takes as were necessary until we got what we needed. Consequently, we did not use any time getting additional coverage of this part of the scene—we didn't need to because we were sure of what we wanted.

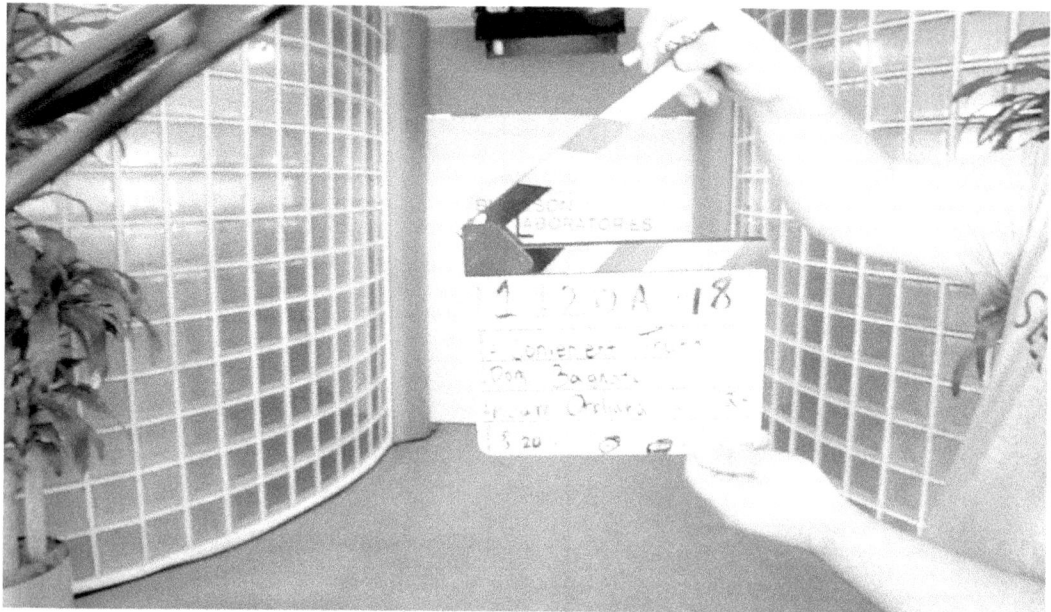

The 18th take is a charm. On location at Tek Park Campus in Allentown, Pennsylvania.

Indie films don't have time to do 18 takes of anything, but imagine how much further behind we would have been that day if we hadn't done all of the pre-visualization prep.

Pre-Laps and L-Cuts—Scene 33

Scene 33 of *A Convenient Truth* cuts back to our interview with Kitty Burleson (Elise Rovinsky)—our introduction to her having come in scene 6. In order to ease the transition from our frenetic moments in the Cycling Room at Burleson Laboratories, we use a pre-lap to get into this scene.

A pre-lap is a device where the audio from the next scene creeps in and over the

Top: Kitty Burleson (Elise Rovinsky) reminisces about her husband's early relationship with energy generation. *Bottom:* A scene in the Burleson Laboratories Cycling Room as Kitty Burleson's audio comes in.

visuals from the outgoing scene. In the case of scene 33, audio from Kitty's interview begins playing while we are still in the Cycling Room.

This pre-lap was not planned at the script stage. In fact, Kitty's interview came directly before the reveal of the Cycling Room in the screenplay, but this is the type of thing that gets changed in editing all the time. When dealing with the actual footage, we knew we couldn't have Coleman lead us up to the doors of the Cycling Room and then cut to Kitty giving an interview. It's not what the audience wants to see at that point. So, we made the change to the order. The problem that was then created by this re-ordering was solved through the use of the pre-lap.

In general, the starting point for most edits is that we want them to be invisible. We don't want the audience to think about or even notice a cut. That said, there are times when you might want to draw attention to an abrupt change. Or, you might find yourself unable to find the cut that you want within your coverage. In this case, it might be worth acknowledging that you don't have it, reversing course, and pushing the edit in the exact opposite direction. From scene-to-scene, the pre-lap is a way to do this. Within a scene itself, you can similarly consider using:

L-Cuts

In scene 33, there were some shining moments of acting by Elise Rovinsky in several different takes. Since this was not an actual documentary (and due to the low budget), we weren't shooting with multiple cameras simultaneously. This meant that cutting together moments from different bits of coverage would have to be done in the more traditional, single camera style. That is, we didn't have the same exact moment in time from multiple angles. (Shooting with multiple cameras is a relatively recent development in film—even though many people assume it's all done that way.)

So, the L-Cut is one stylistic choice that can free a director up to use the best takes for performance—without being a slave to continuity in the editing. This is precisely what we did for Kitty in this scene. There is a wide moment in which Kitty is speaking. This ends in a silent beat. We then begin the audio from her next thought while still on the wide shot before cutting to a close-up. This will not always be a viable option—depending on the style of your film—but we made it work.

The traditional approach would have been to cut on Kitty's movement and to match her action from the wide shot to the close-up. However, the action on the two takes that we wanted to use did not match perfectly. This is a classic decision without an objectively "right" answer, which directors and editors make all the time. Do you use the take that you like slightly less to preserve perfect continuity? Or do you use a device like an L-Cut (or sometimes even a dissolve) to do the opposite? In our case, we used the L-Cut to actually draw attention to the edit in order to use the preferred takes.

Sometimes when you've painted yourself into a corner in the edit, it's best to step back, push in the polar opposite direction of what you've been tearing your hair out to accomplish, and embrace the solution that you find.

Picking Your Shot (and Why Windmills Are Unpatriotic)—Scene 34

"C'mon, boys, let's show the world that Mexicans can be more reliable than the wind!"—Coleman Burleson

Picking Your Shot (and Why Windmills Are Unpatriotic)—Scene 34

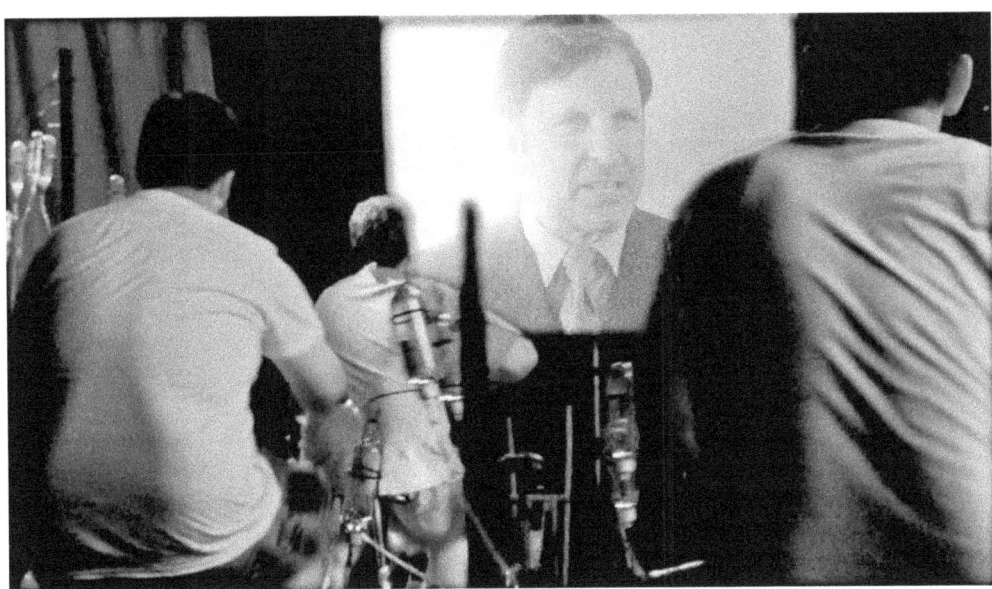

Coleman Burleson (Alan Berman) addresses his riders from the big screen in the Cycling Room.

Scene 34 of *A Convenient Truth* is a single shot, in which Coleman Burleson (Alan Berman) shouts the above at the cyclists in his Cycling Room. On the one hand, a scene doesn't get simpler than being comprised of a single shot. On the other hand, filmmakers will tell you that working without the safety net of coverage makes these types of scenes difficult. If your scene is only going to be one shot, you better pick that shot correctly. And with literally infinite possible shots to choose from, that is easier said than done.

First, why is this scene only one shot? Well, in this case, the entire scene is only one line of dialogue—a total of six seconds. Having even one cut over this duration would seem unnecessary at best, distracting at worst.

Second, how do we begin to frame our shot? Though six seconds is a very short scene, it's actually not an extremely short shot. If we were to pick a boring frame for even six seconds, the audience would feel it. So, we decided to avoid a static frame, and our shot actually tracks left for the duration of the scene. (Side Note: It's important to remember to make sure the dolly is already moving smoothly before you call action in order to be sure you can use the entire shot.) The result is a dynamic shot that gives us a feel for the space and has an energy to it.

That said, this is a small indie film, so it's also important for the shot to be realistically accomplishable. Look at the frame at the start of the section again. What's actually in it? By filling the foreground of the frame with a few extras, we can make the scene feel larger than it actually is. If we were wider, we'd need more extras and to dress more of the set. If were closer, we wouldn't get a sense of context. The central focus of the shot, which is usually the brightest thing in the frame, is a projection screen that we covered in green material. We then filmed Coleman's head separately and composited him onto the screen in post-production.

Finally, the shot is at a subtle low-angle to reflect the subordinate relationship that the listening cyclists have with Coleman. There are technical and story reasons to motivate every camera setup, so you should always know why you've picked your shot.

Why Windmills Are Unpatriotic

The quote above is Coleman Burleson directly comparing his Cycling Room's reliability to that of wind farms, which are competing energy sources. It's unfortunate that the film is already complete. Otherwise, you can be sure that we would have also included a line or two about the fact that wind turbines are actually guilty of murdering eagles in California (that's right: Wind farms actually murder the symbol of American freedom ["No. California Wind Farm Won't Be Prosecuted for Eagle Deaths"]).

Coleman Burleson would eat this news up. Not because he hates eagles, but because it is perfect political ammunition for stirring up support for Burleson Labs.

FOUR CONSIDERATIONS FOR A JOKE IN YOUR FILM—SCENE 35

So you want to write a comedy. Simple, right? You think up a bunch of jokes, string 'em together, and you're good to go. In some ways this is not as wrong as it sounds (comedy does need jokes, after all), but you often hear writers and directors talking about "killing their darlings" or having to cut the funniest part of their comedy. Why would you cut something that makes your comedy funnier? Because jokes have to serve the story. Movies are a combination of moments, but each of those moments needs to progress an overall narrative.

Scene 35 of *A Convenient Truth* was refined like so:

Four Considerations for a Joke in Your Film

1. Is the joke appropriate for your film's genre and form?

As I've mentioned, *A Convenient Truth* is a satire—not a farce. This distinction greatly changes the types of jokes that will work for the purposes of the film. (More on this in #2.) Similarly, our film is a mockumentary, which is formally like a documentary. Because of this, we were able to use the loose style of the documentary to insert jokes at the script stage where they served the overall structure. The first draft of the screenplay was written so tightly that it was actually short. The form enabled me to write jokes into subsequent drafts and have a lot of flexibility for their placement within the film. Scene 35 is an example of one mechanism that I used to do this: question and answer sessions with Coleman (Alan Berman) and his audience members throughout the film.

2. Is the joke consistent with your character?

Scene 35's question and answer session has an audience member directly ask Coleman about the apparently racist nature of his program at Burleson Laboratories. The original joke in the script was Coleman's over-the-top, racist response to this question. However—though it was funny—it was inconsistent with his character to be racist. (Again, it would be a farcical film if we watched a deplorable character doing crazy things

Coleman Burleson (Alan Berman) answers a post-lecture question.

the whole time.) The current version of scene 35 makes sense for our satirical film because the comedy comes from Coleman's earnest cluelessness—which fits his character perfectly. An oblivious politician is much richer fodder for satire than a crazy racist.

3. Does the joke fit the tone of your film?

This question is similar to #2 but includes non-character moments. You should have a sense of where your comedy lands on various comedic spectrums. You don't need to be clinical about this, but do take a step back from time to time to think about what you're trying to accomplish. Is your comedy broad, dry, niche, etc.? Does that bit of hilarious slapstick really suit the rest of the movie?

4. Does the joke help the flow of the story?

The number one reason that filmmakers cut jokes is because they work against the flow of the overall story. A joke can be hilarious and simultaneously negatively affect everything that comes after it. Or, it might come later than it needs to—when the audience is past such a joke. Often test audiences are the best way to determine whether a joke is serving the flow or not. The post-film questionnaires from test audiences were helpful. Sitting in the back of the room during the screenings and noting when people squirmed a bit in their seats was even more revealing.

LOCATIONS: JUST ASK, AND WHEN TO BEND YOUR OWN RULES—SCENE 36

In scene 36 of *A Convenient Truth*, Coleman Burleson (Alan Berman) tells us about the impressive amount of energy that has been generated at his lab so far. The entire scene is only 3/8 of a page and takes just 35 seconds, but every scene needs a location. We decided we wanted to grab this scene in one shot, but we didn't have any firm plans for it yet.

Then, while shooting a couple of other scenes in New York City, we were moving from one location to another on foot. We passed a small bodega and had a little wiggle room in our schedule. Since it was close enough to lunchtime, we walked in and told the clerk that we'd gladly buy lunch for the crew at his establishment if he'd let us get our shot inside. He was happy to agree. (And this was New York City. You'll find that people are even more eager to help out a film crew in other parts of the country.) So, though

Coleman Burleson (Alan Berman) does his best to avoid being "sensationalist."

getting some locations can be arduous, it doesn't have to be. My advice is to just ask. People will often say yes. If you can find a way to patronize their establishment in some way, even better. (Of course, the caveat would be to make sure that the person who agrees to let you shoot actually has the authority to do so.)

We quickly set up and grabbed the shot. Similar to scene 34, we wanted to make sure our single-shot scene was dynamic in some way. However, in order to do this, we had to be willing to:

Bend our own rules.

Stepping back, I should explain that the "rule" we had established with the form of the mockumentary was that interviews were playing out in real-time. This means that the camera should always be reacting to what it is capturing. The cameraperson could never have pre-knowledge of what was about to occur.

We break this rule in scene 36. Why? Because film is an art, not a science, and it felt right.

The scene begins will Coleman saying:

> "In the six months since its local implementation, we—that's our Cycling Room—have generated over 252 million watt-hours. That's 252 million watt-hours."

He then takes a dramatic pause before continuing:

> "I don't think I'm being sensationalist when I say that to ignore these numbers is to accept apocalypse."

Given our established rule, there is no way that the cameraperson would know what Coleman was about to say. However, the camera begins to slightly push in before he says this last line. The effect of the slow push greatly adds to the irony that exists between the

Coleman Burleson (Alan Berman) fails at avoiding being "sensationalist."

content and delivery of the line. Is it a slight cheat? Yes. Is it worth it to land on Coleman's distressed face in this frame?

Yes.

Mini-Lesson: Dressing for Character

It's a small detail, but some people will notice the giant stack of napkins sitting on Coleman's table in the widest version of the frame. Especially since he's only having a bottle of water, this is beyond wasteful and definitely not environmentally friendly. Filmmakers should take every chance to add things to the frame that teach the audience about their characters. In this case, the napkins visually reiterate Coleman's clueless enthusiasm, and it's a small thing for people to notice on second viewings.

FRAMING AND VISUAL MATCH TRANSITIONS—SCENES 37 AND 38

Scene 37 of *A Convenient Truth* is another interview with Leonard Wingmon (Kevin Hauver) in his office. Leonard introduces us to his hamster, Zippy, who inspired the "productivity solution" for the bikes in Burleson's Cycling Room. Since we've already seen Leonard's office in scene 11 and two of Leonard's "disclaimer" scenes (scene 22 and scene 30), we wanted to give the audience something fresh to look at for scene 37. We set up the camera on the opposite side of the room, looked in a direction we'd never seen before, and found some creative framing.

Leonard Wingmon (Kevin Hauver) shows how his pet hamster inspired the bike hydration system in the Cycling Room.

The scene begins with Leonard sitting at a table in his office (absently playing checkers versus himself). As Leonard begins to tell us about Zippy, he moves over to Zippy's tank, which sits atop Leonard's desk. Rather than use several cuts to cover this movement, the camera moves with Leonard. During the blocking of the scene, we realized we could shoot through the glass tank to create the frame-within-a-frame that you see first in this section. The tank both frames Leonard's face and adds depth to the overall frame. The result is an interesting shot with some comedy coming from the unusual nature of its framing.

Similarly, we wanted to find a way to visually represent this "productivity solution." In the script it looks like this:

> LEONARD (CONT'D)
> Then one day I looked to Zippy.
>
> There is a glint of love in his eye for the creature. Maybe even a little admiration mixed in.
>
> LEONARD (CONT'D)
> Thanks to my furry little friend,
> each rider now has a productivity
> solution built into his bike.
> You know, it's a new system. Everything grows,
> and we're learning together. It's a wonderful thing.
>
> CU as Zippy takes a drink from his water dispenser.
>
> MATCH CUT TO:
>
> INT. BURLESON LABS—DAY
> A tube protrudes up from a bike's handlebars, then bends a few inches from each rider's face.

Framing and Visual Match Transitions—Scenes 37 and 38

Leonard's hamster, Zippy, sips water from his cage's dispenser.

As you see in this excerpt, it's important to consider transitions—the movement from one scene to the next—at the script stage. You can achieve a nice effect if you open on a vast landscape if the preceding scene ended on a claustrophobic close-up, for example. In this case, we employed a:

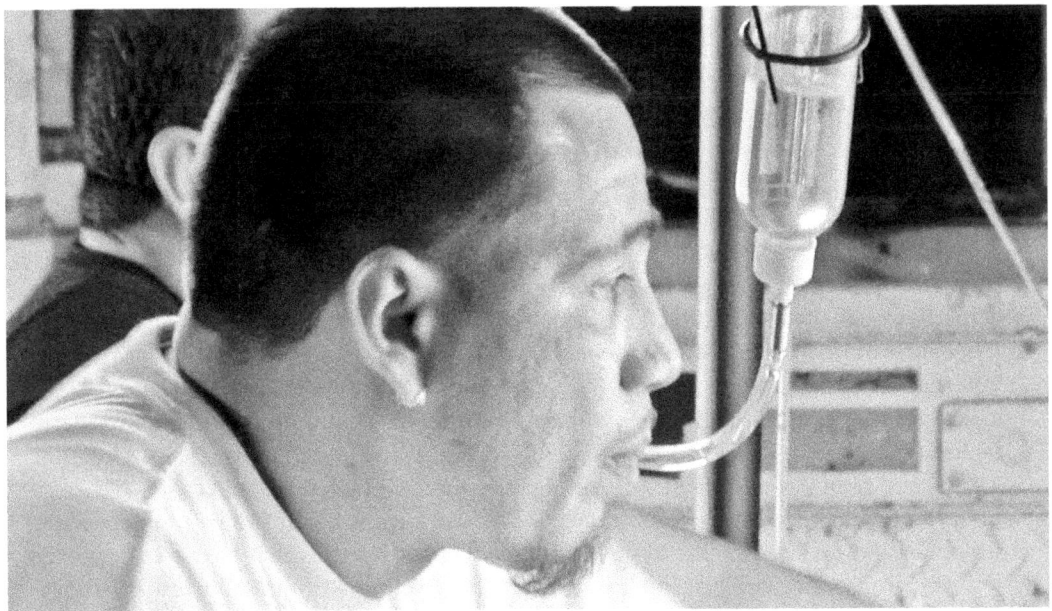

A Burleson Laboratories cyclist (Marcus Rodriguez) sips water from his bike's dispenser.

Match cut images side-by-side.

Visual match transition.
A visual match transition is exactly what it sounds like. The final frame of the outgoing scene closely resembles the first frame of the new scene. Probably the most famous example of a visual match comes from Stanley Kubrick's *2001: A Space Odyssey* (1968) when a bone flying through the air in one scene cuts directly to a spaceship that resembles it in shape.

Scene 37 ends with a close-up of Zippy drinking from the water dispenser in his hamster tank.

Scene 38 begins with a close-up profile shot of a cyclist in Burleson Labs drinking from a water dispensing apparatus built directly into his stationary bicycle. In fact, the dispensers that we used for the art direction of the bikes are actual hamster bottles.

Rather than have Leonard verbally describe the "productivity solution," we're able to visually show the audience what he is referring to. It's a much better way to get the information across, to push forward into the next scene, and—most importantly—it's funnier.

CONFLICT IN COMEDY—SCENE 39

It's widely accepted that conflict is the element inherent in all drama. It should be. It's true. What should be equally accepted is that comedy is simply drama that is funny. That is, conflict is just as necessary in comedy as it is in drama. To the characters in a comedy, the story (and conflicts) are real. As soon as conflict is removed from any scene, it becomes uninteresting—and it then fails to be either dramatic or funny. It's also important that the circumstances themselves are not funny to the characters and that the characters are not trying to be funny. (Is there anything less funny than someone trying to be funny?)

Scene 39 of *A Convenient Truth* is a continuation of what we called the "red chair interview," which we first saw in scene 26. The still here is taken from a moment when Coleman and Leonard bicker about the percentage of bicycles that have been updated with new ergonomically designed seats in the Cycling Room at Burleson Laboratories.

Leonard Wingmon (Kevin Hauver) and Coleman Burleson (Alan Berman) argue over a small detail.

> COLEMAN
> ...we're still completing the transition,
> but uh ... 65% of the bikes–
>
> LEONARD
> 45–50.
>
> COLEMAN
> No, it's like 60–65.
>
> LEONARD
> 60–65.

    I've taken the time to type this out precisely because it doesn't read funny at all, but this character interaction gets a chuckle every time we screen the film. To be honest, I can't remember if I wrote this exact exchange or if the actors went with it, but it doesn't matter. It seems real. The conflict between the two characters adds a brief tension to the scene that makes the audience laugh. It adds nothing overt to the story, but it does make us feel that the story is that much more real. Witnessing a small quibble—the type of conflict that occurs every day between people who spend a lot of time together—makes the characters feel fully realized.

    Another thing worth noting is that the conflict is resolved in a way that is consistent with the characters involved. Leonard is Coleman's friend and essentially a fan boy. When Leonard quickly acquiesces, the audience immediately recognizes that all of Leonard and Coleman's disagreements probably end this way. Even though Leonard is more likely to have the accurate figure about the bike seats, Coleman will always have the last word.

    This is literally the smallest version of conflict that I can think of, but it shows how any amount of conflict adds to a scene—in both drama and comedy.

STRUCTURE IN YOUR FILM—SCENE 40

It's impossible to quickly sum up what a good director does, but somewhere along the way, I picked up the idea that a good director makes you feel like you're in good hands. As an audience, we want to feel like the person taking us on this ride knows what he or she is doing. Sometimes this is done with a stunning visual sequence like the opening to *There Will Be Blood* (2007). Other times, it's a clear, singular voice immediately shining through—like in any Tarantino film. It can be an instant sense of character—like when we meet our protagonist in the bar in *The Social Network* (2010) or through the voiceover in *American Beauty* (1999). It's the sense that we get when we watch the camera float though the kitchen of the Copacabana in *Goodfellas* (1990), even if we haven't consciously registered it as a long Steadicam take. Another (much less sexy) way to let your audience know they're in good hands is through well-considered structure.

Given that *A Convenient Truth* is a mockumentary, I couldn't push the visual style too far without breaking the illusion. I also couldn't rely on traditional character arcs in the way I normally would because I wrote the screenplay with an odd structure. Rather than the traditional three acts, this film has the following structure:

1. Build/tantalize the audience about a proposal
2. Reveal that proposal
3. Show the aftermath and results of the proposal

And then what...

Going back to Jonathan Swift's "A Modest Proposal," I latched onto his structural device of what he calls "collateral advantages." This means he (and I) can introduce the

Coleman Burleson (Alan Berman) takes his proposal even further.

Animated title card to introduce the illegal immigration section of the film.

main benefits of the proposal and then bring up other secondary, or "collateral," benefits that will also follow.

Scene 40 is the point in the film where Coleman (Alan Berman) lets the audience know that there are collateral advantages to his proposal:

> "This proposal would not be nearly as exciting as it is if energy generation were the only positive that came from my plan. There are what I call other collateral advantages. Now, perhaps, there are hundreds of these which I could detail cursorily, but I've chosen to focus on five in depth."

With those three sentences, Coleman has let the audience know what the structure of the rest of the film will be. We're going to see five more situations that are improved by this proposal, and then we get to go home. Armed with this knowledge, the audience can sit back and wait for what's coming. Note, they have no idea what the content of the collateral advantages will be, so they still have the benefit of enjoying the surprises, but they know that someone knows where things are going, and that comfort is important.

It was even important to me to visually support this notion of complete structure with the title card that announces the collateral advantages. Rather than having a single slide for each segment, we added each collateral advantage title to the same card. The result was a cumulative feel. For each new collateral advantage, the audience gets a brief reminder of where we've been. They also see that only five collateral advantages will fit on the title card, which reiterates that there is an end in sight. Think of it as a way of letting the audience check their progress by eyeing how many pages are left in their book.

Immediately added to the structure is:

- Collateral Advantage I
- Collateral Advantage II

- Collateral Advantage III
- Collateral Advantage IV
- Collateral Advantage V
- Conclusion

This isn't a formula; it's structure. It doesn't make the film stale for the audience to know that it exists. This structure still allows me to take the audience wherever I want—because the collateral advantages could be anything—but it also gives the audience something that they can hold on to.

I've created some rules, shared them with the audience, and made an implicit promise to uphold them. I'm not going to randomly flash forward to the distant future, and I'm not taking them on a meandering ride that lasts four hours and includes Coleman's comprehensive list of 342 collateral advantages.

Evergreen Satire—Scene 41

Scene 41 of *A Convenient Truth* is our introduction to the first characters in the illegal immigration section of the film. The two characters, minutemen in Yuma, Arizona, give us one perspective on illegal immigration—one that is certainly representative of a large percentage of the American public. Though the first version of this scene was probably written back in 2007, the beauty of satire is that the issue is even more in the news today. A quick search pulls up a new article for every day of the week.

Minutemen (Scott Boyko and Bill McLaughlin) give their opinions about illegal immigration.

> # I WANT YOU
> ## as a
> ## MINUTEMAN VOLUNTEER
> ## to SECURE the US BORDER
>
> *"The United States shall guarantee to every State in this Union a Republican Form of Government, and shall protect each of them against Invastion."*
>
> —U.S. Constitution Article 4 Section 4

Frame from a tilt down on a minutemen poster insert shot.

Here again, I'll point out the distinction between farce or spoof and satire. So many of the current spoof films that come out rely on the audience's recognition of some other current event or allusion to pop culture. The audiences laugh more because they're "in" on the joke than because what they're seeing is actually funny. The underpinnings of good satire are stronger than that. If done well, the perspective of the minutemen in this scene should be interesting and satirical for a long time. In theory, this scene should be evergreen—or at least relevant until immigration is no longer an issue in America. (I'll take my chances.)

Mini-Lesson: Remember Your Friends

The minutemen play off of each other really well in their scenes. They seem like they're old friends. In reality, they met for the first and only time on the day that we filmed their scenes. Artie Tagis (Bill McLaughlin) is a seasoned actor who we auditioned and loved for one of the roles. We had more trouble finding someone for the other minuteman, Jimmy Reader, though. We cut it so close that I was considering rewriting the scene so that it was an interview with only one minuteman. Then, I remembered my friend Scott Boyko. Scott had been making short videos with me since middle school, and he has always had a great presence in front of the camera. I think I called him with one day's notice, and he showed up the next day ready to shoot.

You definitely don't want to be the guy who makes an indie film with all of his friends in it. If you do, it will only be appreciated by those same friends. Trust me. Looking back at the videos that I made it middle school and high school (which we thought were gold at the time), I realize that they are pure crap—and mostly incomprehensible. Take a look back at your own stuff, if you dare. You made crap, too.

At the same time, don't let your pride or arrogance about how things are "supposed

Minutemen (Scott Boyko and Bill McLaughlin) improvise.

to be done" get in the way of shooting your film. Scott is an actor who could pull off what I needed. Did it matter that he didn't go through the casting process that the other actors did? No. Did it matter that he didn't know anything about the film until the day before shooting? No.

I almost rewrote the scene for one actor, ignored my gut, and constructed a worse scene out of fear that it might be unprofessional to cast a friend.

I'm glad I didn't.

As you'll see in a few upcoming scenes, the funniest minutemen scenes are the ones after this introduction scene—which Bill and Scott largely improvised.

STATIC VS. NON-STATIC FRAMES—SCENE 42

Scene 42 of *A Convenient Truth* introduces us to the would-be California Border Police Initiative. This scene comes right after we meet their rambunctious counterparts, the Minutemen. We filmed this scene at a local YMCA and wanted the feel of a community coming together for a meeting. At first, we set the camera back and had people file in, move around, etc., to capture a dynamic feel, but something just didn't feel right. After some deliberation, we realized that the problem was that the camera was set up on the tripod in the back of the room—static—lifeless.

If we wanted the shot to feel like a cameraman was capturing the beginning of a meeting, then we needed to avoid having the camera fully set up and waiting for things to unfold before him. We'd have to add a level of dynamism to the frame to help our

Static vs. Non-Static Frames—Scene 42

California Border Police Initiative members (Jeff Goldman and Ted Ford) sit center frame as people settle around them.

cause. Naturally, we took the camera off the sticks and went handheld. But then there was too much movement. (I know, I'm a pain in the ass.) Our great DP, Adam Orellana, had the solution:

Use a sneaker.

It sounds ridiculous, but apparently this is an accepted way to get that middle level of movement that I wanted. Adam took his sneaker off, sat it in on top of the tripod, and then laid the camera on top of that. The shoe allowed him to rock the camera back and forth a bit, but the tripod maintained most of the stability. The shot immediately worked the way we wanted it to.

Subsequent shots in the scene were the exact opposite. I wanted to convey in a not-so-subtle way that the ideas of these potential Border Patrol members were similar—too similar—almost interchangeable with one another. To do so, I used the exact same static frame for each of their interviews.

The result is that the only thing that changes visually is the person within the frame. One after the other, the three interviewees jump around within the frame, as if they are all part of the same interview—the same person—the opposite of individual thinking.

Just so you know I'm not making this stuff up on the spot, it was the plan at the script stage:

> INT. YMCA RECREATION AREA—LATER
> The camera stays put. In Polo Man #5's place is now Polo Man #4.

The Polo Men (as I called them in the script because they were all white men wearing polo shirts) were played excellently by Ted Ford, Jake Cassaday, Jeff Goldman, and John Herb, and each brought a unique interpretation to his character. Great actors like this

are another way in which I, as a director, get more out of the material than I, as a writer, gave myself to work with in the first place.

DIRECTING IS LISTENING— SCENES 43 AND 44

If acting is about reacting, then the equivalent behind the camera is that directing is listening. Scene 43 of *A Convenient Truth* is a particularly poignant one to remind me of this lesson—since a breakdown in listening, or a misunderstanding, makes up the entire scene.

In this scene, Coleman (Alan Berman) engages in another one of his man-on-the-street interviews. He begins by asking the interviewee what he thinks about the "anchor baby" situation, which is what some pundits have dubbed the act of an illegal immigrant giving birth to a child in America to ensure that child's American citizenship. (The idea is that the American citizenship of the child will later be used to attain rights for other family members.)

Anyway, the interviewee first thinks that Coleman has said "ankle" instead of "anchor," and the tone for the entire clip is set. Once the word "anchor" is understood,

Coleman Burleson (Alan Berman) conducts another man-on-the-street interview.

Opposite, top: California Border Patrol #2 (Jake Cassaday) talks about the initiative. *Middle:* California Border Patrol #4 (Jeff Goldman) continues the Border Patrol talk. *Bottom:* California Border Patrol #3 (John Herb) shows off the badge prototype that his wife made.

the interviewee says that he does know what Coleman means. He rambles for a bit, and it then becomes clear that he is talking about the "anchor person" on a TV newscast. By the time Coleman realizes this, he can only inject, "No. Anchor ... like on a ship."

And we're out of the scene.

This scene has almost no intellectual merit. The hot topic of anchor babies, which we so desperately wanted to address in the film, gets no actual attention. But ... it's pretty funny. Watching the scene play out made me laugh. And even though that isn't the only thing the director of a comedy has to worry about, it's an important thing to consider. You might ask, "Why can't you have both?" Again, the answer comes back to listening.

Editing a film is in some ways an impossible task. There are literally infinite ways to cut your film. To make your choices finite and workable, you have to listen to the footage in front of you.

This means letting go of what you want to accomplish with the scene or how you hoped the interviewee would respond and taking stock of what you're actually working with. In this instance, when Coleman says, "No. Anchor ... like on a ship," the scene shouts at us to cut away. I realize that saying the scene "shouts" at us is not the most helpful description to someone who might be in a similar editing conundrum, but I can only further explain that weak analogy with a tortured cliché—you'll know it when you see it (or, more likely, your editor will).

The simpler example of the importance of listening for a director comes in scene 44. I've covered the importance of casting actors who can make your material better before, so I won't "re-learn" that lesson here. I've also already described the man-on-the-street interview process, but I do want to point out how listening can help shape your movie's overall structure.

Scenes 43 and 44 here were both unscripted. This means that we had the freedom

Eleanor Burleson (Gilli Messer) tells us what she thinks about people sneaking across the border.

to place them anywhere in the film. It also meant we had the burden of finding a spot for them—which is not an easy thing to do since (if the writing was done well) the scripted scenes should all follow one another logically. Again, wading through all of the unscripted footage quickly became a listening task. Where was the footage telling us it could go? Where would it make sense to place this brief clip? Are themes emerging?

Scene 44 simply came from me asking Eleanor Burleson (Gilli Messer), "How do you feel about Mexicans sneaking across the border?" I won't spoil the answer that she improvised, but I promise that it is funny enough that we knew we needed to include it in the film. Finding a spot for either scene 43 or 44 alone would have been challenging—probably impossible—because either individual scene would have stood out too much from the scenes directly before and after it. However, being aware of all of our footage and smashing these two scenes together allowed us to add both quick scenes (as a neat little bundle) in a way that makes sense within the context and flow of the scenes around them.

JUMP CUT (FOR MY LOVE)—SCENE 45

Back in scene 31, I wrote about how inserts and reaction shots can save your life in the editing room. Since you can't cut from one shot to itself, you can cut inserts and reaction shots into your scene and then go back to the shot you want—when you want it. But what happens if you don't have those shots to weave in? Or what if cutting would just seem out of place? In a traditional narrative, you're pretty much out of luck. If the form will allow it, however, you can employ the jump cut.

Part one of jump cuts with minutemen (Scott Boyko and Bill McLaughlin).

Top: **Part two of jump cuts with minutemen (Scott Boyko and Bill McLaughlin).** *Bottom:* **Part three of jump cuts with minutemen (Scott Boyko and Bill McLaughlin).**

Scene 45 of *A Convenient Truth* is exactly one such situation. We were lucky enough to have a lot of great improv from the actors who portrayed our minutemen. However, this blessing became a curse when we had to find a way to fit it into our film.

That is, imagine you have really funny improv in three takes of the same shot. Let's call them shots A, B, and C. Without something to cut to in between, all you can do is choose which you like the best. You get to put shot A or shot B or shot C into your film. Bummer.

Imagine now that shot C is hilarious at the beginning and ends with the perfect one-liner. The problem is that shot C is 45 seconds long, and you don't want to use any of the stuff in the middle. Bummer #2.

Unfortunately, with the great minutemen footage that we had, I didn't have to imagine these scenarios. I was pulling my hair out trying to solve them. After all, *A Convenient Truth* is a comedy first, and I couldn't bear to cut a whole bunch of funny stuff out. My allegiance to traditional coverage prevented me from seeing a way around these issues.

I couldn't use shot C because it meandered too long—even though it had two parts that I really wanted to include. I'd have to choose shot A or B, which would mean omitting the other—even though I liked it as well.

With a little creative thinking and a willingness to take a big stylistic liberty, the jump cut solved my problem. One part from each of shots A, B, and C. We used all of them—even though the frame is the same.

Sure, jump cuts are not the most elegant choice, but nobody ever walked out of a comedy commenting on how "elegant" it was anyway.

Stepping back, what was truly a difficult decision could have been made simpler by one guiding principle of comedy:

Put in the funny stuff; cut out the dull bits.

The caveat to this would be:

…as long as the funny stuff doesn't undercut the overall film and the dull bits aren't necessary for the spine of the film. (But that just isn't headline-y enough.)

The real lesson I learned here is to not allow pre-conceived formal conventions to stop me from making the film that I know I want to make. No one is going to care that I "cheated" with a jump cut when they're busy laughing.

"CHEATING" MULTIPLE LOCATIONS—SCENE 46

In scene 46, Coleman Burleson (Alan Berman) continues his lecture in yet another location—this time Los Angeles. I mentioned in scene 3 that getting access to great locations though your network is an easy way to add production value to your indie film. I want to explain here exactly how resourcefulness and creativity can make your shooting schedule even easier. Scene 46 begins in the 34th minute of the film, and (in the story world) this is the first time we've seen Coleman in this location. In reality, this is the fourth time we've seen a scene shot in this location.

Resourcefulness comes into play because, once we secured this location, we took stock of everything that was available to us. We then figured out how we could use these to our advantage. Most importantly, the stage had a full lighting grid above it.

Having a great DP, like Adam Orellana, and getting the most out of that lighting grid is where creativity comes in. It's one thing for a producer to say, "Hey, can't we cheat this stage for more than one location?" It's another to have a cinematographer who can actually use available lighting to make one stage stand in for four completely difference places. With some different lighting setups and careful planning of camera angles, we were able to use one stage as four distinct locations.

Above: **Coleman Burleson (Alan Berman) lectures on a new stage.** *Left:* **One stage cheated for four locations.**

I want to include shots of all four lighting setups side-by-side here, as well, in case that is better for some people to view. It really is worth taking a look at how one space can be so drastically transformed.

Mini-Lesson: Find a Location Expert

Once you do find that magic location, my second piece of advice is to find the local person who is familiar with it and recruit her to your team. In our case, since we were shooting at a high school, we met with Nikki Makos, the student who ran the very complex lighting boards for the school. We made her a production assistant, and she saved us hours of fiddling around with unknown equipment. This is also an example of where "indie" shouldn't always mean cheap. By paying someone a little bit, you can often save yourself a lot of time while shooting, which means spending money actually saves money. Especially if you have a complicated location, consider finding someone with some expertise to work with you.

Mini-Mini Lesson: Picking a Specific Shot

If you find yourself pressed for time and have to trim your shot list—one way to cut down is to pick a

Above: One stage cheated for four locations, side-by-side. *Right:* Close-up of Coleman Burleson (Alan Berman) on stage.

specific shot. In scene 46, we stayed mostly wide until the end of the scene. Since I was positive that I wanted to be in close-up for this part of the scene, I could confidently skip it in the wider shots and move on more quickly. I knew we were going to end this scene with a punch in for Coleman's line:

> "My party mates say, build a wall to keep them out. I say, invite them over, and give them each a bell for his bike."

Transition Scenes and Your Film's Spine—Scene 47

Scene 47 of *A Convenient Truth* is a transition scene. It's 11 seconds long. It doesn't have any jokes. It doesn't give us any important new information. That said, it is necessary.

In this scene, Coleman (Alan Berman) sets up that he is about to show the audience (and us) an advertisement for Burleson Labs that is about to start airing nationally. Not only does this short scene prepare the audience for what is about to come next, it also places an important vertebra into the film's spine.

With this simple scene, we have set up a structure that allows for various advertisements to be built into the film (at any point) without audience confusion. This clarity is important for laughter. If the audience has to take a second to figure out what is going on, you've already lost the battle.

There are several Burleson Labs advertisements placed throughout the film, and they are usually some of the best-received bits of the whole thing. Without taking the time to include these dry 11 seconds, I don't think that would be true.

You can see in the wide shot that we even filmed Coleman in front of a screen with a black square on it. The square acts as a visual placeholder for where the advertisement will be played for the audience within the film. It's easy for us to understand what's happening in the film world as we watch the ad ourselves.

Finally, I want to point out one other facet of this transition scene. It is 100 percent consistent with Coleman's character. Just because the scene is dry and exists to serve the overall structure of the scene doesn't mean your character should be ignored within it. As Coleman announces that he's about to show the crowd this new advertisement for the first time, he does so with

Top: **Close-up of Coleman Burleson (Alan Berman) as he introduces an advertisement for Burleson Laboratories.** *Bottom:* **Coleman Burleson (Alan Berman) with screen behind him to help the transition to the advertisement.**

an endearing child-like excitement. He can't help but smirk a little about what he is about to show them. He's happy and proud of this ad (and more than a little pleased with himself).

The director should be looking for ways to infuse character moments like this into every scene. Often, conversations with your actor will be really fruitful toward this end. No one has thought more about that character than the actor who is portraying him.

Mini-Lesson: Trust the Actor's Instincts

In this case, Alan's natural instinct for how to play this scene was dead on. In general, my approach to directing is to see what the actor brings to the scene naturally—without giving him anything. This is obviously a personal choice, but my experience is that actors (who are cast well) often know what to do. (This doesn't excuse you from prepping what you want and being able to answer any questions that will come up. It's just more a matter of adjusting from a baseline that the actor gives you than imposing your will from the start.)

BURLESON LABS ADVERTISEMENT #1—SCENE 48

As I mentioned in the last section, scene 47 of *A Convenient Truth* sets up the first in-film advertisement for Burleson Laboratories. Coleman Burleson (Alan Berman) preps his audience (and the film audience) for the ad that they're about see. Scene 48 is that advertisement.

We get Coleman's setup and then launch directly into seeing the advertisement, which goes like this:

Burleson Laboratories logo caps off the advertisement.

EXT. CHILEAN COAL MINES—DAY
Stock footage of trapped Chilean coal miners.
                    NARRATOR (V.O.)
    In Chile, this is what the subjugation of dozens
    of South Americans for the sake of energy looks like.
Beat.
                      NARRATOR
    In California...
INT. BURLESON LABORATORIES—DAY
Dozens of MEXICANS happily CHEER, give thumbs up, and smile brightly directly into the camera.
A TITLE CARD SILENTLY SMASHES ONTO THE SCREEN.

The background is entirely black.
It reads: BURLESON LABS and contains the familiar energy logo in the center.

FADE TO BLACK.

The advertisement in the film is actually extremely similar to what is scripted here. The image of the Burleson Laboratories logo is what "SMASHES ONTO THE SCREEN." The only real difference is that instead of the title card popping on "SILENTLY," we decided to add the sound effect of a tiny bike bell ringing when the logo comes on. This idea came to us somewhere in the post-production process, and that small addition does a great job of tying the advertisements to each other as the film continues.

This advertisement is also the end of first collateral advantage segment. It grabs our attention and then transitions us out of the illegal immigration portion of the film. Before we've had a chance to think about this capper (of sorts), the next collateral advantage title card pops onto the screen and tells us where we're going next.

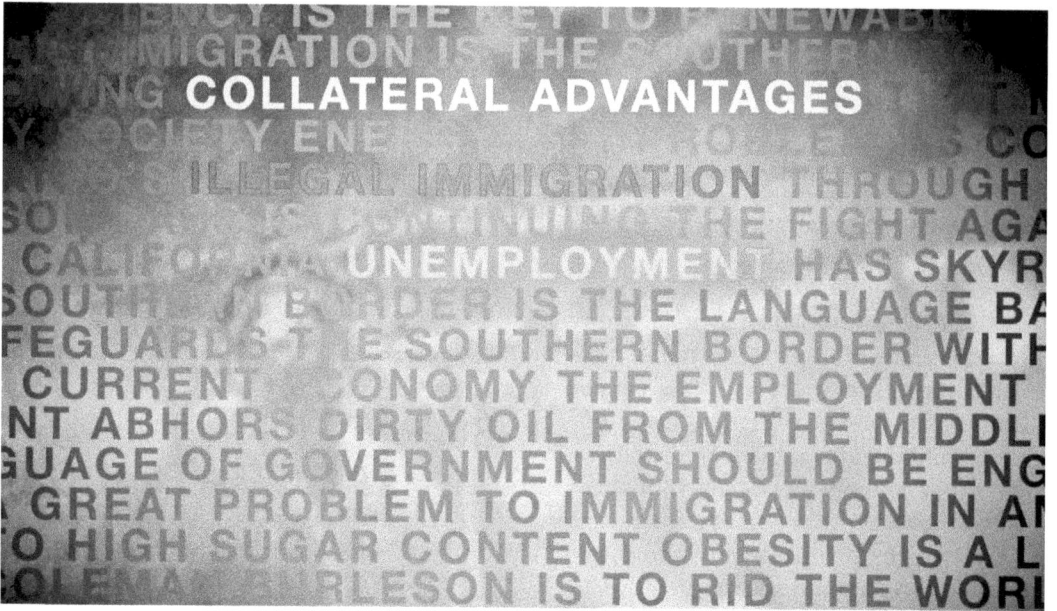

The title card for the unemployment section of the film.

The advertisement is a form within the film that we hadn't seen previously. It's not a talking head character that we know. It's not a part of Coleman's lecture. It's not a man-on-the-street interview. It's completely different and a welcome change. It also serves the purpose of giving us 30 seconds to reflect on the illegal immigration segment that we've just seen.

Since we don't want the audience to think too long about what they've already seen (at least not while the movie is still in progress), we make our goal to entice them about what they're going to see next. The hope is that the title card comes on, and the audience is excited (and maybe a little scared) to see what Coleman's proposal has to say about unemployment.

If the audience is actively wondering about how the proposal will intersect with issues of unemployment, then we've succeeded in engaging our viewers—which is always the ultimate goal.

FREE COLOR CORRECTION—SCENE 49

Scene 49 of *A Convenient Truth* is another sound bite from Cardamom Burleson (Jillian Leigh). This interview setup has already prompted me to talk about the value of casting actors who can write and the benefit that a director gets out of an actor who is skilled at improvising. And now for a completely different lesson I learned from this scene:

Color correction can be done on an indie scale—for free!

Here's the background: This interview was shot on an isolated day—separate from any other shooting schedule. We'd just made the decision to purchase our Panasonic HPX-170, and we wanted to test what the workflow would be like (the number of P2 cards we'd need, the transfer rates, etc.). Our DP, Adam Orellana, wasn't around for this shoot, so Patrick Steward and I decided to try to shoot this interview ourselves. It was, after all, a very basic interview setup, and we only had a couple of lights to work with anyway. This turned out to be a mistake.

We needed a female bedroom location, and a friend of mine was nice enough to let vus shoot in her apartment. The room worked for our purposes, but it was a New York apartment, which means it was small. The two lights that we had at our disposal were

Cardamom Burleson (Jillian Leigh) takes us into the unemployment issue of the film.

too powerful for any real subtlety of lighting design. They were too close to the subject (because we physically couldn't move them any further), and we didn't have any real tools for shaping the light in any way.

All this background is to explain one thing: the footage did not look good.

It was way too hot (overexposed and harsh), and I'm thinking we may not have even white balanced properly because it just did not look right. That said, Jillian's performance was too good to scrap. She made us laugh out loud for most of the night. I have clips that aren't usable for the film that I bet would still make me laugh if I went back to watch them now. Over a couple of hours of shooting, she gave us enough footage for her character to be interspersed throughout the entire film. We couldn't lose all of that great stuff for a technical reason.

We also didn't have the money to pay a colorist thousands of dollars—which would be for smaller corrections to the entire film, not just this one egregious scene.

As we were looking into our options during post-production, Patrick made me aware of the solution to our problem:

DaVinci Resolve Lite

It's possible that every indie filmmaker already knows about this software, and I was just out of the loop, but I wanted to mention it here, in case others are in the same position that I was. The software is also coupled with some of Black Magic's camera lines, so maybe a lot more people know about it from that by now.

Anyway, the lite version of this software can be downloaded for free from Blackmagic's website. This isn't a demo or a trial version. It's a lite version of the full software, which sells for $995, but it includes every basic function that you'll need for color correction on most indie films. (There's also $30,000 version for hardcore colorists that includes hardware, but I assume that's irrelevant to most indie filmmakers.)

Instead of thousands of dollars spent on color correction, we were able to color correct our entire film over three nights in the comfort of Patrick's apartment. It cost a few meals and some time (including some time to learn the software). If you have a computer that runs Avid, Final Cut, Premiere, or whatever your preference, you already have a machine that can run DaVinci Resolve. I mean it. You can probably download it right now.

We took our footage out of Avid and did our color correction on DaVinci Resolve 10. They're already on to version 12, but each new edition only adds more functionality, so the free deal should only get better.

Since *A Convenient Truth* is a mockumentary, we didn't have any really complicated color correction to do. Like most films (hopefully), the color correction was about ensuring consistency from shot-to-shot within a scene and then being mindful of color in transitions from one scene to another. Resolve was also used for titles, transitions, and captions in the film, and each was easy to do as first-time users.

We did put the software to the test with power windows on faces in a few particular scenes, and it was more than capable of handling the tracking on those shots as well. I don't have any vested interest in the software, and you can read/watch all sorts of reviews. Even better, you can download the software and get a sense of it yourself directly. My only goal here is to register the existence of this solution, in case some other poor indie filmmaker is googling "cheap color correction" in the wee hours of the night and might stumble upon this.

Side Note: Free software will not replace the eyes and "know-how" of a skilled colorist. Additionally, you'll need a proper monitor to even be able to use the software once you've learned it, so this is not a recommendation to avoid using colorists all together or downplay their craft. It is an option worth knowing about if you have the time and ability to put into learning it and have no money to pay a colorist.

Building Sequences—Scenes 50–53

Though the rough structure of *A Convenient Truth* was established with the script, we always had the intention of being loose enough to "find" additional scenes to insert. Prime footage for additional scenes came from the man-on-the-street interviews that we grabbed in between other setups.

However, adding these funny or interesting moments had to be done judiciously. Jamming orphan scenes in between scripted scenes would break flow and feel awkward. The way around this was to build sequences by grouping several similar scenes together.

In the case of scenes 50–53, we realized that we had four solid scenes that centered around questions of unemployment. Together these scenes become a sequence to support a theme, and their placement together actually affects our reaction to them.

Part one of the man-on-the-street interviews about unemployment.

Three Helpful Notes for Creating Sequences

These notes are especially true for finding documentary sequences, but they might also apply to narratives. In this case, even though *A Convenient Truth* is a mockumentary, this was exactly a documentary process—since these were real interviews and nothing was scripted or prepared before we captured them.

1. Let the Clips Decide. This means becoming familiar with all of your footage and being open enough to take in what the clips say. They'll begin to talk to each other in a way, and it's your job in the edit room to translate what they're saying. All of the pieces exist, and you must be a responsible curator. (This also means being honest about what's not there. If you love a clip, but it doesn't fit—cut it. Cut it now. You're going to cut it eventually anyway. Save yourself some of the heartache.)

2. Consider Rhythm. I don't have any rhythm whatsoever, but even I eventually began to recognize the importance of the rhythm of clips within a sequence. Sometimes you have the right clips but not in the right order. However, the wrong order might not even be the problem. It might be as simple as having two really long scenes following each other. Try putting a short scene in between and seeing if it helps things. In this sequence, the scenes are all relatively short, but it was important that the scenes got shorter as we moved forward. Especially if the messages are building upon each other in a very similar way, your audience will imagine the later scenes to be longer than they are. This is because they already know where things are going. Keep it short. Don't let them get ahead of you.

3. Create an Arc Within the Sequence. You want the sequence to move your thought forward. Scenes 50–53 can't really be said to have a proper arc, but there is a structure within them. We start the unemployment section of the film with Cardamom improvising about her father firing the cleaning lady. This introduces the topic. Then, this sequence gets supporting evidence as Coleman interviews regular people on the street about how hard it is to get a job. The first two clips of the sequence handle that really well. Importantly, the third and fourth clips aren't two more people talking about the problem of unemployment. They're about the solution. The sequence transitions into Coleman's daughter, Eleanor, asking people if they'd be interested in a job riding a bike that generates electricity. Instantly, we've gone from defining the issue to showing how Coleman's proposal can help fix that issue. As always, the sequence looks forward to what comes next: a full exploration of how Coleman's proposal solves the unemployment crisis.

Opposite, top: **Part two of the man-on-the-street interviews about unemployment.** *Middle:* **Part three of the man-on-the-street interviews about unemployment.** *Bottom:* **Part four of the man-on-the-street interviews about unemployment.**

Creative Character Introduction— Scenes 54–56

I covered character introduction in scene 29 with Juan "Pepe" Blanco's montage. Here I want to point out another way we did it. Meet Horace Cullen (Joshua Ryan).

Horace Cullen (Joshua Ryan) gets introduced while half asleep.

The distinction with this character introduction is that we meet Horace by not meeting him right away. We begin by talking with his mother Tess Cullen (Vicky Kramer).

Like any proud mother, Tess begins by saying what a blessing it has been for Horace to get a job at Burleson Laboratories. She slips and mentions that it has historically been difficult for her son to keep a job. When pressed by the cameraman, Tess alludes to some alleged lewd acts, which resulted in Horace's termination. Now our interest is piqued. This is a character introduction worth its screen time.

Though on its face the film crew is following Horace to document how working at the lab has bettered his life for the unemployment section of the film, the audience immediately has another interest: lewd acts?!

The scene plays out exactly as it was scripted:

INT. KITCHEN—DAY
Horace's mother, TESS, leans back on the kitchen counter. She is 41 but dresses like she's 19. Her halter top struggles to cover her breasts with her cleavage proudly on display.

         TESS
    It's a blessing what they're doing
    over at Burleson. My Horace couldn't keep a job

Creative Character Introduction—Scenes 54–56   101

Tess Cullen (Vicky Kramer) expresses her appreciation that Burleson Laboratories employs her son.

                before they opened up the plant.
                Food service mostly.
                        CAMERAMAN (O.S.)
                Why do you think he couldn't keep a job?
                             TESS
                         (tentative)
                He had a little trouble.
                        CAMERAMAN (O.S.)
                What kind of trouble?
Tess leans in closer. Her cleavage completely in view.
                             TESS
                Something about lewd acts in the food preparation zone.
                        (Short pause)
                Twice.
Leans back.
                         TESS (CONT'D)
                Anyway, that was the reason he couldn't
                keep a job and, after word got around, it got to be
                the reason he couldn't get a job.
Shakes her head disapprovingly.
                         TESS (CONT'D)
                Wendy's, McDonalds, Burger King,
                these people all talk. It's all politics.
Refocuses.
                         TESS (CONT'D)
                But not now! Now my little angel has a steady job.
                One where they accept him. They're just good
                people over there.

The scene accomplishes exactly what we wanted it to do. It then leads us to seeing Horace in action. The film crew asks him how he feels about working at Burleson Laboratories while actually watching him perform his cycling duties.

Horace Cullen (Joshua Ryan) answers questions while cycling at Burleson Laboratories.

Horace's voice exclaims how much he loves working at Burleson Labs. His face, and general fatigue on the bike, however, tell a different story visually.

In general, whenever you can have a character saying one thing and expressing the opposite, you'll find some fun things to play with. (You have to trust your actor to be able to play it this way and not fall into the trap of overwriting.) If I'm ever stuck on how to write or direct a scene, I've often found that playing with these opposing messages is a good way into something more interesting.

In the edit, we decided to add ten seconds of b-roll that we'd grabbed over the very beginning of Tess Cullen's dialogue about her son. The b-roll is simply Horace half-asleep in a messy room, and the image at the top of this section is extracted from it.

We actually see the person being described (Horace Cullen) before we see the person who is talking (Tess Cullen). It's easy to work it this way around because there is no risk of the audience being confused about who is talking once we see Tess on screen.

This is worth noting. The alternative would have been to open on a woman we haven't seen before talking about someone else that we haven't seen before. By showing Horace on screen first, we're able to achieve the delayed introduction effect that we wanted without confusing the audience.

The scene with Horace cycling in the lab then gives us our first direct interaction with him. Scene 57 will continue this introduction with Horace's talking head interview, but it will feel much fresher than if we had started with yet another talking head interview introducing us to yet another new person.

SHOOT THE SCRIPT AND THEN CHECK YOUR GUT—SCENE 57

After the build-up to our introduction to Horace Cullen (Joshua Ryan), it's crazy to me to think that the character was only scripted to have half a page of dialogue:

INT. BURLESON LABS—DAY
Horace pedals away. He attempts sincerity as he speaks:

> HORACE
> Yeah this job is great. First job
> I ever had where I felt at home.

Shakes his head up and down as if mostly trying to convince himself.

INT. HORACE'S BEDROOM—DAY
Horace sits on his bed.

> HORACE
> I really need a car. A 17-year-old guy needs a car.
> So yeah, I love working at the plant.

Realizes the camera.

> HORACE (CONT'D)
> I'm very happy with the opportunity which Burleson Labs
> has provided me. So, yeah, what I mean is, Burleson has
> enabled me with a job that will allow me to achieve
> my goals. Er ... my goal ... of getting a car. Oh and
> other things. All my goals really.

Smiles brightly directly into the camera.

> COLEMAN BURLESON (V.O.)
> (deliberately)
> Burleson labs has helped him achieve all of his goals.

After this small scene, Horace disappeared, and we moved directly on to meeting another character in the unemployment section of the film. (I don't know what the screenwriter was thinking.)

I knew I wanted Joshua in the film as soon as he finished up his audition and, like any professional actor, he came prepared to shoot on the day. He knew his lines. He'd given thought to the character's inner life. So, huddled into a small office in my brother's basement, we shot the scene as expected.

Horace Cullen (Joshua Ryan) puts a positive spin on his job at Burleson Laboratories.

But there came a moment as I was directing that I realized I was underusing a great collaborator. We'd gotten the scene as written, which is always good practice, but I could feel that there was so much more there. I had to step back and check my gut.

Rather than rush off to shoot the next scene, which is what the schedule will always demand, I reminded myself that my job was to make the best film I could—not slavishly

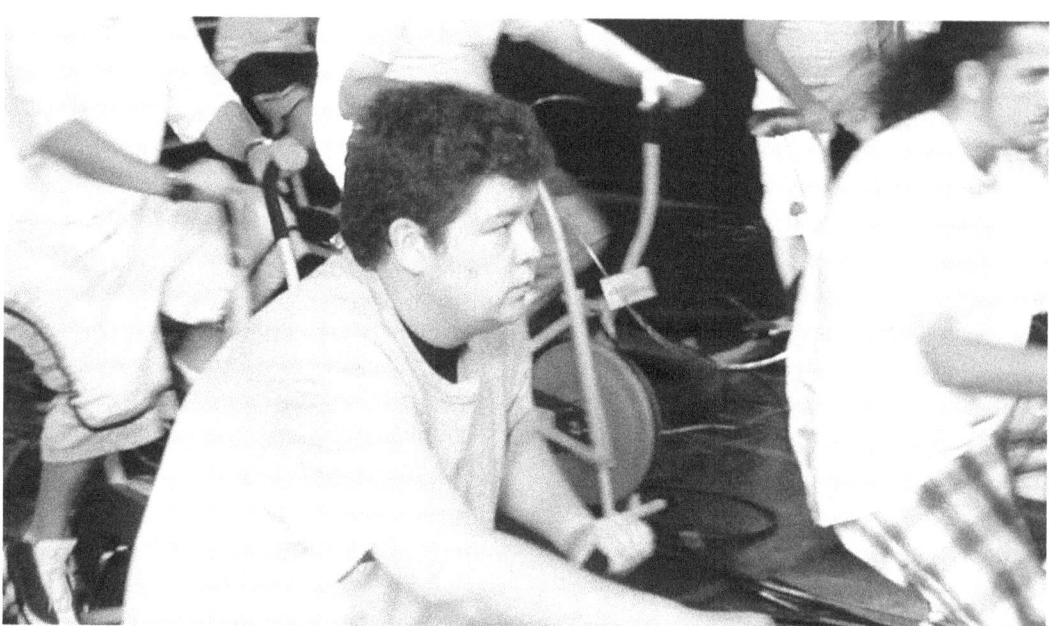

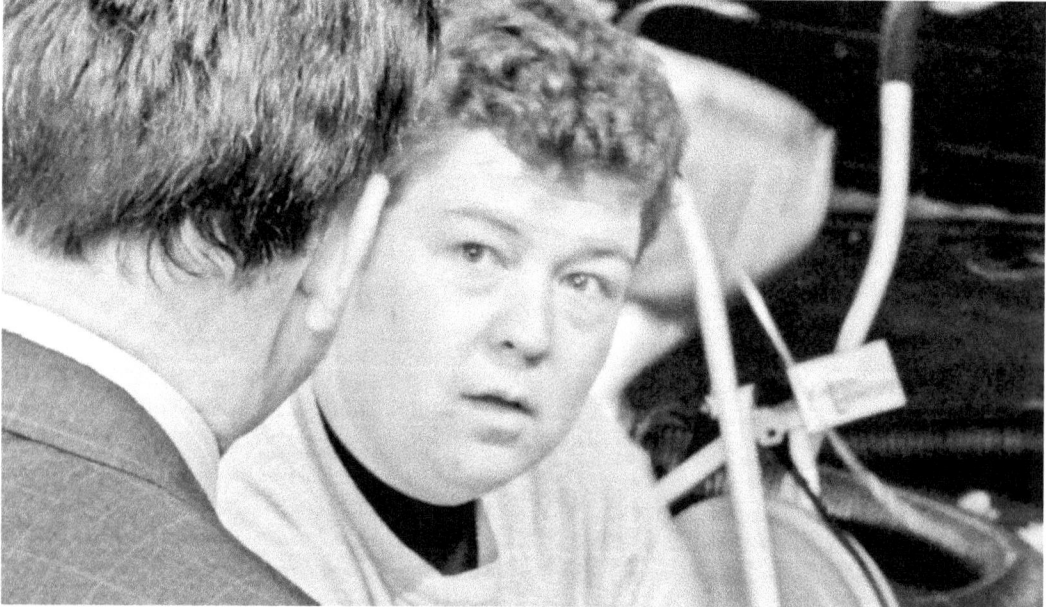

Top: Horace Cullen (Joshua Ryan) looking less than thrilled about his job pedaling at Burleson Laboratories. *Bottom:* Coleman Burleson (Alan Berman) interacts with Horace Cullen (Joshua Ryan) in the Cycling Room.

cross things off of the schedule or be beholden to the script (which I made up in the first place, anyway). With the script in the can, I decided to take advantage of Joshua's improvising skills, which we'd tested in the audition.

Here was the setup for the improv:

I told Joshua that I, as the interviewer in the film, was going to press him about the "lewd acts" that his mom mentioned in her scene. His goal was to avoid telling me the details of those "lewd acts" at all costs. Of course, my goal was to get the story out of him.

Naturally, this was an unfair setup, since I was the director. And, therefore, I was the one who decided when the camera would cut. The result was a very lengthy exchange. Horace really didn't want to tell me about those "lewd acts." But I really wanted to know.

Eventually, after the scene had gone on long enough, Horace got the sense that the director was not going to let him off the hook, and he begrudgingly told me the story of the lewd acts. More on this at a later time, but for now I'll just say that I cracked up laughing. In fact, the scene cuts out quickly because I started laughing so much that I nearly ruined the take.

We eventually covered the talking head scene (the part that was actually scripted) with more shots of Horace in the lab as we hear his interview.

Given how much I loved the improv, after we got done shooting I announced that the scripted bit was the most dull, and we'd probably wind up omitting it and using everything else. We didn't cut the scripted part all together, but we did wind up using most of the improv that my gut was telling me we should do.

The next few sections will explain how we employed editing to allow us to use so much of this long scene and how we decided how much of it was the right amount to keep in the film.

Side Note: Independent film shoots are always behind schedule. There's no money. There's no time to play around. That said, studio filmmakers always fondly talk about doing "little indie movies." This is because indie budgets actually do allow for the flexibility to play around—to follow an interesting thread when it comes up—to have fun and adjust as you go. Yes, more money means more time to do things, but it also means there are a lot of people standing behind you who are invested in how you're spending that time. Listening to my gut served the film, and I'm glad I took advantage of one of the positive aspects of independent film. Lord knows we had to deal with all of the negative aspects.

Long Takes—Scene 58

Covering our introduction to Horace Cullen (Joshua Ryan) in scene 57, I talked about how the short scene expanded substantially with some improv. One way to use only the parts that I wanted from that improv was to intercut the pieces with other scenes. As a result, scene 58 acts as an interlude between two different parts of scene 57.

In scene 58, we meet another character, Mitch Heron (Jesse Wakeman), who was similarly down on his luck before he landed his job at Burleson Labs. This scene is 2.5

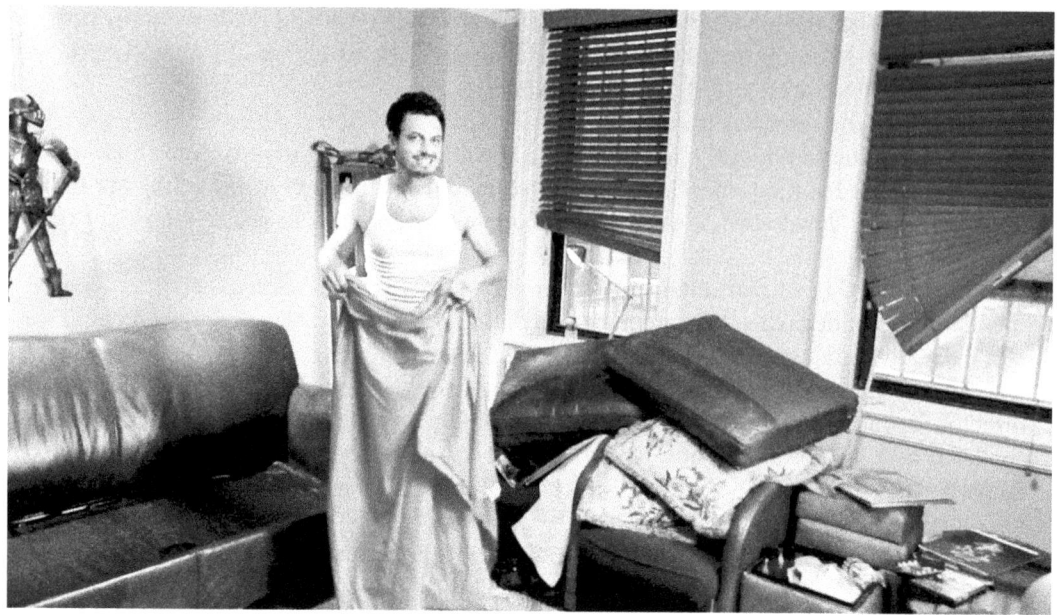

Mitch Heron (Jesse Wakeman) makes his sofa bed as he gives his interview.

scripted pages. Which means it's roughly going to be about 2.5 minutes long. That's a long scene. To make things more difficult, I decided I wanted this entire scene to be one long take. This wasn't an arbitrary decision. The scene is meant to feel like Mitch is talking to us as he goes about his daily routine. We find out that he has three jobs, and it makes sense that he'd be too busy to sit down and do an interview with a film crew. This way, we are encountering Mitch, and he tells us his story almost as a by-product—there's someone there to listen as he goes about his chores, so he talks. This is much different from someone sitting down to give an interview, and it feels more dynamic. We're also able to learn about Mitch by viewing his surroundings in the frame.

Now, we knew that shooting a 2.5-minute scene in one take was a bad idea. But I also didn't want to shoot the scene from several different angles, as it would ruin the casual nature of the scene to have two or three cameras all pointing at Mitch in the small room. We compromised by shooting a ton of insert shots of different items in the room and even other items that weren't in the frame but would illustrate Mitch's lifestyle. (I recall shooting an insert of him making a grilled cheese sandwich on his radiator, for example.)

However, the reality of the edit was that all of these inserts were useless. Mitch's monologue was so engrossing that any cutaways seemed unmotivated and actually a little annoying to the viewer. (Why are we looking at that pile of papers? I want to see the guy who's talking to us.) At best, the insert shots felt rude. At worst, they seemed like forced editing by someone who was trying to cover a long take—that is, exactly what they were. They drew attention to themselves in a negative way and tried to "fix" something that didn't need fixing. Jesse was so engaging in the scene that it didn't feel long. Even though it is a long take, no one has ever noted to me that it feels slow.

I could have saved myself (and our editor) a lot of headaches if I hadn't been too afraid to simply let the engaging scene play out. Messing with inserts and coverage sequences came out of an insecurity about such a long scene, in general, rather than a reaction to what I was actually watching—which was always an enthralling performance that easily held up against the pressure of the long take.

With all that said, I did have it both ways by using pieces of two different long takes. There's a moment when Mitch is making his sofa-bed and he punctuates what he's saying my pounding on the couch cushions. In an instant, we get a glimpse into the anger bubbling just below the surface. Charlie Pinto, our editor, used this moment as a perfect place for a cut. We were then able to continue the scene using a different take and maintain the illusion of the same—if not continuous—moment in time.

Top: Mitch Heron (Jesse Wakeman) sits for the remainder of his interview. *Bottom:* Wider shot of Mitch Heron (Jesse Wakeman) as his surroundings visually comment on his verbal statements.

The long take continues with Mitch sitting down on the couch that he has just transformed from his bed. And even though his entire monologue has been about how his life took a turn for the worse with the economic crisis, his focus turns to explaining how working at Burleson Labs has helped him turn his life around.

Collaboration Makes Your Film Better

There's a great moment in this latter part of Mitch's monologue that is entirely created by our DP, Adam Orellana. As Mitch sits on the couch in a medium shot, the film director asks him, "So you have three jobs right now, is that right?"

Mitch's response begins with, "Hell yeah, I have three jobs." It ends with, "You gotta be willin' to work, if you want to attain a certain kind of lifestyle."

At that exact moment, which was improvised, Adam zoomed out and re-focused to create a wonderful moment of visual irony.

Here's a guy who—by all accounts—has had life shit on him repeatedly in recent memory talking about "a certain kind of lifestyle," and Adam pulls back to not so much reveal as remind the audience of the way he's living. The visual reality is telling us exactly the opposite of what he is trying to convey to us with his words.

That's a found moment. A moment that Adam created instinctively. And, most importantly, a moment that only exists in the film because I had a collaborator who is great at what he does.

How to Know When You're Done Editing—Scenes 59–61

In scene 57, I described our introduction to Horace Cullen (Joshua Ryan). Rather than retread the situation, I'll assume you've read that section. The most important thing to know is that Horace Cullen's introduction became a very long improvisation that I loved. This immediately created an issue for editing. How do we include as much as possible of this great improvisation? The other question is how much do you include?

Scene 59 is the second time that we see part of the improvisation. It's another 41 seconds of the interview that we started in scene 57. Our introduction to Mitch Heron in scene 58 then comes in between scene 57 and scene 59 to give us a way to break up the improvisation into digestible parts.

In the script, Mitch continues his monologue from scene 58 in a totally different location—as he is on his way into work at Burleson Laboratories. To give us another edit point instead, that scene now becomes scene 60, which is a walk-and-talk scene that is

Opposite, top: The interviewer presses Horace Cullen (Joshua Ryan) for an answer to the question on the audience's mind. *Middle:* Mitch Heron (Jesse Wakeman) about to enter the Cycling Room for his next shift. *Bottom:* Horace Cullen (Joshua Ryan) finally tells the audience what they want to know.

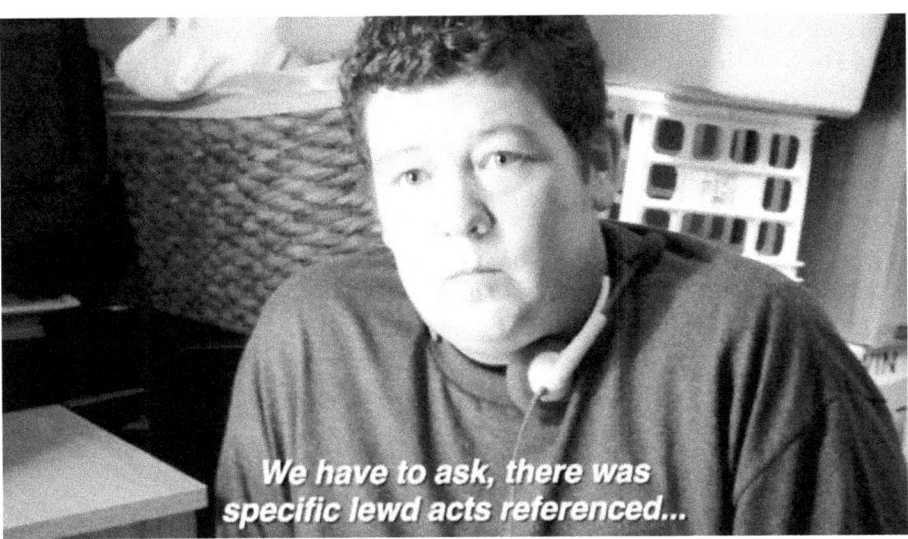

actually 56 seconds long. Another long scene. In this case, we're owning that our scenes are long and cutting back and forth between them. Since we're only away from Horace's improvisation for one scene, it helps for that scene to be almost an entire minute long. We then return to Horace for a third time to complete the improvisation in scene 61.

We wrap us Horace's improvisation with a final 40-second clip. Even though 40 seconds is longer than the average scene—it's short relative to the scenes leading up to it, and the audience will experience it as such.

I've included the timings for each of these scenes to draw attention to the rhythm of the editing. It was extremely difficult to settle on the right length for each of these scenes and, ultimately, it was only possible when viewing the scenes in context—both within this sequence and within the film as a whole.

Test Screenings Can Help You

That's right—test screenings. Some filmmakers love to complain about how studios, investors, or some other entity forces them to hold test screenings of their films. The implication is that they resent making changes to their film based on the opinions of a few audience members—audience members who know nothing about making films. But let's step back. The audience does have experience watching films. Their opinions are valid.

Does that mean a filmmaker should slavishly listen to the notes on the post-film questionnaires? Of course not. But we held two test screenings for *A Convenient Truth*, and they were extremely helpful to me in the following ways:

1. Watch the audience, not the film.

By the time you're screening your film for test audiences you can see the film with your eyes closed. You know it. You don't need (and in fact might dread) another viewing. So, what I found helpful was to sit in the back row and pay attention to the people as they watched. Of course, every time there was a laugh I was happy to take note. However, I was also watching every time someone whispered to a friend or shifted in her seat. Little behaviors like this might be a sign that there is more editing to be done at that point in the film.

2. Read the problems, ignore the "fixes."

Audiences earn their disdain from filmmakers in certain respects on the post-film questionnaires. (View the form we used at the end of this section.) Audiences don't know what goes into making a film, so the questionnaires will be filled with responses like "what if the main character was a woman?" "What if this film wasn't about climate change?" "What if his wife came with him for the entire film?" These types of "fixes" are unhelpful. They would often entail re-shooting huge portions of the film or simply making another film altogether. There's no choice but to ignore them. However, what is useful is to group the responses by the parts of the film that they are trying to address. Though the suggested "solutions" will be irrelevant, these groupings can signal points that the filmmaker needs to take a harder look at. It's then up to the filmmaker to come up with the fix.

3. Don't ruin your drawing.

I often go back to this analogy because it's personally resonant. When I was a kid,

I'd often draw things—like most kids. And sometimes I actually liked what I made. I was proud of it. But then, in an effort to make it even better, I'd take out the crayons and add to it. And add to it. I'd only stop after I looked down at my drawing and realized it was hideous—barely resembling what I originally liked so much. The problem of editing is this exact problem—magnified in importance and done in a vacuum of literally infinite potential combinations. I could tinker forever. How do I know when to stop?

Test screenings are one answer. In our first test screening in New York, one grouping of the comments on the post-film questionnaire related to this improvisation with Horace. At that point, there were about two to three additional minutes of the improvisation in the film. In response, we trimmed the improvisation scenes way down in the next cut. Our second test screening in Pennsylvania showed that we had solved the pacing issue related to these scenes, but the comedic response to the scenes was also not nearly as strong. We were able to calibrate optimal timing for the scenes by trimming them down but also adding back in what was absolutely essential to obtain the laughs.

In general, the final cut of A Convenient Truth is actually closer to the cut that we used for our first test screening in New York. There were a couple of sequences that worked better for the Pennsylvania test screening, but we realized several changes that we had made actually hurt the film as a whole. That realization was what allowed me to stop tinkering with the film. We'd reached a point where our work was actually making the film worse—so I put down the crayons. (Thank God Avid is more forgiving than Crayola.)

A CONVENIENT TRUTH
– Test Screening Questionnaire –

1. Did you like the film? (Circle One): YES / SORT OF / NOT REALLY / NO
2. Is there anything you'd cut out?
3. Is there anything you'd like to see more of?
4. Were there any moments/scenes you particularly liked? (Please list)
5. Were there any moments/scenes you particularly disliked? (Please list)
6. Was there anything that frustrated or confused you? (Please list)
7. What did you think about the use of voiceover/narration?
8. What did you think about the use of montage?
9. List your favorite characters: _____
10. List your least favorite characters: _____
11. Which was your favorite advantage of the proposal?
    Energy Generation / Climate Change / Illegal Immigration / Unemployment / Obesity / Language / Foreign Oil
12. How would you characterize your political leanings? (Optional)
13. How would you rate the following elements? You can elaborate in the margins, or the space below. (5 = Excellent, 1 = Poor)

The concept	1	2	3	4	5
The humor	1	2	3	4	5
The pacing	1	2	3	4	5

The music	1	2	3	4	5
The story	1	2	3	4	5
The characters	1	2	3	4	5
The beginning	1	2	3	4	5
The middle	1	2	3	4	5
The end	1	2	3	4	5
The politics	1	2	3	4	5
The immigration section	1	2	3	4	5
The unemployment section	1	2	3	4	5
The obesity section	1	2	3	4	5
The language section	1	2	3	4	5
The foreign oil section	1	2	3	4	5

Any other comments or suggestions? (We really want them. It's why we're here).

Thanks very much for filling this out.

CREATING A STYLISTIC LOOK—SCENE 62

Scene 62 of *A Convenient Truth* is the second Burleson Laboratories advertisement in the film. This ad, which caps the unemployment section of the film, opens on a home-

High angle shot of Homeless Mexican (Anthony Montana Silot) from the second Burleson Laboratories advertisement.

less Mexican man panhandling as a white woman walks by. The narrator admonishes, "Don't peddle for change." A happy cyclist pops onto the screen and triumphantly adds, "Pedal for change!"

As with all of the advertisements, we took this as an opportunity to create a stylistic look that separates the footage from the documentary look of the rest of the film. This immediately signals to the audience that the scene they're watching is different from the one preceding it and allows us to have some visual fun that would have been out of place in the documentary form.

The first shot is high angle, panning, and involves a rack focus—all visual elements that indicate a planned shot, rather than trying to feel like they're "capturing" something live. In addition to the angle and camera manipulation, we also created a "look" in post-production that made the footage really stand out. The colors and contrast have been manipulated so that all of the shots within the ad feel cohesive with one another and completely different from the baseline "normal" footage of the film.

Homeless Mexican (Anthony Montana Silot) begs for change in the Burleson Laboratories advertisement.

Continuing the trend of the first shot, the second shot tilts up on an extreme close-up of the Mexican man. Again, this shot would be much too staged for a documentary and hopefully stands out from the other scenes in the film. We also took the opportunity to find beautiful frames for our shots, concentrating on what looked best and not having to be constrained by what would be plausible for a documentary crew to capture. It was great fun to be able to construct images like the one that starts this section on a shoot that was otherwise very practical in its visual choices.

Finally, even though we shot the button for the ad on the same built lab set as the rest of the lab footage, we shot it under different lighting conditions than the rest of the scenes that we see there. Within the story world, this clip has been shot with the intention

Burleson Rider #1 (Samelo Moraes) announces, "Pedal for change!" to conclude the Burleson Laboratories advertisement.

of being used in an advertisement. The filmmakers would want a perky lab worker to convey their message, "Pedal for change!" with an enthusiastic glow. Therefore, even though it would be funnier to have a downtrodden Mexican struggling to say the words under the strain of pedaling his bike, it would undermine the logic of the film and be inconsistent with the stylistic look that we created for the ad.

The specific look that we created is not so important. However, it is important that we bothered to create a look—and that we honored that decision once it was made by not ditching it for a cheap laugh.

FILM ARCS—SCENES 63 AND 64

I discussed the structure of *A Convenient Truth* in scene 40. Essentially, the film has a first act that culminates in a reveal. There are then five "collateral advantages" that make up the second act. And the third act resolves things. In traditional narrative film arcs, the second act is always the toughest. For this reason, it can be extremely helpful to study the middles of films, which is a lot less sexy than looking at the beginning or end. If we accept that this is the structure of our film, then scene 64 represents the middle of the middle—collateral advantage 3 of 5. It comes almost nearly in the middle of the film's duration, as well.

Kitty Burleson (Elise Rovinsky) discusses her husband's personal ties to obesity.

Collateral Advantage III: Obesity

A title card represents the entirety of scene 63. This section of the film opens with another clip from Kitty Burleson's interview. It's a familiar sight that we chose to continue the film with. However, the way we chose to progress the arc is to allow things to get a little bit "bigger" than they have been up to this point. Kitty is increasingly drunk as she says:

> "The 'fat thing' is very close to Coleman's heart. 'Cause his mother died from being fat. She was just … a whale."—Kitty Burleson

These are a few very broad lines of dialogue—lines that would be out of place in the subdued satire of the first act. Similarly, the obesity section of the film, in general, will take more comedic liberties with its characters and form than what we've seen thus far.

An arc means that the second act escalates in some way. If all five collateral advantages were equally intense in tone, there would be no build to the overall feeling of the film. The diagram of that structure would flatline at the first collateral advantage and then stay at that level until the film began to resolve. It wouldn't be satisfying. I knew this at the writing stage, and it was helpful in deciding what order the collateral advantages should be presented within the film.

So, right around the middle of the film: Kitty gets a bit drunker, the collateral advantage topic gets a bit sillier, and (hopefully) the audience is ready for a bit of broad humor to join the established dry tone. Any combination of structure and tone can be accomplished, but it's important to put a lot of thought into where things land in the film arc in order to pull it off well.

Title card to begin the obesity section of the film.

If you're ever about to make a decision for your film that seems like it could be arbitrary, consider the arc, and a reason for the answer will be waiting.

Tempo and Sequences—Scenes 65–67

With the end of the unemployment section of *A Convenient Truth* being comprised of several long takes (see scenes 57–61), I learned just how important the tempo of scenes can be to the overall feel of the film. It's obvious that scenes need to be looked at in context—at the very least, how they relate to the scenes directly before and after them—but it took creating a feature film for me to understand the full weight of this.

With those long takes behind us, the film really called for a change of pace. The third collateral advantage section on obesity opens with a brief intro from Kitty Burleson to set the stage. We then really ramp things up. We hear Coleman's lecture continue about the obesity issue as some related images cover the dialogue. Six images in total appear on screen—each holding for only two seconds before dissolving into the next.

When we finally settle on Coleman giving his lecture, he only continues for ten seconds before we cut away to the next scene.

Scene 66 lasts only another 24 seconds, as we watch Coleman field a post-lecture question about the potential damaging effects that riding a bike for so many repetitive hours might have on the health of the workers. (Spoiler Alert: he handles it with expert ignorance that results in unintentional comedy.)

Scene 67 then gives us a medical opinion on the matter, which naturally focuses on

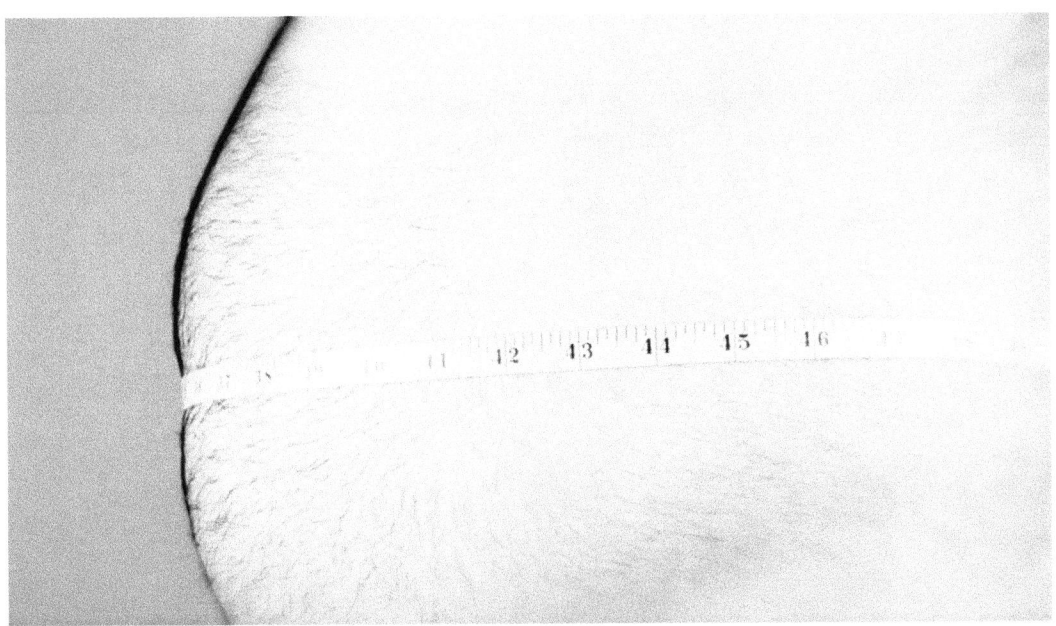

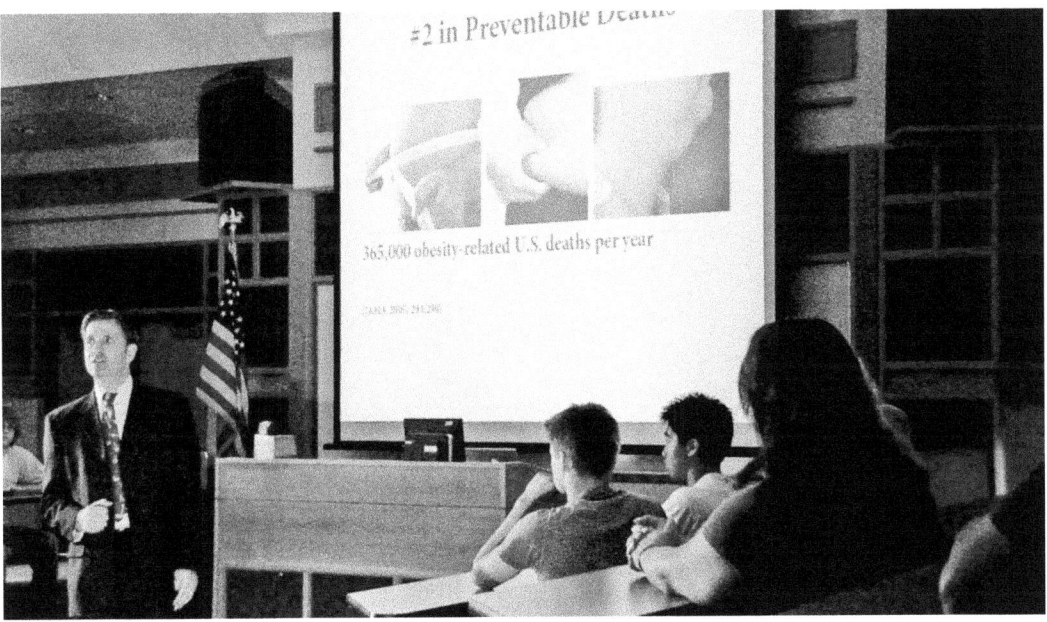

Top: **Stock footage used to introduce the obesity issue.** *Bottom:* **Coleman Burleson (Alan Berman) tells the audience about America's obesity epidemic.**

the positive effects that are attributable to regular cycling exercise. This scene is 18 seconds long.

I'm giving the timings here to show that in less than a minute we get a mini-montage with a short tail scene and two additional scenes.

Side Note: Consider this on the page when writing. If the general rule of thumb is that one script page equals one minute of screen time, it's likely that most of your pages

Top: Coleman Burleson (Alan Berman) defends the potential health risks of extended bike riding during a post-lecture Q&A. *Bottom:* Dr. Julius Monroe (Joseph Caputo) explains the positive health effects of bicycle riding.

should contain parts of more than one scene. If your script is comprised of scenes that all spread out over several pages, you likely will have a pacing/tempo issue. (If it's an intentional style that's one thing, but most scripts won't be laid out like that.)

Following this up-tempo series of scenes, the audience will (hopefully) be ready to settle back into the film and be introduced to the main character of the obesity section of the film—Thomas Corpolant (Nick Magliocco)—which will occur in spectacular fashion in scene 68.

Serendipity in Filmmaking—Scene 68

There are certain moments in filmmaking that cannot be planned. Moments that are unscripted and unexpected—children of serendipity. Filmmakers continue the crazy struggle of creating films because at some point they tasted this serendipity, and they need to taste it again. Scene 68 of *A Convenient Truth* is an example of this. In this scene, we are introduced to Thomas Corpolant (Nick Magliocco) as he is … for lack of a better word … abducted by Burleson Laboratories. Thomas's mother has contacted the lab about getting him to work in the Cycling Room—almost like a paid fat camp.

The vague idea of this abduction was written into the script, but I could not have anticipated exactly how it would play out. This is part of the fun! If it wasn't, I could stop at the writing stage. Or I could storyboard what I wrote and call it a day. The specialness of filmmaking comes precisely from what happens on set—when you're dealing with unknown factors and collaborating with other skilled people.

The scene begins at the front of the house as the camera follows the two goons from Burleson Laboratories. As they approach, Mrs. Corpolant signals for them to go around back. They do as they're told—going through the gate into the backyard and approaching the house from the rear. We spy Thomas eating at a table through sliding glass doors.

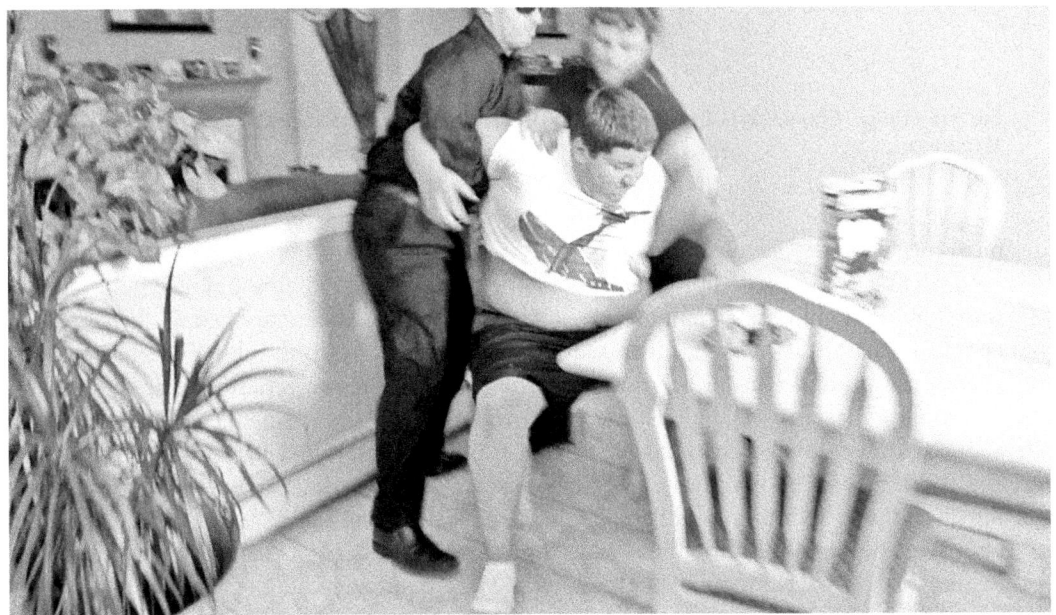

Burleson thugs (Frank Davis and Matthew Magliocco) descend upon Thomas Corpolant (Nick Magliocco) as he eats.

The goons barge in through the glass doors to surprise Thomas. The cameraman attempts to capture all of this action as it occurs.

So what happened to surprise me?

In all of the commotion of the scene (the goons bursting in, Thomas yelling for his mother to help, and his mother telling the goons that they're doing "God's work"):

Thomas grabs some more food off of the table and shoves it into his mouth! This is while he is physically being dragged away by two strangers who've just taken his house by siege. The character's priority in this outrageous moment is the piece of doughnut that still remains on his plate. It was comedic genius on Nick's part.

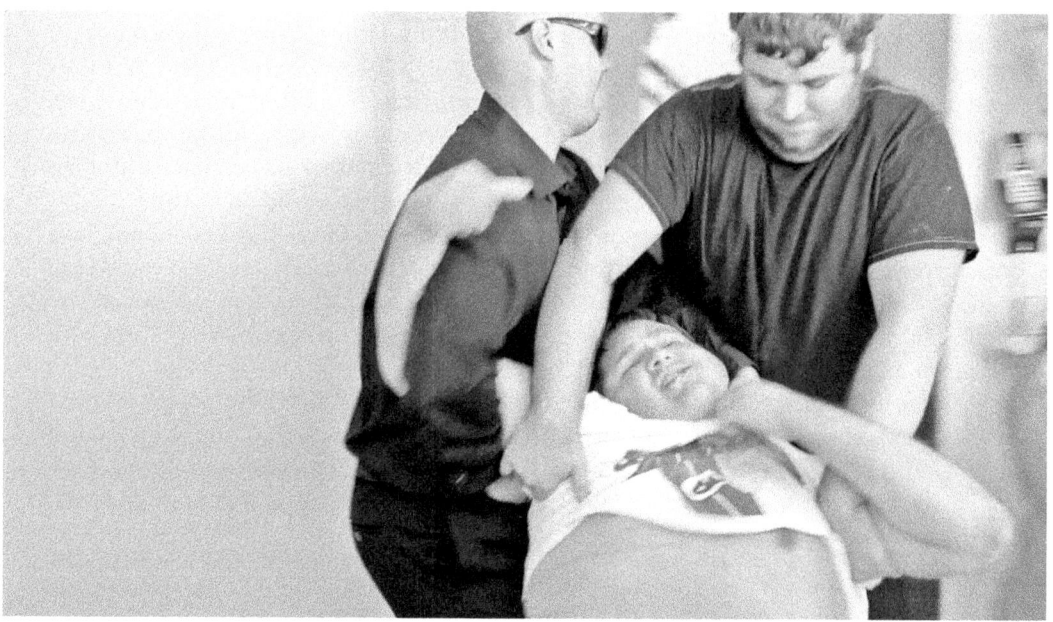

Burleson thugs (Frank Davis and Matthew Magliocco) struggle to abduct Thomas Corpolant (Nick Magliocco).

What's more, Adam Orellana instinctively zoomed in on Thomas at this exact moment. I couldn't have planned it better. And that's the point.

I define this as serendipity because it connotes the magic of filmmaking. If the actor wasn't living within his character, this action would have never surfaced. If the camera operator wasn't really tuned in and reacting to what was in front of him, the audience's attention would have never been drawn to focus on this action. These are the moments that make a director smile after he calls cut. They're also the moments that I feel guilty about getting credit for, since they're instances of others making what I imagined better.

With that said, I'll add that good filmmaking involves a certain amount of priming for serendipity. Working with professionals who are taking their craft seriously greatly improves the possibility for these serendipitous moments to occur at all. In that way, casting and crew selection can be thought of as choices that create the most potential for serendipity.

The other reason that I consider these moments of serendipity is that they can almost never be recreated. As much as I loved this moment, or other moments of improv within

Burleson thugs (Frank Davis and Matthew Magliocco) approach the Corpolant house.

the film, the first take is almost always the one that is used. I'm sure that on subsequent takes I asked Nick to make sure he shoved some bit of food into his mouth as he was abducted and that I told Adam how much I loved the push in on that moment. But it was exactly that: a moment. A combination of fleeting factors that were special and won't be reproduced. I don't understand it, but I know that it's true. And I'm happy about that.

Mini-Lesson: Timing

As I mentioned above, the scene begins at the front of the house and wraps around to the back. For a real documentary feel, we covered this entire walk in one long take. The abduction played out in real time. Though I love the idea of this, the actual experience (not the idea) is what has to be taken into account when editing. Put simply, it was boring to watch two guys walk around a house. The solution was to jump forward three times within the same take. This still established the geography of the scene but added a sense of urgency to the abduction and saved precious seconds.

RULE OF THREES—SCENE 69

Scene 69 of *A Convenient Truth* is the third and final installment in what I call "Leonard's Disclaimers." The basic idea is to allow the documentary (but really us) to show scenes ranging from off-putting to downright heinous while maintaining the film's logic. How do we have it both ways? By immediately having Leonard (Kevin Hauver)

Leonard Wingmon (Kevin Hauver) delivers his third disclaimer on behalf of Burleson Laboratories.

pop onto the screen to acknowledge the shock of the preceding scene. And, to frame it in a way that makes it more palatable—more politically aware. Notice that I say politically "aware," not "correct," because the politically correct thing would be to never show the offensive scene in the first place. It turns out being politically correct is spectacularly unfunny.

Many people who know a lot more about comedy than I have talked about the "rule of threes." So, rather than try to present some overarching theory, I want to briefly talk through *A Convenient Truth*'s use of the rule of threes here. I, personally, love finding case studies when I search for things. Specifics to supplement theory are always welcome. So, here is how "Leonard's Disclaimers" use the rule of threes:

1. Scene 22 is our first of "Leonard's Disclaimers."

Context: Coleman finally reveals his controversial proposal during his lecture in scene 20. The blowback to this proposal directly confronts Coleman in scene 21—when his opponent brings up all of the reasons that it's politically incorrect in a local debate.

Function: So, in scene 22, Leonard pops onto the screen invoking Einstein. "Great spirits have always encountered violent opposition from mediocre minds," he says. He manages to ground the film in reality by admitting that this proposal is not easy to accept but also acts as a spin man—a public relations manager—a cheerleader. In essence, he tells the audience, "Don't worry. We know how it sounds. Trust us. We get it. Soon you'll get it, too."

2. Scene 30 is the second disclaimer.

Context: Scene 29 is a montage as Juan "Pepe" Blanco—freshly plucked from gardening in Coleman's backyard—gets suited up to work at Burleson Laboratories.

Function: Scene 30 allows us to deliver a punch line without the setup. Leonard again pops onto the screen and assures the audience that:

> "…at the time that Juan 'Pepe' Blanco was a landscaper in the employ of the Burleson family, Assemblyman Burleson was unaware of his illegal status. The correct paperwork has been filed to rectify this oversight."

We didn't know in advance that Juan was in America illegally, but we don't need a scene that tells us that before Leonard pops onto the screen. The punch line alone fills in the first part. Also, since we've established that Leonard has this politically aware role, many audiences already know what's coming when they see Leonard again. We've just seen a Mexican gardener working for a politician and then coerced into working at Burleson Labs in an overtly staged montage. Chances are there's going to be something that needs to be disclaimed after that…

3. Scene 69 (this scene) is the final disclaimer.

Context: Scene 68 might be the most visceral in the film. It therefore is in dire need of a disclaimer. We watch as two thugs abduct an overweight teenager to bring him to work at Burleson Labs. (I mean, it's no *Funny Games* [1997], but: What? How is this happening?)

Function: As with everything in the structure of the movie, these scenes escalate. Here we're only allowed to pull off an abduction scene in the middle of a mockumentary while both getting the laughs and staying logically believable because of Leonard's disclaimers. In scene 69, he once again pops onto the screen—hopefully with the audience still slack-jawed at what they've just witnessed. He calmly assures the audience that this "abduction" was actually requested by the teenager's mother, which jives with what we know, since she is shouting that the thugs are doing "God's work" as they pull her son out of the house.

I want to stress something visual here. Leonard could have also given us a set of three disclaimers using three completely distinct scenes. He could have shown up in each of the offensive scenes directly—like Slugworth whispering in the ears of the golden ticket winners. Or we could have had Leonard doing various interesting activities as he delivered us these bits of information. However, in this case, I can unequivocally say that these disclaimers are more effective because we chose to use identical framing for each of them.

That split second that is saved as the audience orients themselves at the beginning of the second—and especially third—disclaimer works wonders. The rule of threes does its job. The comfort and familiarity with the frame allows for the comedy to come more crisply into focus from the start. The result of this choice is clear and observable: more laughs.

ACTING IS REACTING—SCENES 70 AND 71

Following the abduction of Thomas Corpolant (Nick Magliocco) and Leonard's disclaimer informing us that we have not, in fact, witnessed an abduction, we get our first

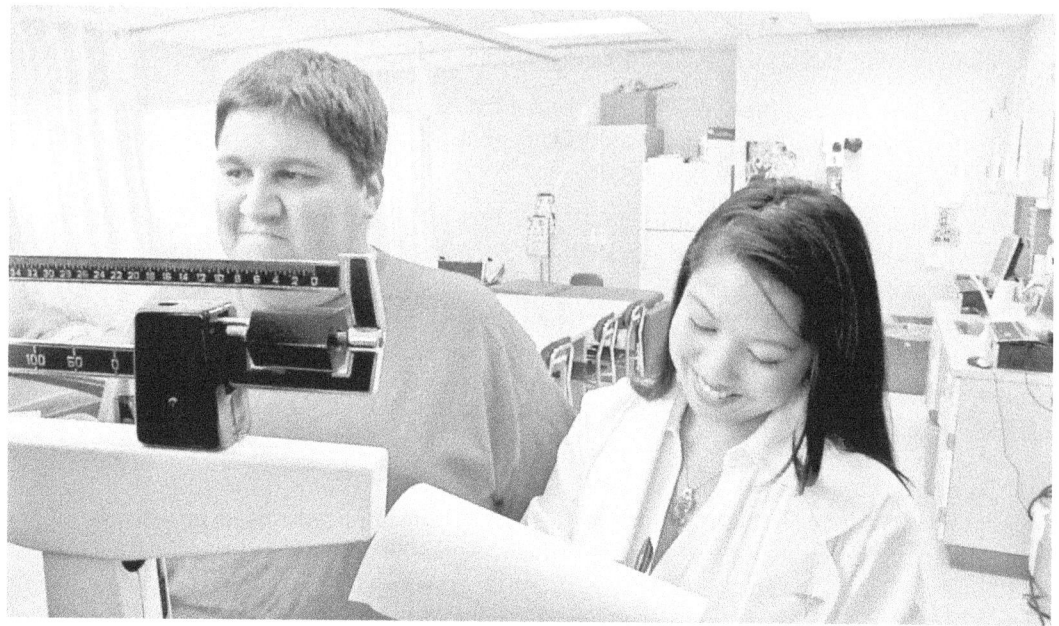

Thomas Corpolant (Nick Magliocco) gets weighed in by the Burleson Laboratories nurse (Pamelalynne Ramirez).

non-hysterical glimpse at Thomas in scene 70. In this scene and the one that directly follows it, we get a sense of who Thomas is without him uttering a single word. It's trite to say that acting is reacting, but I wanted to point out these two specific examples here.

In scene 70, Thomas steps up onto Burleson's scale for his first weigh-in. The nurse informs him that he's "got some weight to lose." Thomas doesn't have a response line in the script, but he doesn't need one. His face says it all.

Take a look at the still of Thomas and the nurse, and you'll see the beauty of the moment. In one instant, the nurse's face lights up. She smiles, so pleased with herself, while Thomas' face drips with disgust.

This is one of those moments that you hear about all the time. One of those moments when directors realize that they don't need nearly as much as is often written into the script—because they have actors. This is precisely what good actors do. They express more with less. They let us know what is going on in the character's inner life without making it seem like that's their goal.

I don't think Nick was worried about making sure the audience knew how his character felt in that moment. I think he was in the moment and reacting to the situation naturally. These are the takes when I'd call cut and literally feel like I'd just been given a gift. And, in some ways, I had. Directly after the weigh-in, Thomas gets another silent, reaction-heavy scene.

In scene 71, Thomas gets a pep talk from the Burleson Laboratories's trainer before his first day on the job. The trainer will be working with Thomas on all of the non-bike-riding elements of his training while he works at the lab. Here, Thomas is once again reacting to the trainer.

As the trainer hands Thomas his punch card, he explains to him that he's handing him much more than that. He's handing him a "ticket to a better life." Thomas' body lan-

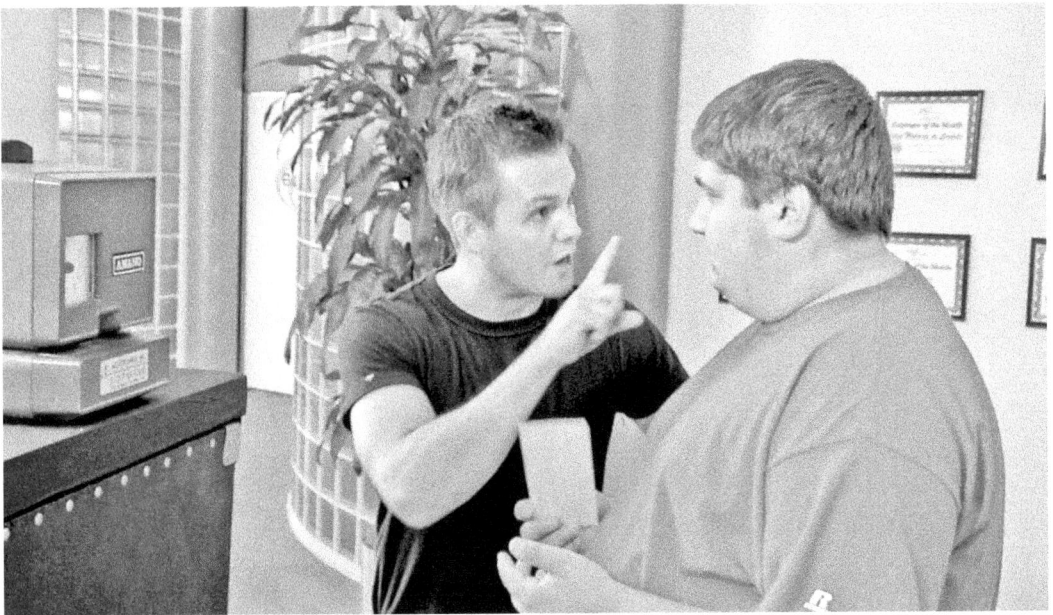

The Burleson Laboratories trainer (Kent Wykoff) begins Thomas Corpolant's (Nick Magliocco) training session.

guage and reactions to the trainer let the audience know that he's not buying what the trainer is selling. Since the audience is also not buying it, it endears us to Thomas to know that the character is a good proxy for us. That said, the character is also in a situation that is not entirely voluntary, and he is about to begin work at Burleson Labs.

It's hard to explain, especially with a still image, but there is something funny about a character who thinks the person talking to him is full of shit but still listens—and, ultimately, still goes along with it. At the script stage, the comedy from this scene was meant to come more from the insults that the trainer spews at Thomas as part of his "pep talk," but the final scene works more because of Thomas's reactions than anything else.

In short, don't forget to consider the potential for comedy that can arise from your straight man's reactions to a comedic situation and/or another overtly comedic character.

Four Lessons from a Montage—Scene 72

What I'm terming "scene 72" from *A Convenient Truth* is actually a montage. Following Thomas Corpolant's (Nick Magliocco) introduction into the Burleson Laboratories workforce, we immediately get a sequence that shows him working at the lab and getting into shape.

Thomas Corpolant (Nick Magliocco) generates watts while getting fit.

Four Things I Learned Creating This Montage

1. Use a funny actor.

The overall idea of this montage is funny because of how absurd it is, but most of the individual clips are heightened because a funny actor brings a little something extra. The faces, moans, and groans that Nick added to these shots are really what make this montage work.

This isn't so much a new lesson as another example of an old one: work with talented people.

2. Use locations to your benefit.

Most of the clips in this montage (all of the shots that use workout equipment) were shot in the weight room of the same high school that we used for the main lecture hall locations. Additionally, the medical room in which we see Thomas get his weigh-in is the high school infirmary. Taking stock of the resources in one location can add production value to other scenes in your film and actually make your shooting schedule easier.

3. Use time to your advantage.

Circumstances meant that we shot the various pieces of this montage over a long period of time. Large gaps in our production schedule created issues, but they also allowed us certain advantages. In this montage, we weren't able to get Nick to come to the Cycling Room stage at the time that we filmed on it. However, we were able to take one of the Burleson Labs bikes from the Cycling Room to another space and film Nick on it at a later date. We were also able to take a look at the shots that we did have for the montage and selectively shoot specific shots that we wanted to fill it out. (The shot at the top of the section is a composite of a watt-hour insert that we shot and Nick on a Burleson Labs bike.) I was also able to get some additional shots of Nick jogging by shooting out of the back of a convertible to allow for a sense of build that we wanted for the montage. (Stylizing the entire montage allowed us to match several disparate shooting conditions into one cohesive whole.)

4. Cutting to music.

With many montages, and certainly with this one, the montage is built upon the underlying music. This is a standard strategy. However, it's also a standard strategy to edit to temporary music for early cuts. When it comes to something specific like this, I'd caution against this. We originally used a theme from a *Rocky IV* montage, and it is really easy to fall in love with your temp music. More importantly, it makes the job of the person who is tasked with creating the music after the fact incredibly difficult. Luckily, our scorer was up to the task, but in the future I would make sure that creating that score begins much earlier in the post-production process.

RESOURCEFUL FILMMAKING— SCENES 73 AND 74

Scene 73 of *A Convenient Truth* essentially repeats the framing of scene 70. This sequence has a very simple structure: Thomas (Nick Magliocco) gets weighed in before he starts working in the Burleson Labs Cycling Room and then after. The montage in

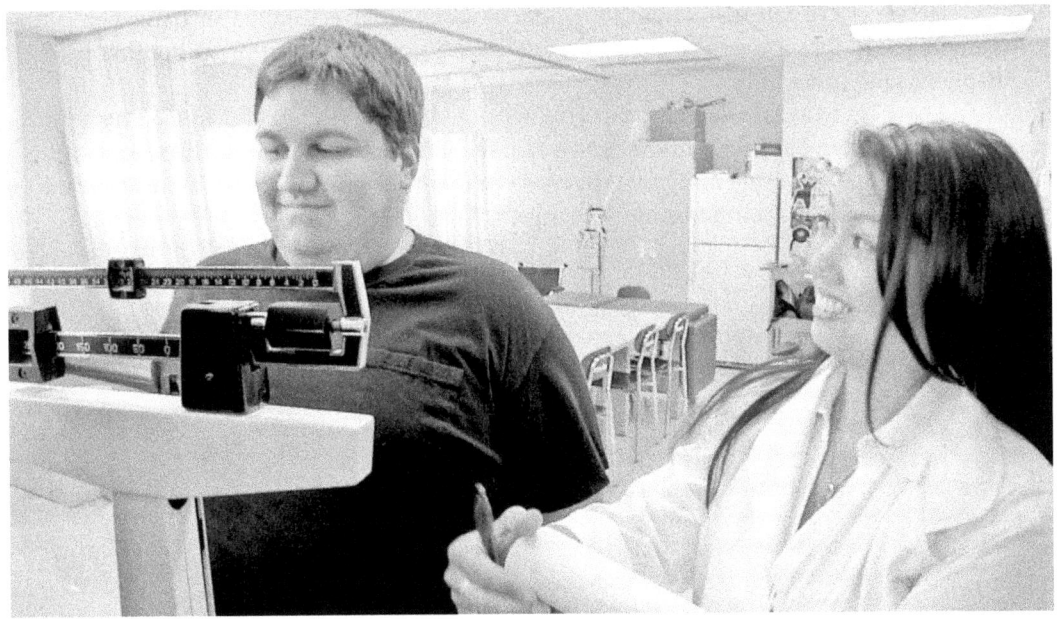

Thomas Corpolant (Nick Magliocco) gets re-weighed by the Burleson Laboratories nurse (Pamela-lynne Ramirez).

between shows us that progress. Because we were filming these scenes back-to-back in reality, the best we could do was to put Thomas in a black shirt that fit him better to make him look like he'd lost a lot of weight. In practice, the eyes see what we want them to. So, when the nurse says that Thomas has lost 40 pounds, it sort of looks like he has. Within reason, cheats like this are believable. However, scene 74 will show us that being resourceful can eliminate the need for such cheats.

Scene 74 was originally filmed at a similar time as the re-weighing one shown here, and it involved Thomas talking to the camera about how happy he is to have lost so much weight over the summer. In the shot, Thomas curls a barbell and thanks "Mr. Burleson" for helping him through the cycling program.

However, as I've mentioned before, shooting this movie over an extended period of time did have some advantages. In this case, the actor who played Thomas actually lost about 100 pounds over the year following filming!

This is where being resourceful comes in. All independent film has to manage its limited resources well, but the less obvious part of being resourceful is recognizing the resources that you do have at your disposal. Here, even though we already had a version of scene 74 in the can, it was actually resourceful to go back and re-film the scene. We got tremendous production value out of recognizing what a gift it was that the actor who we were pretending lost weight really lost weight. All it took was a quick afternoon with equipment that we had on hand to re-shoot scene 74.

Plus, the original version of scene 74 did not go to waste. We were able to insert a brief clip of the original version into the new one to make the contrasting weights perfectly clear.

I want to stress here that we can't take credit for most of what made this work. Nick lost the weight on his own, and we were lucky that both he and the location were still available to us.

However, we can take credit for understanding what had fallen into our laps and going back to film a scene that was already crossed off the list—something that rarely happens with indie film.

There isn't any advice that I can give about how to be resourceful, since every situation is different, but I do think it's important for filmmakers to constantly be evaluating (and re-evaluating) everything that they have at their disposal and to never be too scared or lazy to react when circumstances change.

Thomas Corpolant (Nick Magliocco) in before and after shots to illustrate his weight loss.

OFFENSIVE SATIRE—SCENE 75

Scene 75 is the third in-film advertisement for Burleson Laboratories. (Read about the first in scene 48 and the second in scene 62.) Now—even though this is a film about taking undocumented workers and hiring them to ride bikes that generate electricity—I consider scene 75 to be the most offensive in the entire film. And it has nothing to do with Mexicans.

The advertisement is a parody of those ASPCA ads with Sarah McLachlan. (Not familiar? Need a good cry? YouTube it.)

Parodying those ads is offensive enough, since they cover a very serious and emotionally charged subject. But this is also exactly what makes them ripe for satire. The comedy is possible because we are working with an existing commercial that pulls at the heartstrings. We're playing off of that pre-existing notion and using the familiarity of our audience as a shorthand. This allows us to save time and deliver only the punch line of a joke because the audience's shared knowledge of pop culture takes care of the setup.

However, this is not the most offensive aspect of the ad. In our ad, the images that we see are not mistreated animals. Rather, the images are of (and I'm cringing even as I write this) the recent devastation of Fukushima.

The overlaid text reads:

In Japan, this is what a core meltdown in the name of energy production looks like…

Later text points out:

Burleson Rider #2 (Robert Konczyk) caps off the advertisement in the film's obesity section.

In California, a core meltdown is...

The music changes to techno as we cut to the low angle shot that you see above of a Burleson Labs cyclist slimming down his "core" by pedaling the pounds away.

This whole thing is offensive. It makes me shrink down in my seat a bit every time I watch the film with an audience. But does that mean I shouldn't have created it? I don't think so.

If I had made this film for the sake of being offensive, then I'd be the first person to call bullshit. But I didn't. There is something uncomfortable about satire. It's what gives it its power. If it's not offensive, you're not taking any risks and—most importantly—it probably won't be funny.

It's really hard to find the appropriate "line" when creating satire, but I've learned that if I don't constantly feel like I'm skirting that line, I'm likely writing something that is boring. Worrying about offending my audience is a surefire way to deliver bland comedy with a bland message. (And—though comedy is not about delivering a message—I do think this is important here: If I didn't have the intention of raising awareness about these issues through comedy, and I was just being offensive to be offensive—I'd be a dick.) Maybe I'm a dick anyway, but at least I know why I did it.

So, yes, this ad is offensive. People should be angry when they see it. They should react strongly. But they should react more strongly to over 100,000 people having to evacuate their homes because of nuclear cores melting down.

A Scene in Three Shots—Scene 76

Scene 76 of *A Convenient Truth* is a transition scene between two of the film's collateral advantage segments. The obesity segment of the film has just ended, and Coleman (Alan Berman) is easing us into the next segment. The scene is less than a minute long and is covered very simply. However, that doesn't mean there's a lack of intention behind the editing. The scene plays out in three shots—each of which serves a purpose.

The scene opens with a medium shot, which would generally be an odd choice. There isn't much information in the frame, and it certainly doesn't establish where we are for the audience. We can get away with beginning with this shot though because the audience has seen this location before. They know the situation and won't be confused or distracted. The medium shot also gives the audience the feeling of joining in the middle of a larger scene, which is the case. It's also better at demanding attention.

When Coleman is ready to reveal what the next collateral advantage will be to his lecture audience, we also reveal it to the film's audience by cutting to a wide shot.

We cut to a wide shot at the exact moment where we need to see it. It's used to emphasize the new information in the frame. Coleman's slide changes from displaying something about obesity to a new one: Collateral Advantage IV: Language Barrier.

We've now gotten the information that we wanted, so there's no reason to linger in the wide shot. We punch in with a medium close-up. We finish up the remainder of the scene in this medium close-up to add weight to the thoughts that Coleman imparts about

Top: **Medium shot of Coleman Burleson (Alan Berman) as he continues his lecture.** *Bottom:* **Wider shot of Coleman Burleson (Alan Berman) as he continues his lecture.**

his solution for the language barrier between English and Spanish speakers in California. This part of the scene is more character-driven than informational, so it makes sense to "save" the close-up for it. That is, the close-up is used as a tool for emphasis, but it only works if used in that way. (You can shoot a whole scene in close-up, but it would be for a reason other than this effect. Imagine writing an entire paragraph with exclamation points.)

Medium close-up of Coleman Burleson (Alan Berman) as he finishes the scene.

Mini-Lesson: Sequence Rhythm

This scene is helpful to the overall rhythm of the film because it adds variety to the ways in which the collateral advantage segments interact with each other. A couple of previous collateral advantages end with one of the Burleson Labs advertisements and then go directly to the collateral advantage title card that introduces each segment. This scene breaks up that pattern and prevents the rhythm from becoming stale.

Planning a Scene—Scene 77

In scene 76 of *A Convenient Truth*, Coleman (Alan Berman) transitions us into the film's next collateral advantage segment. We immediately see the title card for Collateral Advantage IV: Language Barrier.

This is followed directly by an actual advertisement that Pat Buchanan ran in 2000 as part of his presidential campaign. The ad features a choking man attempting to call 911 only to collapse while waiting for the automated phone menu to cycle through the language options. (One can only wonder how a choking man was going to communicate over the phone anyway, but let's put that aside for now...)

"For Swahili, press 12," the phone voice declares, as the choking man's dog stands atop his now lifeless body. (Why make something up if reality is so bizarre?)

The film then transitions from the advertisement back to Coleman's lecture. I want to take a moment to point out four small ways in which forethought helped create an illusion on a small budget.

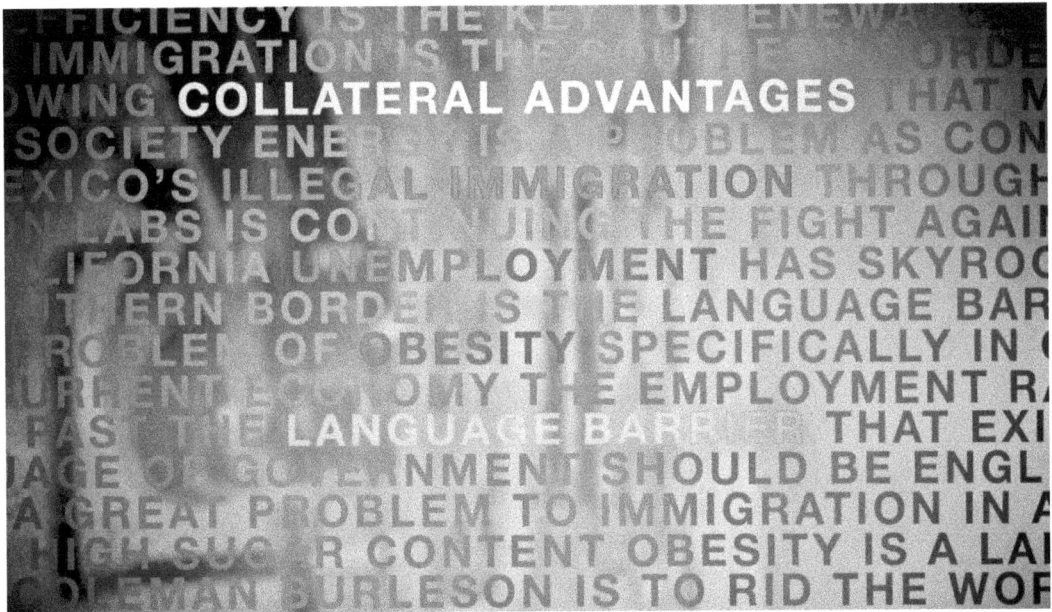

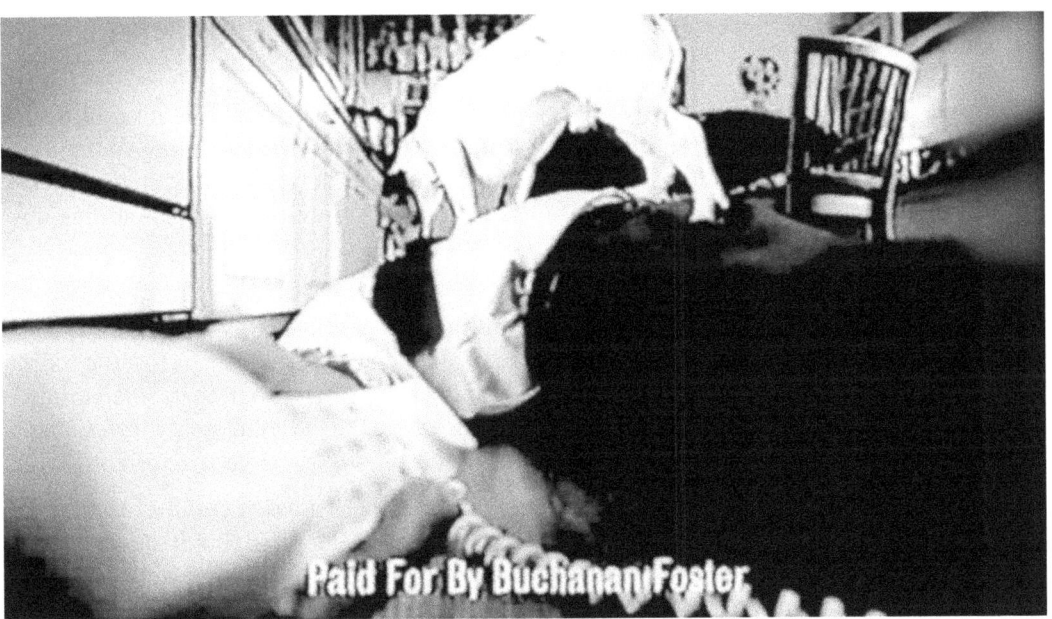

Top: Title card to begin the language barrier section of the film. *Bottom*: Closing still from Pat Buchanan campaign advertisement from 2000.

Four Low-Budget Film Tricks within the Frame Above

1. Know your transitions.
Thinking like an editor from the script stage will save you time and money. In the situation above, we anticipated an issue: how will we make it clear to the film audience that Coleman has just shown his audience the advertisement that we've just seen? Simple,

A cameraman on stage captures Coleman Burleson (Alan Berman) as he delivers his speech from within pools of light.

we see the last frame of the advertisement on Coleman's projector before he continues talking. The solution here is not difficult. What was important was planning enough to know that we'd need a solution before shooting. (Could this have been done in post? Yes. But indie film means relying on post as little as possible—prevent little costs adding up with a little planning.)

2. Sweat the details.

Notice the cameraman on the far right of the frame? Within this scene, we quickly cut to a close-up of Coleman. Placing the cameraman in the wide shot means that the audience understands where the close-up shot is coming from when we cut to it. Small things like this help sell the documentary feel of the film and make the frame more interesting.

3. Consider the edges of the frame.

One of the magical things about being on a film set is taking in all of the crew, equipment, etc., that sit just outside the frame. It's remarkable to have simultaneous visual access to what the film audience will eventually see and all of the elements that go into creating that shot. In this case, we used this to our advantage. We didn't have money for the hundreds of extras that it would have taken to fill the seats in our auditorium, but we wanted the place to feel full. By cutting off the bottom of the frame at the first row of the audience, we were able to establish Coleman on a stage with an audience, but we only needed a dozen or so cast and crewmembers to sit silhouetted in the first row to create the illusion. The film audience assumes that there are more people sitting behind the ones that can be seen. There aren't. (We had so few people that I'm probably directing from one of those seats in this frame.)

4. Use lighting creatively.

As mentioned in earlier sections about shooting in this location, we were lucky enough to have the full stage lighting grid at our disposal, and we used this to great advantage by creating multiple locations within one actual physical space. In this frame, we kept the lighting minimal to create three distinct pools of light that Coleman could wander in and out of. This made for an interesting look and in a strange way keeps the audience's attention. I feel like it's human nature to actively want Coleman to find himself back in the light when he's in the space in between pools. Anything that keeps an audience actively engaged is a useful tool.

Mini-Lesson: "Finding" Focus

Similar to the use of pools of light in number four above, we used a long lens for Coleman's close-up coverage of this scene. Within the shot, the camera operator has to adjust the focus as he follows Coleman. This is exactly how it would be in a real documentary, but it also makes the shot more interesting. As you can see here, the single shot transforms quite a bit, and the result is more engaging to watch than a single pristine shot. We actually have several shots that are miraculously entirely in focus, but we preferred this shot.

Four frame grabs from a single shot that add to the documentary feel of the film.

GET AN IMPOSSIBLE SHOT ... WITH TWO SHOTS—SCENE 78

One of the big disadvantages of our video camera was its lack of latitude within the frame. That is, for example, the daylight coming through a window can read as completely

Coleman Burleson (Alan Berman) points to something outside of the overexposed window.

blown out and lose image information (whereas the latitude of shooting film would capture more definition within the bright spots). Our video sensors couldn't handle the nuances of visual information the way a film camera could.

In this scene, Coleman (Alan Berman) points to something outside and across the street, but I wanted to capture both what he's pointing to and the lead up within the convenience store in a single shot. This essentially involved four difficult maneuvers for the camera operator in a very short time:

1. Follow the actor to capture the first part of the scene.
2. Snap-zoom a great distance to capture a sign across the street.
3. Adjust the aperture to properly expose for the outdoor conditions.
4. Focus properly on the distant sign and hold without shaking (which is a task on such a long lens).

We tried this for a few takes, but it was a longish scene, so each take was eating up our day. We eventually decided to make sure we captured all of the elements that we needed separately and to figure it out in post. If you've read much of this book, you'll know that I think indie filmmakers should be very leery of "figuring it out in post," but the situation called for it. The solution:

If you have fast enough motion in a shot, you can bury a cut.

After the blur occurs, we're able to cut in a totally different shot in which we've already changed the aperture, so the outside is no longer blown out. The motion blur is so great that the audience won't be able to distinguish it from the motion blur of a completely different snap-zoom. So we're able to take the tail end of a snap-zoom that we like and combine it with our favorite take for the first part of the scene. No one who has

Top: **Blur from the snap-zoom allows us to hide a cut.** *Bottom:* **A restaurant marquee across the street from the location that allowed us to post a message for the film.**

ever seen the film has noticed that we "cheated" here. We got exactly the "shot" that I wanted—even though that shot is actually two shots.

We got permission to post marquee letters on a sign across the street with a message that was written into the script. (Here's where location scouting is so important. We found a convenience store that would let us shoot in it and that had a sign across the street that we'd be allowed to use—all for free.)

Coleman Burleson (Alan Berman) tries to play the lottery with the Spanish-speaking cashier.

Mini-Lesson: Listen to Everyone

At the beginning of this scene, Coleman is attempting to give the clerk the lottery numbers that he'd like to play, but the clerk doesn't speak English. In the script, I'd written for the clerk to say, "No comprendo," which roughly translates to "I don't understand" and is exactly how someone who learned Spanish in a school might say it. However, the actor, who is a native Spanish speaker, pointed out that he would say, "No entiendo." Of course, this is a better response, so we went with it. Another instance where listening made the movie better.

LANGUAGE SEQUENCE—SCENES 79–88

Scenes 79–88 are best thought about as a sequence. This sequence is comprised of ten scenes and plays out from minutes 53:51 to 55:55 within the film. In all, these ten scenes cover a total of 2 minutes and 4 seconds. I've written about sequences more generally twice before—about building them in scenes 50–53 and in terms of tempo for scenes 65–67—so I want to focus on this particular sequence here.

Scene 79 further cements the film's transition from concentrating on obesity to the issue of the language barrier. Since this collateral advantage section began with an old advertisement from Pat Buchanan's presidential campaign and we've just seen Coleman in the informal convenience store setting, scene 79 brings us back to his presentation. The audience can settle back in and be ready for the many quick scenes that are about

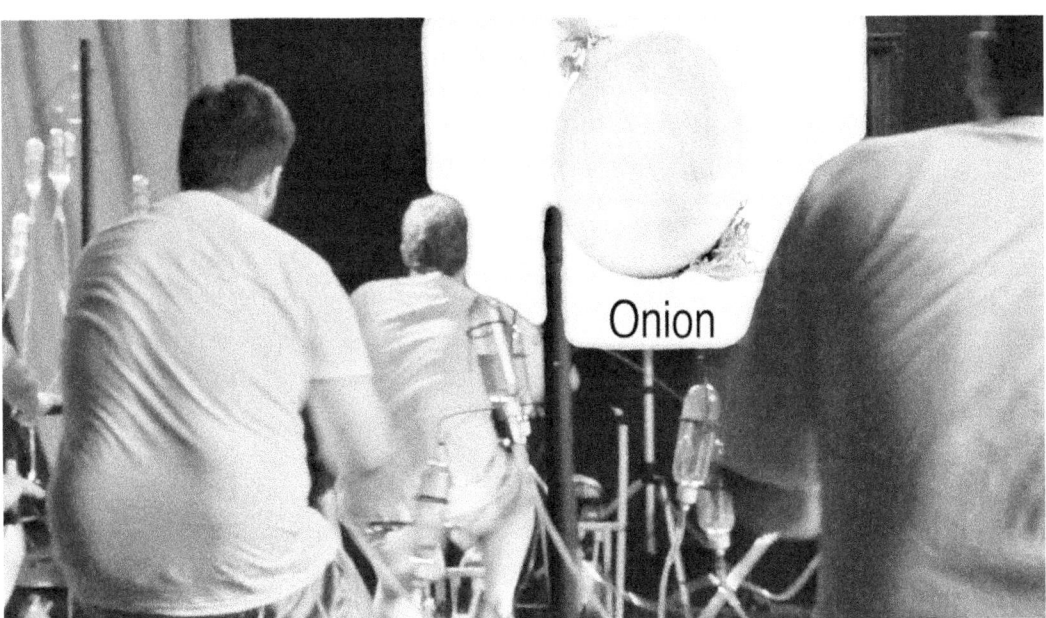

Top: Coleman Burleson (Alan Berman) officially introduces the language barrier section of his lecture. *Bottom:* Burleson workers get language lessons on the big screen in the Cycling Room.

to come their way. Coleman's last words in the scene are spoken definitively: "In America, we speak English."

The cut immediately reveals how Burleson Labs deals with the language barrier issue. A tracking shot from the back of the Cycling Room shows a picture of an onion displayed on the room's large screen. The word "Onion" is written below it, as a disembodied voice pipes into the room, "La cebolla. Onion." "Onion," the cyclists repeat back aloud

140   Part Two: Production

with varied degrees of fluency. Out of context, this scene would have almost no meaning, but it works well within the sequence.

Side Note: An old trick employed here is filling the foreground of the frame. The still only shows three cyclists, but creates the feeling that more people are outside the frame.

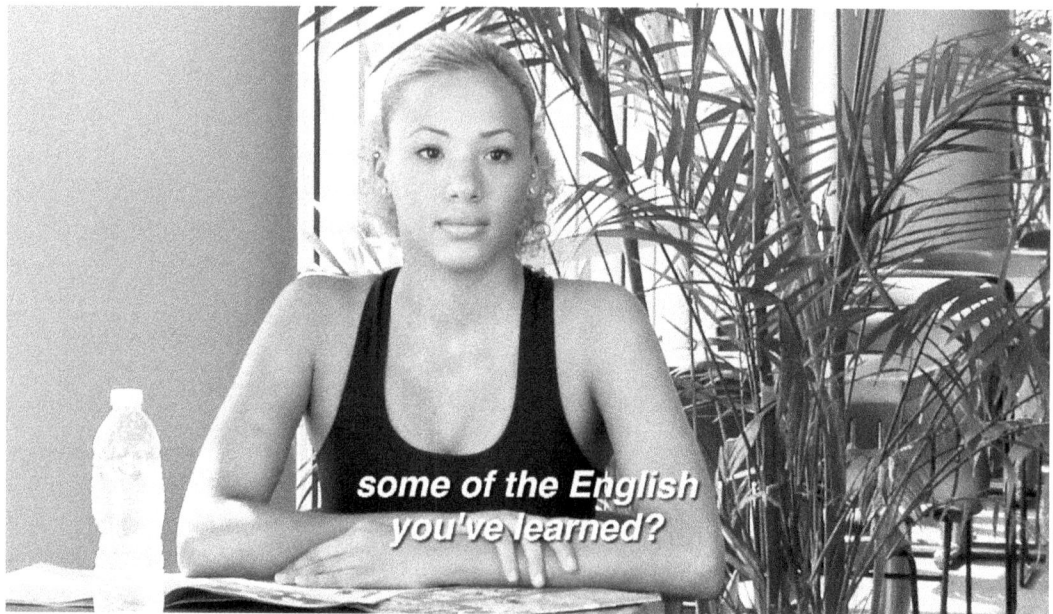

Top: A Burleson rider goes through some of the English that she's learned while working at Burleson Laboratories. *Bottom:* Coleman Burleson (Alan Berman) explains the language lessons at Burleson Laboratories.

Since the logical progression of seeing this type of language training is to want to hear from the workers in the program, scene 81 cuts directly to one such worker. The cyclist is asked if she can tell us some of the English that she has learned while working at the Lab. We take this opportunity to get a few laughs out of some of the phrases that she has learned. However, more importantly, we use the scene to introduce her character, so that we can quickly cut back to her for comedic moments without confusion.

Burleson riders repeat English words back at the screen in the Cycling Room.

Scene 82 once again gives Coleman an opportunity to explain himself. We never want the audience to be ahead of us, so—as with many scenes in the film—we preempt their questions by giving Coleman or Leonard a chance to advocate for Burleson Labs. Within this short (9-second) scene, Coleman explains that these language lessons occur on the big screen before and after their "stories," which refers to the telenovelas that can be seen in the Cycling Room at other times. He is also hilariously condescending, saying that the cyclists are "learning at a remarkably fast pace"—to his clear astonishment.

Finally, we use the scene to tie the location of this interview to Burleson Labs by playing a loop in the background that shows the Burleson Lab shield and various slogans that we see throughout the film. (This loop was created in After Effects in about 15 minutes, but it's an example of why location scouting and thinking about framing in advance is crucial. Why not use a television that exists in the space for production value? Again, we were constantly looking for ways to make talking head frames more interesting.)

Scene 83 gives us the reverse angle of scene 80. We now get to see the faces of the cyclists as they stare up at the screen and repeat back the English names of vegetables. This shot also mirrors scene 80 in that it similarly tracks across the cyclists. It's only 11 seconds long, but it makes complete sense because of the context of the sequence.

Scene 84 cuts back to the cyclist that we met in scene 81. We've established her as the interviewee who will represent the first-person account of learning English in the

We return to some of the English that has been learned.

Lab, so we waste no time getting into the scene. The cyclist struggles to say the word "onion," which directly calls back to scene 80. Again, this seems basic—because it is—but without the context, we'd have a random scene of a woman struggling to say the word "onion."

Cardamom Burleson (Jillian Leigh) recounts her father's ideas about the importance of learning English.

Scene 85 slows things down a bit as we return to Cardamom's (Jillian Leigh) interview. This scene allows someone other than Coleman to comment on the ridiculous nature of the scheme without undermining the film's satirical tone. It's also an example of how an actor's delivery can make your script so much better than you ever imagined. Jillian delivered the line in the script verbatim. However, as she did, she laughed a bit at the truth of what she was telling her interviewer. We instantly knew this was the take that we were going to use, and it was another one of those moments of true collaboration when an actor elevated my script above anything I'd imagined.

Top: Coleman Burleson (Alan Berman) defends the practice of language lessons. *Bottom:* We return again to the English that has been learned in the Cycling Room.

"These are not stupid people," Coleman continues in scene 86—seemingly picking up from and doubling down upon his condescending statement in scene 82. "This program is about breaking down barriers and that includes the language barrier," he declares.

Our final look at a language lesson in the Cycling Room comes in scene 87. The cyclists all repeat back, "For English, press one," with pride. We've earned this moment by building a sequence that leads to it and escalates along the way. That is, if we had gone directly from Pat Buchanan's ad with the 911 recording saying, "For Spanish, press one" to this, it would have been on-the-nose and unfunny. (Whether or not our version is funny is subjective, but I believe the structure of the sequence leads to a more successful joke.)

Finally, as a button on the end of the sequence, we cut back to our cyclist interviewee in scene 88. This time she's practicing saying a new phrase, and she finishes up by saying it with authority. This gives closure to her mini-arc. (Beginning = introduction with some phrases, Middle = struggling to say "onion," End = succeeding in confidently speaking English.)

The sequence is capped with a return to the interview about English learned at Burleson Laboratories.

MINING FILM LOCATIONS—SCENE 89

In indie films, when it comes to locations, you often have to "use what you got." This doesn't mean that every film that you shoot needs to take place in your living room (or dorm room). As long as you're not lazy, you'll realize that the locations that you have at your disposal are pretty expansive. For my first short film, *Awkwardly*, I got free access to a swanky office building in midtown Manhattan—because our producer had a con-

Coleman Burleson (Alan Berman) gets a resume from someone who learned English at Burleson Laboratories.

nection, and we asked. For my senior thesis film, *Initial Conditions*, a town in New Jersey let us shoot in a huge open field and even brought the fire department out to let us tap into their hydrants for use in our makeshift rain machines (jerry-rigged PVC pipes).

Scene 89 of *A Convenient Truth* was shot in a beautiful, historic home in North Plainfield, New Jersey. We needed an affluent look for the home of our protagonist, but we didn't have the money for proper set decoration. The solution was to shoot in a place that already looked the part. Ordinarily, that type of place would be expensive, but we put feelers out to our network and found a couple that allowed us to shoot in their home for free.

In this case, shooting with "what we got" was actually a joy. It no longer meant we had to figure out how to make do with subpar settings. Instead, it meant taking stock of the space and being inspired by it. Location scouting became a fun logic puzzle in this scenario. We walked through the amazing home and marveled at all that was available to us. This also helped the schedule take shape because obviously we wanted to group together scenes that would be filmed in the same physical location.

We were completely open to the possibilities of the space and made the most of the location. This one house served us well for four distinct locations within the film:

One house, four locations

1. We first see a room within this house in scene 5 (a gorgeous dining room).
2. This space ties directly to the sitting room in which Kitty Burleson (Elise Rovinsky) gives her interview throughout the film (beginning with scene 6).
3. Scene 89 makes use of a local politician's office that was temporarily on an upper floor of the house. We added a California flag and were pretty much ready to shoot Coleman's office.

4. Finally, the house had a really interesting attic space, which inspired us to improv a scene about the creation of Burleson's prototype bike. The scene was ultimately deleted from the film for pacing, but it looked great.

Whereas these scenes could easily have been spread out over four separate days, the proximity of all of these locations meant that we were able to shoot them all in one weekend and be comfortable doing so.

Top: Coleman Burleson (Alan Berman) and Leonard Wingmon (Kevin Hauver) test a bike prototype in a deleted scene. *Bottom:* Insert shot of the resume that Coleman references.

Mini-Lesson: Motivating the Macro

Within this scene, there's a moment when I really wanted the audience to be able to get a close-up of a résumé that Coleman holds and references. Given the mockumentary style, a traditional close-up would have been a bit clunky, so I solved the potential issue with a character moment. In the scene, Coleman tells the camera operator that he may have to "use that macro"—meaning a separate lens that will allow for shooting an extreme close-up. It explains the cut but, more importantly, it gives us another bit of insight into Coleman's character—namely that he's been around a film crew for a little while now and arrogantly thinks he knows what he's talking about. I don't think anyone would argue about that being consistent with his character.

SLAPSTICK COMEDY—SCENE 90

Scene 90 of *A Convenient Truth* is the fourth Burleson Labs advertisement in the film. (Earlier ads are scene 48, scene 62, and scene 75.) In it, one man (Jason Boyle) breaks some bad news to another. The second man (José Alvarez) has had a tracheotomy and talks with the use of a speaking device. As this second man pleads his case, the first man slaps the speaking device away—rendering the man with the tracheotomy unable to speak. It's a slapstick moment (with a literal slap) as the clank of the plastic device hits the ground and the man with the tracheotomy futilely tries to continue talking. The first man laughs uncontrollably at the second man's impotence. The whole thing is extremely

Man #2 (Jason Boyle) and Man with Tracheotomy (José Alvarez) in Burleson Laboratories language advertisement.

broad and more farcical than much of the rest of the film. However, it gets laughs, and we've previously established an over-the-top tone for the in-film advertisements.

It's very kind to say this scene was "problematic" from the start. The script version included a parrot—as if notions about the importance of the ability to speak needed to be pushed even further. It also jumped right into the middle of an intimate conversation between two new characters in a new space. The whole thing was just strange. We cut the parrot bit from the script, and—to be honest—I still wasn't even sure if we'd be able to make the scene work when we were setting up to shoot it.

It was my first time shooting on a "cyc," which is essentially a wall that curves at the bottom where it meets the floor. That curve creates the sort of infinite distance that you see in many commercials. I was excited to be able to shoot in the space, but I worried about the content. This is where I relied on my actors. I had to hope that they'd bring something to the scene that was better than the script. They didn't disappoint.

Each of these actors, Jason Boyle and José Alvarez, were day players who had submitted headshots to our Pennsylvania casting session. Their entire experience with the film was comprised of that audition and the half-day that we had to shoot this advertisement. With so much going on in an indie film, it would have been easy to neglect these relatively small roles, but these situations are precisely why a director should always be working hard and paying attention.

The laugh that Jason brought to the scene worked perfectly—better than I had imagined on the page. (It's actually really hard to fake laughter.) The physicality and timing of the slap also made a real difference in terms of the comedic action. It elicits a visceral laugh from audiences every time.

Similarly, José brought an intensity and vulnerability to his character that is the reason the scene works. We only know his character for about five seconds before we feel sincerely bad for him—an emotion that enables the comedy of the scene. (José was so prepared he even came to the soundstage with a tracheotomy collar tied around his neck.)

I feel completely confident in saying that this advertisement was a good candidate to be a deleted scene before we began filming it, but clutch acting elevated it to one of the heartiest laughs in the film.

Now, although we allowed the film to get progressively broader as it went on, we still needed to maintain the overall tone of the reality that we created in it. How could we have such a broad, crass scene in our little dry satire? Simple: Coleman immediately acknowledges the outrageous nature of what we've just seen and doubles down on his sincerity. Within the ad, Coleman wipes onto the screen—sharing the same white cyc background.

Coleman Burleson (Alan Berman) wipes onto the screen to end the language advertisement.

"This was a harsh scene. But, in many ways, these are harsh times. Learn to speak up. And never let anyone take your voice away again."—Coleman Burleson

This button at the end of the scene squeezes a bit more comedy out of the ad and brings us back to the world of the film—which is heightened—but not nearly as heightened as this advertisement.

Mini-Lesson: Repeat Watching

Many friends and family members have now seen the film multiple times, and several have remarked that they enjoy it even more upon repeat viewing. This is because they catch little things that we've implanted that most audience members won't or couldn't catch the first time around. There are tons of these in the film, but one example to mention here is that Mitch Heron (from the unemployment section of the film) credits the tracheotomy ad with inspiring him to work at the Lab (before we've seen what he's talking about).

Audiences like to pat themselves on the back for recognizing things like this, and it's also evidence that the filmmaker has put in additional thought—always a good sign.

As a viewer, especially with comedies, repeat watchability is important to me. So, as a filmmaker, I should do my best to make sure my films have that attribute.

PACING: THE ONE-HOUR MARK—SCENES 91–93

Pacing is one of the most interesting considerations in editing any film. It's something that you really can't consider until everything is laid out in front of you. In general, as the audience gets to know the film, the pace has to pick up to prevent the viewers from getting ahead of you and getting bored. This certainly held true for *A Convenient Truth*.

Collateral Advantage V: Dependence on Foreign Oil came right around the one-hour mark of the film. At this point, the audience knows the drill. This is collateral advantage 5 of 5. They've seen four other collateral advantage sections, and they know that this is the last one. So, by design, this is the shortest collateral advantage section. It seems basic (because it is), but we could have easily fallen in love with this collateral advantage, made it longer, and killed the pacing of the film.

So, this section begins with three short scenes that combine for a total of 76 seconds. No need to dally. One after the other.

In fact, this section originally began with a whole chunk of voiceover about America's oil usage that we realized we didn't need once we were in the editing room. We cut it and got right into our three scenes.

First, we get a conservative opinion from a man-on-the-street interview about how the price of oil affects him. Scene 91. Second, we get a liberal opinion about how we need an eco-friendly alternative to fossil fuels. Scene 92. Third, we get a scientific opinion for an impartial documentary feel. Scene 93.

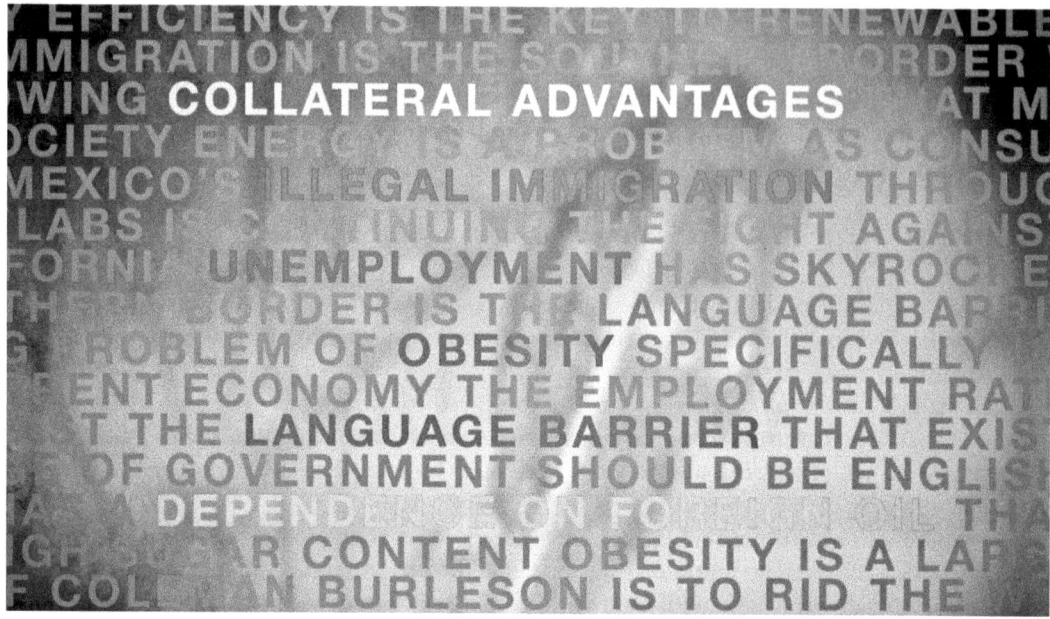

Top: Title card to begin the foreign oil section of the film. *Bottom:* Coleman Burleson (Alan Berman) conducts a man-on-the-street interview about gas prices.

Scene 93 holds two important lessons for me:

1. Always be open to casting opportunities.

The actor portraying Ethan Mayes is Richie Warmkessel. One night after a long day of shooting, we were all exhausted and returned to our hotel. We'd driven around a lot that day, and no one was particularly keen to get back into the cars to travel to a cast and

Top: Eleanor Burleson (Gilli Messer) gets an environmentalist opinion in a man-on-the-street interview. *Bottom:* Ethan Mayes (Richie Warmkessel) gives a geological perspective on oil dependence.

crew dinner. The hotel complex happened to have a Cracker Barrel restaurant in it. I'd never heard of Cracker Barrel, but it's indie film, we're not going to high-end restaurants anyway, so we went.

We spoke about the next day's agenda over dinner and many of us had scripts, schedules, etc., out on the table. Our waiter that night was no one other than Richie Warmkessel, and he noticed. He asked about our film and let us know that he's an actor. We had a day player role that we hadn't yet been able to fill, and Richie seemed serious enough, so we gave him the scene. Of course, if he hadn't had any acting ability, we would have cut the scene, but if we didn't give him the chance, we might not have been able to even give the scene a try. He came to set a few days later and nailed it. He was assertive enough to let us know he was an actor, and we were flexible enough to take a chance. I'm really glad we did.

2. There's always something to do on a film set.

Since, as I mentioned, we were originally unable to find someone we liked for the role of Ethan Mayes, it meant that scene 93 was never fully incorporated into the schedule. It always hung by on the side as a potential scene that we might fit in somewhere. However, once we cast Richie, it meant that we now needed to find time for it. How did we do it? You might recall that scene 32 was a particularly difficult one to shoot. We shot in a beautiful industrial complex that doubled for Burleson Labs, and the scene involved using almost all of the lights that we rented. It also involved a camera move and a blue screen behind practical doors that we built and brought in. All of this is to say that it was complicated.

Rather than sit around as the DP lit the scene and worked out the camera move, I ran over to an adjacent part of the complex with the camera and a sound person. We filmed Richie's scene (which was a simple walk and talk) literally as another scene was being prepped.

Normally, I would have loved to be there as scene 32 got set up, but I would have essentially been sitting and waiting. There's no time to sit and wait on an indie film set—especially as the director. By recognizing this possibility, we were essentially able to "create time" in the schedule and get more pages shot in the same amount of time.

OFFENSIVE SATIRE, REVISITED—SCENES 94-96

I first talked about offensive satire in relation to scene 75—the Burleson Labs advertisement in the obesity section of the film.

Scene 94 is a quick transition scene to lead us into the next Burleson Labs advertisement, which we've come to expect for each collateral advantage section by now—based on our experience viewing the film.

Coleman dances around the topic of foreign oil dependence. He is hesitant to draw a link between foreign oil and the war on terror—but he does allow himself to show an ad. This prepares the audience to see something that is likely going to be highly offensive—since even Coleman is thinking twice about it. The ad doesn't disappoint.

We are immediately confronted with a stark, black-and-white image. The man is calmly speaking (though we don't hear any words), but the music is terribly over-the-top. We immediately recognize that the man is being presented as a gross stereotype. Coleman sits across the desk—nodding along, but not really listening to him. We cut back and forth a few times, until Coleman finally slams a Burleson Labs nameplate onto the desk, shakes his head, and waves goodbye to the man. The narrator announces, "Burleson Labs, not funding terrorism since 2007."

Obviously, this is horribly offensive and is an extremely broad joke. That is, it would

Above: Coleman Burleson (Alan Berman) introduces the final collateral advantage section of the film. *Right:* Close-up of Arab (Jesus Melendez) in Burleson Laboratories' bank ad. *Below:* Coleman Burleson (Alan Berman) denies a loan in Burleson Laboratories ad.

be a broad joke if the film were making it. The real joke, within the context of the satire, is obviously on Coleman and Burleson Labs. By simply presenting how ridiculous their notions are, we are able to get our point across without needing to separately comment. (Sometimes it's more effective to simply show something offensive than to get on a soapbox and preach about prejudice.)

As I mentioned when I wrote about scene 75, it's precisely this type of dangerous, cringe-inducing offensiveness that tells me I'm in a place that is ripe for satire.

The advertisement immediately turns into a sort of double advertisement, and we get another ad directly on the back of this one. Scene 96 opens with devastating images of animals affected by the BP/Deepwater Horizon oil spill of 2010. They are tragic and affecting. The narrator comes on, "In the Gulf of Mexico, this is what a greasy living thing looks like thanks to BP."

Oil covered pelican after the Deepwater Horizon oil spill in 2010.

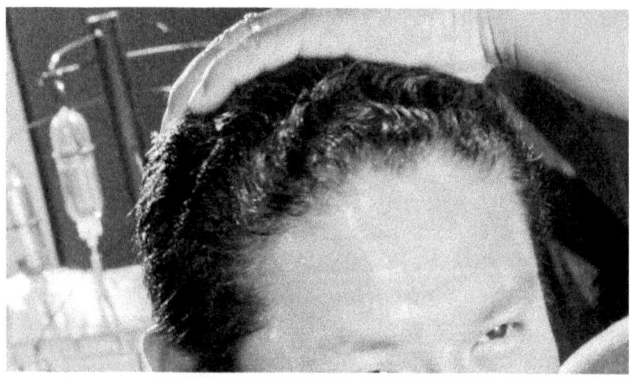

Extreme close-up of greasy hair in Burleson Laboratories advertisement.

The narrator then continues, "In California…"

And we see that at Burleson Labs a "greasy living thing" is nothing more than a Mexican who has been riding a bike all day.

Again, these ads are offensive. People should be offended by them, but they should be more offended by the rampant racism and horrific oil spills that are real and occur daily.

Mini-Lesson: Letting the Film Evolve

Scene 96 was obviously not in the first draft of the film—since the events hadn't happened yet. However, since we followed related news items and were always open to improving the film, we were able to add this advertisement to the film and draw attention to yet another injustice within our existing scope.

FIVE WAYS WE FIXED A DULL SCENE—SCENE 97

(Warning: This section is much longer than the others, but that's because this is the single scene from which I learned the most.)

Scene 97 was the one that killed my movie. It came right after the fifth (and final) collateral advantage section of the film. The audience was primed to move on to the next bit—to see where this was going. But scene 97 was a recap. In general, recaps are never good. Filmmakers shouldn't give the audience information that they already know. However, even though I knew this general guideline, I felt that the audience had been bounced around so much in the first hour that they would need some scene that brought it all back together. After the first test screening of the film, scene 97 jumped out at me. It was beyond dull, and it needed to be fixed. There was something about seeing it on the big screen that made this very clear.

The main issues with the scene arose because we had covered the scene in a very

Coleman Burleson (Alan Berman) begins the recap of his proposal.

standard way—with three different shots (wide, medium, and close-up)—but there was not much continuity in the action from one take to another. This meant that we had to cut more with an eye for continuous movement than performance. It also dictated the length of the scene.

To clarify, imagine Coleman talking for a few minutes and pacing the stage as he does. This is fine, and the movement actually makes the shot more dynamic. However, if he doesn't pace in a precisely choreographed manor, he might be on the right side of the stage when he finishes up a sentence in take one and somewhere in the middle of the stage when he completes that same sentence in take two.

Now imagine that there are several takes of each shot (wide, medium, and close-up), and remember that we're not shooting multiple cameras simultaneously. The result is that we were extremely limited in the takes that we could actually use without Coleman magically hopping all around the frame. In practice, it meant that scene 97 actually cut very rarely because we had to let each clip play out as long as we could—each edit represented a matching challenge.

The scene was essentially about five minutes of Coleman talking about the six advantages of his proposal alternating between a wide and a medium shot. Riveting…

But how could we fix it? I'll show you.

1. Sound-ups

After much deliberation about how to fix this catastrophic scene, a big part of the solution was to stop thinking of it as a scene at all. What if scene 97 were actually a sequence?

This opened up a whole new world. Now, not only could we cut away from the problematic recap, we'd have a place to insert some of the clips that we loved that hadn't made the cut of the film. We called these inserts "sound-ups" internally—though I'm still not

Wide shot of Coleman Burleson (Alan Berman) giving his recap.

Five Ways We Fixed a Dull Scene—Scene 97   157

Top: Stock footage of light bulb used as b-roll. *Middle:* Stock footage of lights going out in a cityscape used as b-roll. *Bottom:* Burleson Laboratories cyclists hard at work.

Back to the wide shot of Coleman Burleson's (Alan Berman) recap.

sure if that's actually the right term—or a term at all. So, when Coleman is recapping all about how Burleson Labs is the solution for the energy crisis, we can continue to hear him but see more interesting things that complement his speech. Alternatively, we can cut in with entirely new clips that we both see and hear to support Coleman's statements.

2. Visual and character callbacks

We were always looking for ways to bring back characters that we'd met earlier in the film, but the structure made this difficult. In many cases, characters would be introduced as part of a specific collateral advantage segment, and it didn't make sense to see them outside of that context. However, here we were able to solve two things at once. Since Coleman was recapping his proposal, we could also visually recall characters from the sections of the film as Coleman referenced them. For example, we get another look at the Burleson cyclists, which we hadn't seen for a while.

Coleman continues his recap, reminding us of the proposal's alleviation of immigration woes. Rather than being forced to watch Coleman talk about immigration in this wide shot, we get to again see the Minutemen (along with some other interesting coverage). In fact, this solution allowed us to use a clip of the Minutemen that we had considered lost. The clip was the end of a lengthy improv, and I called cut before I knew that the next line was going to be hilarious. The camera cut without capturing the end of the line. However, the microphones did pick up the audio. Since the editing format of the sequence was now fluid and fast-moving, we were able to see the first part of the scene and use other coverage over the part of the line that was not captured by the camera.

Next, we get to see Cardamom for a few seconds. In addition to making the sequence more dynamic, we again were able to accomplish our goal of integrating characters from earlier in the film into this latter part.

Top: Minutemen (Scott Boyko and Bill McLaughlin) provide a callback to break up the recap. *Bottom:* Stock footage of Mexico/Arizona signage used as b-roll.

3. Shortened it

This one is obvious but still worth pointing out. If a scene is dull, the first instinct should be to cut it entirely. If it can't be cut for some reason, the second goal should be to make it as short as possible.

By adding all of this complexity to the sequence, we were able to make a lot more edits, which also meant more freedom to cut out entire chunks that we didn't need. Since

Top: **Stock footage of children crossing a river.** *Bottom:* **Cardamom Burleson (Jillian Leigh) provides a character callback to further break up the recap.**

we no longer had to look for cuts that visually matched for continuity, we could keep the minimum acceptable amount of dialogue. (Whereas in the first version we would have been forced to keep an extra sentence or two because we had to wait until Coleman landed on the spot that we needed him to be in to make the edit to the next shot.)

My opinion is that shorter is always better when it comes to scenes, but that's especially true for comedy. (You can think I'm full of shit, but you're beefing with Shakespeare if you don't think "brevity is the soul of wit.")

Top: Stock footage used for the obesity portion of the recap. *Bottom:* A slight digital zoom added to the wide shot of Coleman Burleson (Alan Berman) to add some dynamism.

In fact, we moved on to the next part of the recap without even cutting back to Coleman at all. We continue with alternative coverage as we hear him begin to talk about obesity. We then come back to Coleman after a few more shots. This is where I'll mention:

4. *Added movement in post*
We added a very slight digital push-in to almost all of the clips in this sequence—

including the boring wide shot of Coleman. This added cohesion to all of the diverse clips that we were now mashing together for the recap and actively lets the audience know that they're all part of the same thought.

You definitely don't want to overdo techniques like this, but they can be very effective if used subtly. At the beginning of the sequence, it probably takes audiences a few moments before they even realize that we're employing this zoom tool. And that's a good thing. It's about creating a feel, not drawing attention to the editing.

It's also worth noting that this is the first time that we see Coleman's slide as he recaps the obesity section of the film. It reads, "Fatties," and gets a laugh from astute

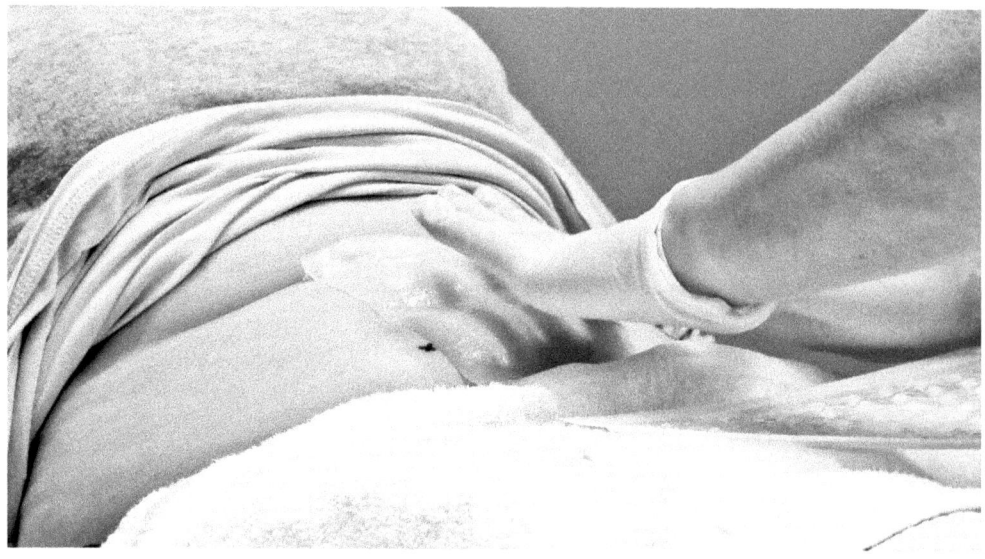

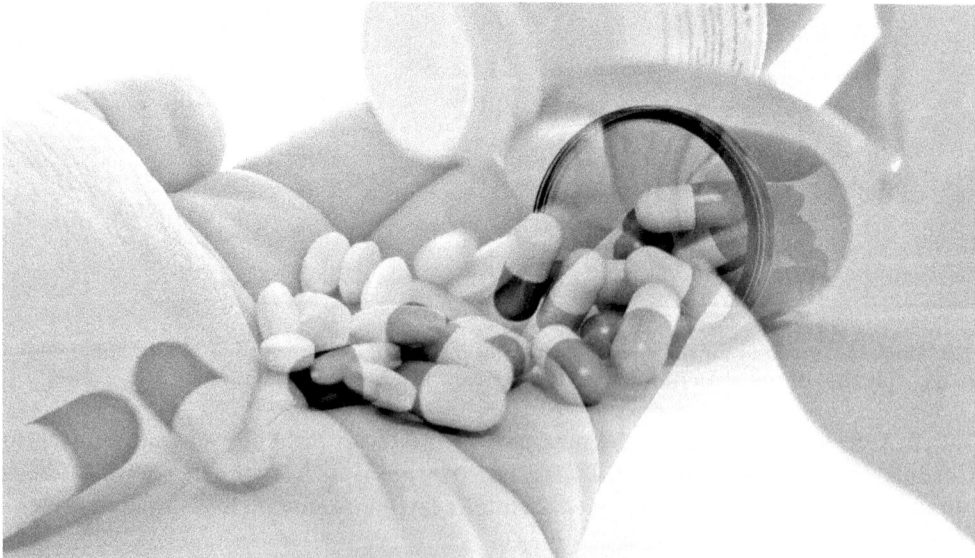

Top: **Stock footage of liposuction surgery used as b-roll.** *Bottom:* **Dissolving layered stock footage of pills used as b-roll.**

viewers every time—a reveal that wouldn't have existed without this new sequence approach.

We then see more shots that fall into the "Visual and Character Callbacks" fix. In some cases, we inserted several shots very quickly to ramp things up. And then we see a sweaty shot of Thomas Corpolant as Coleman talks about solving obesity with "good old-fashioned sweat." Yay for more character continuity.

Top: **Character callback of Thomas Corpolant (Nick Magliocco) working out.** *Bottom:* **Coleman Burleson (Alan Berman) recaps the language advantages of his proposal.**

Top: **A character callback reminds us of the language lessons at Burleson Laboratories.** *Bottom:* **Coleman Burleson (Alan Berman) reaches the last part of his recap.**

Coleman begins to talk about how his proposal teaches his Mexican workers English, and we cut back to the worker that we met in that section of the film. "Avocado," she repeats a few times, trying to perfect the pronunciation—until we punch in as she says it confidently, triumphantly even. This briefly seen character has now been given a mini-arc that the audience enjoys. Further, a layer of connection is added because Coleman talks in his recap about "getting what you ordered at the drive-thru," and we realize that

Top: **Horace Cullen (Joshua Ryan) offers a gasoline-related conspiracy theory.** *Bottom:* **Dissolving layered stock footage of oil drilling and gas pumps used as b-roll.**

a lot of what we've seen the cyclists learning is the names of various foods. (It also ties in nicely with Cardamom's earlier scene, which explicitly mentions Mexicans and fast food.)

Before we know it, we've reached the foreign oil part of the recap. We barely need to see Coleman by this point in the sequence. Instead, we get more interesting coverage and callbacks for Horace Cullen and Eleanor Burleson.

Above: Character callback of Eleanor Burleson (Gilli Messer) speaking about fossil fuel alternatives. *Left:* Dissolving layered stock footage of a gas pump and meter used as b-roll. *Below:* Coleman Burleson (Alan Berman) walks away as he rests his case.

When we finally come back to Coleman, he wraps up his recap and turns his back to the audience. He begins walking away. He's resting his case—dropping the mic without literally dropping the mic.

5. Scoring

Finally, I can't remember if the original version of scene 97 had no scoring or temp scoring, but it doesn't really matter.

Don't fall into the trap of hating your sequence without a score or loving it with a temp score. You have no idea what it will ultimately be like until someone has written a score specifically for your images and you've laid it in.

Music won't make a deadly scene amazing all by itself, but it can be a huge part of improving something that feels dull or lifeless. If scoring isn't appropriate, try music of some kind. If the music isn't working, try a genre that you would never have imagined for the scene. Playing around with music can really do wonders. In this case, the great driving score that we created really gave us that extra help that we needed.

I haven't even included images from all of the shots that we used in scene 97, but it should be clear how we exploded the idea of a static scene through the use of dozens of other shots to create a sequence.

EDITING CHOICES—SCENE 98

In their simplest form, editing choices come down to two types of problems. In one case, you don't have the coverage that you want to properly cut the scene. In the other, you have plenty of great coverage, which means you're essentially faced with infinite

Medium close-up of Leonard Wingmon (Kevin Hauver) listening to the interviewer's question.

choices. Where do you start? Scene 98 of *A Convenient Truth* is a clear illustration of how we approached one such scene.

This scene is another excerpt from our "red chair interview." (Other clips were used in scene 26 and scene 39.) The scene has standard coverage for this type of interview. We have a two-shot that establishes the space and allows us to see the interaction of the two characters. We also have medium close-ups for each speaker.

The most basic order of such coverage would be to begin with the two-shot and then move into the singles as the scene dictates. However, in this scene, it was important to not let convention trump performance and storytelling. Additionally, since we'd already seen this location earlier in the film, we didn't need to establish the location with the two-shot in the same way. The audience knows where we are. No one is going to be confused.

So how did we choose how we wanted to cut the scene? We worked backward. We found the shots that we wanted to be on for certain key lines and then let pacing help us decide from there.

We knew that we had one specific take of Coleman's medium close-up that we wanted to use for his response to the interviewer's question. We also knew that we wanted to end the scene on the two-shot because there was a great interaction between Coleman and Leonard that we needed to see.

Matching medium close-up of Coleman Burleson (Alan Berman) listening to Leonard's response.

This was fine and only presented one small problem. Namely, we heard Leonard talking off screen for part of Coleman's response. Since we'd be using Coleman's single, Leonard would seem like a disembodied voice to the audience.

The solution was to begin the scene on the shot of Leonard. So we actually see Leonard as the question is being asked—even though Coleman is mostly going to be the one responding. It's a small thing, but it means that when we cut to Coleman's single for

Wide shot of Leonard Wingmon (Kevin Hauver) and Coleman Burleson (Alan Berman) in their familiar interview setup.

his response we don't have to worry about any confusion taking the audience's attention away from listening to what Coleman is saying.

We can then end the scene with the two-shot, which is what we wanted for performance, and it doesn't seem odd at all. This order would not have ever been the first to come to mind—or how I'd expect the scene to play out—but listening to the footage and thinking outside convention led to smart editing choices. Ultimately, this allowed us to cut together the version of the scene that uses the best takes for each angle.

STAGING THE CASUAL—SCENES 99 AND 100

Scenes 99 and 100 of *A Convenient Truth* presented the same interesting challenge that we'd faced many times in the film. How do we best go about "staging the casual"?

In most movies, but especially in mockumentaries, there is a certain amount of staging the casual that has to be done. The completely planned and rehearsed scene playing out in front of the audience needs to feel natural.

The reason I say "especially in mockumentaries" is because audiences for these films do the least amount of suspending their disbelief. The conceit is that they're watching something real unfold—like in a documentary—so we can't get away with something feeling fake. Again, no movie wants to feel fake, but audiences going into an epic fantasy film have a different expectation and relationship with the film, so we need to honor that as filmmakers. (Or purposely subvert the conventions, but that's another topic.)

170 Part Two: Production

Coleman Burleson (Alan Berman) answers a post-lecture question while sitting on the edge of the stage.

In scene 99, Coleman is asked a simple question from the audience after one of his talks. Even though Alan Berman knows exactly what's about to happen before I call "action," Coleman Burleson and the crew don't. There are a few small things we did to make it feel spontaneous.

1. Find your frame.

Begin with the camera in motion and then "find" the person asking the question as he stands up. "Finding" the frame is a good way to start.

2. Lose focus.

The camera zooms from the speaker to Coleman as he gives his response, but we also see it lose focus along the way. In a non-mockumentary film, this scene would be rehearsed and re-shot until the zoom and focus pulling were perfectly in sync, but that wouldn't make sense here.

3. Imperfect audio.

You have to be really careful with this, as bad audio is one of the most common and frustrating issues with independent films. However, in this scene (in addition to using a lavalier microphone), we recorded the feed from the prop microphone that Coleman used. Coleman is so incredulous in his answer to the question that he waves the microphone around a bit as he answers. The performance is great, but we also decided to use this slight audio wavering in the film. It added a sense of reality without detracting from the audio quality too much.

4. Think of the crew as characters.

How would they react to capturing the scene if they had no prior knowledge? Even

Delivery boy (Michael Melendez, Jr.) on a bike delivers food to Coleman Burleson (Alan Berman).

small non-reactions from your crew can ruin the illusion of spontaneity. Similarly, any anticipation on the part of the crew is a dead giveaway that something is staged—the camera should be moving with the action or slightly behind it, not ahead of things that could not be predicted. Similarly, the boom operator should be genuinely reacting to what's occurring in the scene. You may even consider making the actors vary certain things within each take to keep everyone honest.

Scene 100 was a similar situation. Coleman and the crew are mostly idle in a hotel room. How do we make that seem natural and not boring? In a regular narrative, we generally get into scenes as late as possible and get out of them as quickly as possible. We want the audience to only see the most important bits. However, in a mockumentary, sometimes more context is necessary because that context is what makes the scene funny.

As we shot this scene, we had some fun with the crew. The DP casually set the camera somewhere; the sound guy decided he wanted to come out of the bathroom. Then we let Coleman and the sound guy have an impromptu exchange. Additionally, the delivery person on the other side of the door would vary the amount of time that he would take before knocking. This meant that Coleman, the DP, and the sound guy would all be genuinely reacting to a knock because they couldn't predict exactly when it would come.

Don't Mistake "Casual" for Lazy

I want to reiterate that each of the casual scenes were still approached professionally. The clearest line I can draw here comes with lighting.

I could imagine some filmmakers taking this idea of staging the casual to mean that they don't need to light a scene at all. (What's more casual than using available light?) However, that was not our approach for any of our scenes.

Anyone can be casual when making a film. Remember the "staging" part. Each of these scenes was carefully lit to get the look that we wanted. Filmmakers are always lighting their shots, but they almost never want them to look lit. It's about creating an illusion that the space actually looks the way it does, and that illusion does not draw attention to itself. So, in my opinion, this is not something that mockumentaries can get away with, but rather something they have in common with purely narrative films.

Mini-Lesson: No Man's Land in Structure

These two scenes, as well as scene 98 before them, fall into the "no man's land" of the film's structure. With the structure being: intro, five collateral advantage segments, recap, and third act.

This "no man's land" in between the recap and the third act is originally where we stuffed all of the scenes that we thought were funny but didn't otherwise fit into the film's structure. This is never a good idea.

Ultimately, even though the scenes were funny, we had to cut this "no man's land" down to just these three scenes to keep the film moving forward. In our experience of watching the film, this was what we found to be the tolerable limit before needing to move into the third act.

CONTEXT CHANGES EVERYTHING—SCENE 101

Scene 101 of *A Convenient Truth* looks familiar when it pops onto the screen. It's actually the second half of scene 21. One of the biggest epiphanies we had while editing was that we could break up scene 21 into these two distinct scenes. Why was making this leap so enticing? Because context changes everything. Nothing exists in a vacuum, and the meaning behind a scene is altered based on what an audience has seen before it—as well as retroactively by what directly follows it. In this case, there were four advantages to splitting the scenes in this way.

Four Reasons That Context Created Scene 101

1. Bookending.

Scene 21 showed Senator Harris's direct reaction in opposition to Coleman's proposal. It falls in the 13th minute of the film, and it served the function of giving voice to the audience's outrage. It also kept the film anchored in reality by showing someone who would express the audience's thoughts.

The end of Senator Harris's speech is a perfect ending to a scene. So, rather than letting the rest of the scene (Coleman's response) play out, we cut away. However, coming back to Coleman's response in scene 101 (in the 65th minute) adds a great structure to the film. We can now return to the debate scene and listen to Coleman's response with the information that the body of the film has given us.

Coleman Burleson (Alan Berman) and Senator William Harris (Michael Anderson) engage in a local debate, as a continuation of scene 21.

2. Avoiding redundancy.

Scene 22 is Leonard defending Coleman's proposal by explaining that all great leaps forward are controversial. Since we have that scene directly after scene 21, we don't also need to hear Coleman defend himself in the debate scene.

3. Different reading of the scene.

I've always been fascinated by the idea of using the same exact footage in order to create an alternate feeling or meaning. (Putting a pop song under a dark scene or focusing on different details within the same image, for example.) Since we've already seen part of this scene before, we get back into it with an extended fade up. We don't actually need to see it again. We hear just enough to get across that we're returning to something that we have seen before.

However, the first time we see the scene, Coleman seems worried as he listens to Senator Harris—and we're mostly focusing on Senator Harris. The second time around, with most of the film under our belt, our reading of Coleman is different. If he seems antsy, it isn't because he's caught having to answer to Senator Harris's accusations. It's because he can't wait for his turn to rebut them. When we finally do get to hear Coleman speak, it actually sort of makes sense, whereas it would have completely come off as more clueless propaganda if it were still part of scene 21.

4. Two shorter scenes.

This one is fairly self-explanatory but is worth noting. In most cases, two shorter scenes are better than one really long scene—especially when the scene is static. Scene 21 weighs in at 1 minute and 10 seconds; Scene 101 is a whopping 1 minute and 41 seconds. These scenes are actually quite long as they are, but combining them would have created a single scene just under 3 minutes long. That's just too long. (The scene plays out almost exactly as written, but it was less than two script pages. This is more proof that the page-a-minute guideline is just that—a rough guideline.)

Mini-Lesson: The Kuleshov Effect

I've been obsessed with this idea of re-using the same footage to achieve alternative readings since a high school psychology class, in which I read about the Kuleshov effect. In essence, this effect establishes that the reading of identical footage is altered by the other footage with which it is intercut. A quick web search will turn up many videos that show this effect of context at the most basic level, including a clip of Alfred Hitchcock talking about its use. Take a look.

YOUR TIME IS LIMITED—SCENE 102

Your time is limited. Putting existential jokes aside, scene 102 of *A Convenient Truth* taught me that—regardless of how much I want to ignore it—time is limited in film.

This scene comes directly after we've seen Coleman handle himself very well in the local debate. He sits in the back of the car with Leonard—smug and accomplished. Since smugness is such an integral part of Coleman's character, this was a particularly juicy situation. We reveled in it: Coleman and Leonard riffing with each other in a moment of justified confidence. The possibilities were seemingly endless. The trouble is:

The useable scene is finite.

I happily climbed into the car with two actors raring to go in the backseat. We must have improvised ten takes as we drove around the city. And many of them were excellent. However, some of the takes were hilarious primarily because of their length—a long story comes full circle, or a reference comes back around and lands beautifully. Takes like that were great for our own energy and amusement, but they were not helpful for the film.

For many reasons, but especially the momentum of the film, we weren't going to dump a four-minute scene into the film at this point—no matter how funny it was.

Additionally, it was important for me keep in mind as we shot that the slate was wiped clean every time I called cut. Because this was a single camera mounted in a car, there was no coverage. I couldn't keep bits of other takes in mind and then try to stitch them together. It was all or nothing.

And anyone who has played around with improv will tell you that it's usually futile to try to recreate an improvised moment. I'd recommend moving on without even trying it.

None of this is groundbreaking, but I had to go through it to really learn it. You can get a lot of great stuff, but you don't get to keep it all. You have to choose one. Internalizing this now will save you a lot of future grief. To a certain extent, you're making a film on the film's terms. (Think of it like going to an animal shelter and playing with a bunch of cute kittens or puppies. It's great! But don't forget that you only get to take one home.)

Leonard Wingmon (Kevin Hauver) and Coleman Burleson (Alan Berman) debrief about the debate performance.

Mini-Lesson: Shooting in a Car

The proper way to do this scene would be to mount cameras and tow a picture car with the actors in it. Sometimes in indie film, you can't be completely "proper." As long as you're safe, that necessary invention can be part of the fun. It's also why you have to surround yourself with a crew of people whose attitudes are naturally oriented toward problem-solving, rather than lamenting how things "should be."

In our case, the car held four people: two actors in the backseat, a driver, and me. Since the driver had to focus on not killing us, this meant that I was also running the camera and sound. The tripod was mounted between the driver and myself, and the audio recorder was in my lap. Again, this is not an ideal way to shoot anything. That said, we got what we needed.

Finally, you'll notice that the view out of the back windshield is occluded by rain. We didn't plan this, but it actually helped us. The rain meant audiences wouldn't be able to tell if we were driving around the same few blocks. The view was enough to show that the car was moving, but the level of detail was not quite there. It also ensured that the background didn't distract from our characters.

If I'm ever in a similar situation in the future, I'll keep in mind that a little rain can have this effect, and we can recreate it, if desired.

SAYING NO TO MY ENTIRE FILM CREW—SCENE 103

Scene 103 of *A Convenient Truth* is the only time I can remember when I found myself saying no to every other person on set.

It was the first or second day of shooting, and we were filming one of the audience questions that Coleman answers throughout the film. The questioner is of Asian descent, and he asks a pointed question about the use of Chinese immigrant labor in the building of American railroads—as it relates to Coleman's proposal to use Mexican immigrant labor. The scripted response, like all of Coleman's responses, is dry. The humor comes from subtle satirical comment.

This Is Not What the Cast and Crew Wanted

Somehow, as often happens on a fun set, someone threw out an idea. "What if Coleman responds to the question in Chinese?" "We could subtitle his response like the jive talk scene in *Airplane*," another spouted. "The Chinese guy would be so taken aback. It would be hilarious," a third crewmember said confidently.

The suggestions got even wilder: "What if he responds in Korean—just because?" Before long, Alan (Coleman himself) was getting into the idea and was thinking up all sorts of funny responses to the question. (Maybe he wanted to put on a karate display. I can't remember the specifics years later.) What I do remember was that things were spiraling out of control—and away from the tone of the film that we were making. The suggestions being offered were farcical. One was more ridiculous than the last. You would've thought we were making a cartoon if you listened without any context. I laughed at first, but it quickly became apparent that the cast and crew were serious about their jokes. They wanted us to film these versions of the scene. They were sure that their versions of the scene were funnier than the one I had scripted. They urged me to try a few takes. And even though it's possible that some of those scenes could have been funnier…

I said "no."

I had to say no. The cast and crew wanted to shoot a farce, not a satire.

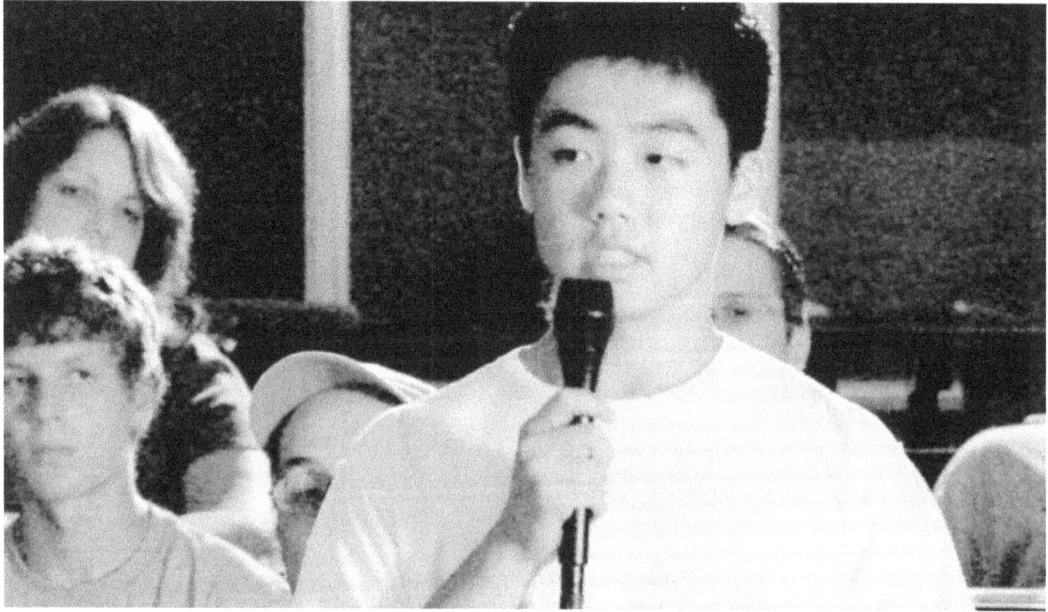

A post-lecture Q&A scene that caused an issue on set.

Again, this was the first or second day of shooting, which is important for two reasons:

1. The situation arose because the cast and crew didn't yet have a feel for the tone of the film.
2. By taking a strong position, it showed that I had a clear vision for the film, which I would defend when necessary. This prevented similar situations from arising later in the shoot.

Collaboration with a Leader

Film is a collaborative medium. It's one of the reasons that I love it. However, collaboration is only great until it hinders the final product. The position of director exists for a reason. Ultimately, there is one person who is responsible for the vision of the film. He or she has the responsibility of remembering the context that each scene exists within (even when that context hasn't yet been shot) and the purpose that it serves (even though that might change in the edit).

Side Note: One of my theories about why bands break up so often is because of the sticky situation of band leadership. I'm glad no such ambiguity exists on a film set. I'm pretty damn liberal and about as anti-hierarchy as they come in life, but films need directors.

As the director, I could potentially take a lot of the credit for making a good film, but I will certainly take all of the responsibility for making one that's less than great. Knowing that, it's my job to protect the film in its entirety—which sometimes means protecting it from its cast and crew.

Coleman Burleson (Alan Berman) readies his response to the questioner.

Mini-Lesson: Seeing the Listener

The actor pictured at the beginning of this section was essentially an extra that we pulled for the scene. His delivery was adequate but not tremendously engaging. To cover this and also show the audience what they're more interested in seeing, we only briefly see the questioner as he begins his question. We mostly see Coleman's face as he intently listens and mentally prepares his answer. Watching Coleman listen to the question becomes a rich experience and helps the scene deliver a hearty laugh when he finally does respond.

CHANGES FROM SCRIPT TO SCREEN—SCENE 104

I already talked briefly about the setup for this scene when I discussed using green screen in scene 4. So, what I want to talk about for scene 104 is the changes that occur from the script stage to what goes on the actual screen. This scene is a good one to look at because the dialogue itself is nearly identical to what it is on the page, but dialogue is only one of the changes that come from the choices a director must make along the way.

Coleman Burleson (Alan Berman) nears the end of his speech to the House of Representatives.

To make this clear, here is what the scene looked like on the page:

INT. ASSEMBLY PROCEEDINGS—DAY
Coleman addresses the entire legislature from a raised podium in the center of his colleagues.
                    COLEMAN BURLESON
    It is not improbable that some scrupulous people might be apt
    to censure such a practice, although indeed very unjustly.
    I have now taken the time to exactingly detail the many ways
    in which my proposal has proven itself. I would like to challenge
    my opposition to respond with equal care and reasoning in this matter.
Turns to speak to the other side of the room.
                 COLEMAN BURLESON (CONT'D)
    I implore you all to respond with thoughtful input and commentary.
    Knee-jerk reactions, reactionary propaganda, and ad hominem attacks
    may be the status quo around here, but I urge you to not let them rule

>   over this dire matter. In fact, please don't comment at all
>   if you have no proposal that can trump this one. We're talking
>   about our children here. That's the children of both Republicans
>   and Democrats last time I checked. This is the future.
> Beat.
>   COLEMAN BURLESON (CONT'D)
>   So again, before you run screaming about how off base ole Burleson is,
>   take the time to consider what I'm proposing. And actually try
>   to answer the question—what is really so wrong about letting
>   our undocumented workers pedal their way into
>   our economy, our environment, and our hearts.

If you actually took the time to read the dialogue, the first thing you should notice is that no one on earth could pull off that first line. It has no business being spoken out loud. Perhaps I knew this at the writing stage, but the writerly side of me wanted to push the homage to Jonathan Swift as far as I could. It's the director side's job to quash the writerly side when he pushes too far.

So, the scene immediately becomes:

INT. ASSEMBLY PROCEEDINGS—DAY
Coleman addresses the entire legislature from a raised podium in the center of his colleagues.

>   COLEMAN BURLESON
>   ~~It is not improbable that some scrupulous people might be apt
>   to censure such a practice, although indeed very unjustly.~~
>   I have now taken the time to exactingly detail the many
>   ways in which my proposal has proven itself. I would like
>   to challenge my opposition to respond with equal care
>   and reasoning in this matter.
> Turns to speak to the other side of the room.
>   COLEMAN BURLESON (CONT'D)
>   I implore you all to respond with thoughtful input
>   and commentary. Knee-jerk reactions, reactionary
>   propaganda, and ad hominem attacks may be the
>   status quo around here, but I urge you to not
>   let them rule over this dire matter. In fact, please
>   don't comment at all if you have no proposal that
>   can trump this one. We're talking about our children
>   here. That's the children of both Republicans and
>   Democrats last time I checked. This is the future.
> Beat.
>   COLEMAN BURLESON (CONT'D)
>   So again, before you run screaming about how off base
>   ole Burleson is, take the time to consider what I'm proposing.
>   And actually try to answer the question—what is really so
>   wrong about letting our undocumented workers pedal
>   their way into our economy, our environment, and our hearts.

The fact that the dialogue still makes complete sense with the first line eliminated means that it can (and probably should) be eliminated. This is a good test for your entire script.

One Page Doesn't Always Equal One Minute

Let's call the scripted scene 6/8 of a page. By the general rule of one page equaling a minute of screen time, this scene should play out in about 45 seconds. Since it's entirely dialogue, some might even estimate that it will be quicker. However, that is usually true of dialogue with two or more people because of all of the white space on the page between characters.

In this case, what we have is a dense monologue. Coupled with the weight of the situation and the necessary deliberate delivery, the scene actually times out to 85 seconds. That's nearly twice the length! And it matters.

Forty-five seconds turning into 1 minute and 25 seconds meant that coverage was necessary. The focus of the scene is Coleman's performance. However, we need to help the audience continue to pay attention to him by giving them some visual variety.

The solution was to cut away to other people listening to Coleman's speech. This breaks up the scene nicely and also creates an illusion that they are reacting to what he's saying—which, of course, they're not.

Emotional Barometer

As a director, there are two masters to serve for each scene: the emotion of the scene itself, and the scene's role within the larger arcs of the story, character, plot, etc.

Reading this scene alone (if it wasn't part of a larger film), the goal would be to achieve the strongest emotional reaction possible by the time Coleman says "and our hearts." However, I know that we are going to come back to a later part of this speech in scene 110. So, the goal changes.

The barometer tells me that at the end of this scene we want to be at the level of emotion with which we want to begin scene 110. That knowledge changes the preparation, direction, and performance of the scene.

ADDITIONAL PRODUCTION WRITING—
SCENE 105

One of the big benefits of a protracted shooting schedule was that we were able to look at issues with our cut footage and do additional production writing to fix those problems. Scene 105 of *A Convenient Truth* was not in the original screenplay and was specifically crafted to solve one such problem.

The original screenplay contained two distinct sequences:

1. Coleman and Leonard meeting with the U.S. Ambassador to Mexico.
2. An occurrence outside of the U.S. Embassy in Mexico.

It was clear after shooting that this was going to be confusing to audiences and unnecessary.

The script also included a scene in which Leonard flirted with the receptionist before meeting with the U.S. Ambassador, but we couldn't make the schedule work for all of

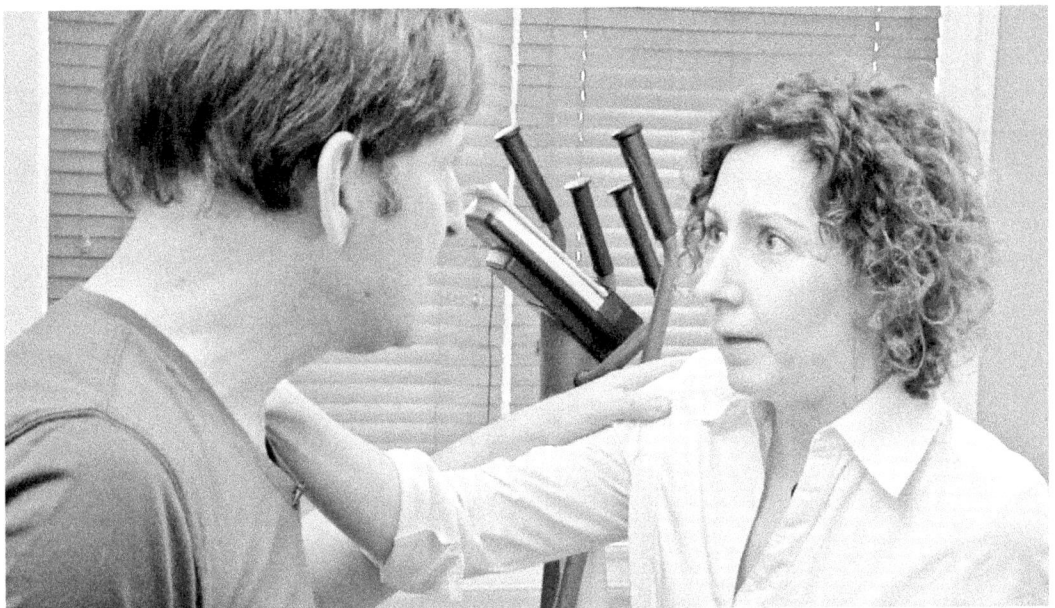

Coleman Burleson (Alan Berman) and Kitty Burleson (Elise Rovinsky) discuss an upcoming trip to Mexico.

the actors, so we tried shooting the scene with Coleman alone. It didn't work for various reasons—but mostly because the scene was meant to reveal Leonard's character, and that possibility was lost.

The solution was to combine these two sequences into one trip within the film. The receptionist scene was omitted, and the occurrence outside of the Embassy becomes the moment directly before the meeting with the ambassador.

In order to make this clear, I wrote a scene between Coleman and Kitty. The new conflict for the scene is that Kitty is (very understandably) worried about Coleman going down to Mexico. Whereas Coleman is clueless and sure that the ambassador simply wants to thank him for all the work that he's doing for the Mexican people.

Similarly, the following scene (scene 106), which takes place in the airport before the Mexico trip, was re-written to include Coleman and Eleanor, rather than Coleman and Leonard.

Scene 105 now accomplishes:

- Setting up a sense of foreboding around the upcoming trip to Mexico.
- Acknowledging Kitty's internal conflict (wanting to support her husband vs. having a better grasp on the reality of the situation than him).
- Planting the fact that Leonard can't make the trip with Coleman, even though the audience would expect him to be there.
- Setting up that Coleman will go to D.C. to see Eleanor before his trip to Mexico.

Importantly, we worked to make sure that this fill-in scene was not solely for problem solving. We were constantly looking for ways to add family interactions in the later parts of the film, and we were able to use this scene to create nice character moments while fixing our exposition issues.

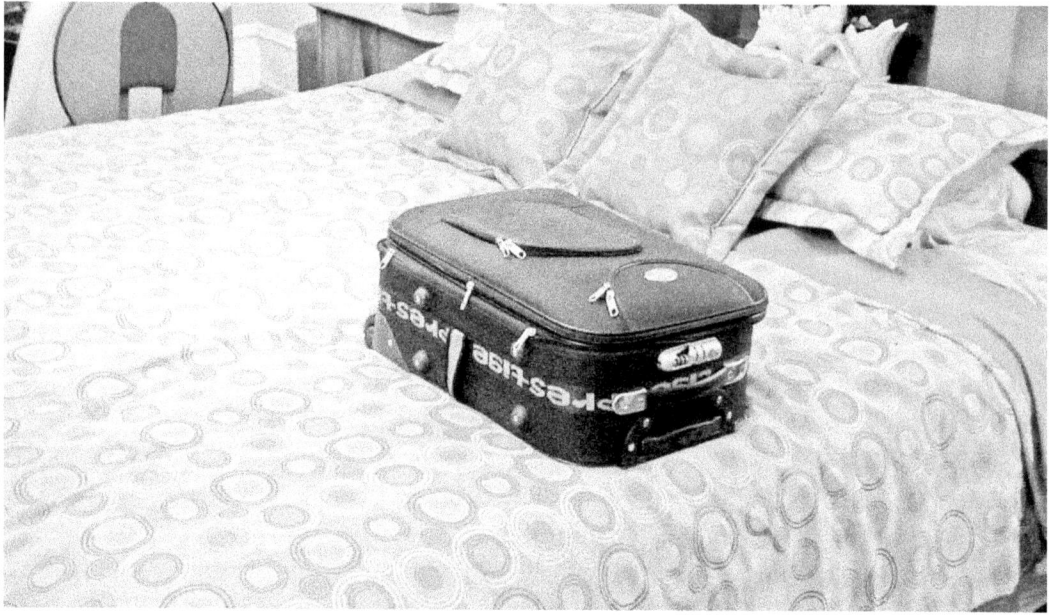

Coleman's suitcase on the bed helps the transition to the next scene of baggage at the airport.

Mini-Lesson: Visual Match

I've written about visual matches before, but I want to add here that we used a visual match of Coleman's luggage to transition from this scene to the next. Since we knew that this was an added scene, we did everything we could to make sure it didn't feel like one. By ending the scene on a shot of Coleman's suitcase and beginning the next one on shots of luggage, we are sending the message that this was planned all along.

SCHEDULING CAN BREED CREATIVITY—SCENE 106

Scheduling, and particularly scheduling conflicts, can be looked at as creative challenges—after the initial swearing and lamenting that no one cares about the film as much as you is over, of course. Scene 106 of *A Convenient Truth* is one example in which a scheduling issue changed the characters in a scene, but its purpose was maintained.

In the screenplay, Coleman and Leonard are supposed to be in the airport for a short scene before they travel to Mexico. Since we filmed over such a long and crazy schedule, the actor who played Leonard was (understandably) unavailable to shoot this scene. However, we were scheduled to shoot the scene while the actress who played Eleanor (Gilli Messer) was on the east coast to complete filming of her other scenes. Naturally, we inserted her into this scene and allowed for the different character dynamic.

Instead of a scene between colleagues, it's now a scene between a father and daughter.

Coleman Burleson (Alan Berman) and Eleanor Burleson (Gilli Messer) meet at the airport.

Coleman is allowed to make the same error that was originally scripted (grossly overestimating the time difference between Washington, D.C., and Mexico City), but the way in which Eleanor responds to him is different.

We also allowed for Eleanor's coquettish nature to sneak in as she flirts with the camera (cameraman?) at the beginning of the scene.

Interestingly, this worked expressly because we adapted the scene to fit the new characters and didn't simply ask one character to say another's words. (We tried that in another scene that was ultimately cut because it didn't work.)

As long as your characters are clearly defined in the script and your actors have internalized their roles, this can actually be a fun experiment—as it was in this case. Alan Berman (Coleman) and Gilli Messer (Eleanor) understood—and even helped create—the dynamic between the father and daughter pair during callbacks, so I always knew this would work.

In fact, the resulting scene works even better than scripted and accomplishes our goal of getting more family interaction into the later parts of the film.

This is just one small example, and this solution obviously won't work for every circumstance. But, my hope is that it might help one future filmmaker as he or she frantically tries to figure out what to do when an actor pulls out or a location falls through at the last minute.

Yes, it sucks. Complain about it for a minute. Then, thank your significant other for listening to your frustrations and make a mental note to minimize that. Then, do what you do best, and creatively solve the problem.

Yes, it's a scheduling problem. For the line producer or assistant director, right? Wrong. If you're the director of a film, ultimately, it's always your problem—so you may as well resign yourself to solving it.

If someone else magically finds a solution—bonus! But don't bank on that or waste time sweating over everything being ruined.

Be creative. Solve it.

Seven Images, Seven Lessons—Scene 107

What I'm calling "scene 107" here is actually a montage of very short clips that come between scene 106 and scene 108. Rather than write at length about any one lesson that I learned from this montage, I'm going to mention one small lesson that I learned for each of seven still images from the sequence. In a few cases, this montage represents lessons that I've expanded upon in earlier scenes.

Use setting to reveal character.

In the first still, Coleman has just pushed his way through an alarmed door to make his special entrance to his private jet. The empty hallway further makes it clear that he is not flying commercially. More on why this is important after the next still.

Need a plane? Just ask.

I'd written a scene in which Coleman takes a private jet down to Mexico. This was funny to me to because of the irony involved in someone burning so much fuel to travel around the world to preach about the environment.

Coleman Burleson (Alan Berman) in silhouette as he begins his trip to Mexico.

On our small budget, renting a plane was impossible. It turned out that we didn't need to. We simply asked the very helpful people at a local Pennsylvania airport if we could film there, and they suggested that we use one of their planes. Granted, we only went as far as the plane steps, but the shot added production value to the film at a cost of exactly $0. This lesson about props is really a cousin of an earlier lesson about locations.

Top: Coleman Burleson (Alan Berman) waves in front of the private plane that he's chartered for his travel. *Bottom:* Stock footage of takeoff used to create a sequence.

Cut to music.

The plane in the previous image is actually one still from a single, continuous shot of the plane taking off. However, rather than choosing one section of this clip to fit the duration that we needed, we jump cut on the beat of the accompanying song. The effect is that the plane leaps forward in the frame, which is more interesting to watch and allows us to use exactly the parts of the clip that we want.

Don't be proud, grab it when you can.

We needed another clip to fill the plane montage for Coleman's travel to Mexico, but we couldn't find any stock that worked for what we wanted. So, on one of my flights I used my iPad to shoot a brief bit of video through the plane window. Is it the same quality as the rest of the movie? No. Does it serve its purpose? Yes.

Quick footage taken with an iPad during a flight to help the sequence timing.

Stock footage (again).

The frame at the top of the next page is another example of stock footage helping us out. After the plane shots, we establish Mexico quickly and easily. I talked more about stock footage in scene 2.

Be smart about using your locations.

The still at the bottom of the next page, which is supposedly outside of the American Embassy in Mexico, is actually an empty lot that was attached to the production studio in which we built Burleson Labs. In our location scouting we made sure to assess everything that was at our disposal, and we were able to add a couple of scenes like this to the scheduled days in the studio. It's always helpful to have as many locations in close proximity to each other as possible.

Visual buttons.

As the car rolls through the angry mob in Mexico, Coleman interprets the crowd's

Stock footage of Mexico used as establishing b-roll.

Coleman Burleson (Alan Berman) reacts to the "rock star" treatment that he believes he's receiving from the Angry Mexican Mob Woman (Kelsey Lynn Schepise).

reaction as if they're giving him the type of excited welcome normally reserved for rock stars. The banging and yelling goes on for a few seconds, but it's always helpful to have a "button" or witty ending for a scene. In this case, the rolling continues until the background reveals smoke, an angry shirtless boy climbing on the other side of a fence, and

Visual button of a burning effigy at the end of the scene.

a burning effigy. All together, it forms a nice extra visual laugh for anyone still paying attention.

Serendipity in Editing—Scene 108

Scene 108 of *A Convenient Truth* involves Coleman Burleson (Alan Berman) meeting the U.S. Ambassador to Mexico (Ricardo Aguilar). This is a big (and seemingly unavoidable) moment based on the premise of the film. The audience cringes at the thought of what the ambassador might say to Coleman, whereas Coleman expects nothing but praise for the positive effects of his proposal on the Mexican people. The scene plays mostly as written but is bolstered by a magic moment of serendipity in the editing room.

I've written about serendipity before for scene 68, but that was within the moment of filming a scene. In this case, we stumbled upon some fun accidentally while cutting.

The coverage for scene 108 is as basic as it gets (a medium shot and its reverse), so the editing was the only real way to spice up the presentation. As we were going through our options in the edit, Charlie Pinto (the film's editor) was in trim mode and began looping a clip in which Coleman said the word "Arabs." We immediately began laughing.

Sometimes this laughter can be the result of slowly going crazy in the tenth hour of staring at editing screens, but sometimes the stuff is still funny the next day. Instead of moving on with the original plan for the edit, we incorporated this repetition into the sequence as Coleman explains his proposal to the ambassador.

Serendipity in Editing—Scene 108

U.S. Ambassador to Mexico (Ricardo Aguilar) greets Coleman Burleson (Alan Berman).

It's also worth noting that you never want to tell an audience something that they already know. In this scene, Coleman's entire purpose is to tell the ambassador what we already know—having watched the entire film leading up to this scene. The solution is to show funny snippets that let the audience know what Coleman is imparting to the ambassador without actually having to hear them. Happily, the scene becomes a sequence entirely comprised of funny phrases in quick succession.

Coleman Burleson (Alan Berman) waits for the opportunity to launch into his prepared speech.

When Coleman is done recounting the details of his proposal to the ambassador, there's nothing left to do other than to show the ambassador's shocked reaction.

The ambassador doesn't know what to say. How could he respond to Coleman's ridiculousness? Naturally, Coleman (ever the optimist) interprets the ambassador's silence as speechless adoration. He even directly addresses the camera and asks the cameraman if he's "getting" the amazing reaction.

Top: U.S. Ambassador to Mexico (Ricardo Aguilar) listens incredulously. *Bottom:* Coleman Burleson (Alan Berman) can't believe that he's left the ambassador speechless.

Three Mini-Lessons

1. A good crew is priceless.

When we scouted this scene, the office location was operational. However, when we arrived on the shooting day, the office was largely empty. The crew scrambled to get appropriate set dressing from local stores and businesses. This saved us from shooting against bland, bare walls.

2. Local casting.

We cast Ricardo Aguilar through our local casting efforts for the Pennsylvania portion of our shoot. He came prepared and knocked the scene out of the park. It's always helpful to consider this option.

3. Some scenes need to be deleted.

I've previously mentioned a scripted scene that was supposed to go directly before this one. That scene leads into this one and takes place in the reception area of the office building.

The main purpose in the script is to get some comedy and character development from Leonard's character as he flirts with the receptionist. Since the scene had to be reworked without Leonard (due to scheduling), it simply didn't work. We shot a version, but it wasn't good. More importantly, the audience wouldn't be confused if we went directly into the ambassador's office, so it wasn't necessary for the story. It lifted right out and that was the right decision.

BEGINNING OF THE END—SCENE 109

There comes that point in every movie when it's about time for it to start winding down. The key as a director is to recognize this point before the audience feels it. Scene 109 of *A Convenient Truth* is that point—the beginning of the end of the film. We see Coleman (Alan Berman) giving a bit more of his C-SPAN speech—the last bit that we'll see.

It's important to note here the power that I was given (or took) by deciding that what we see in scene 109 was the last part of this speech.

Let me explain: We see this speech in three or four different parts throughout the film. From an editing standpoint, they could have easily been used in a different order, or different spots. We had the freedom to use them in any way we wanted. However, from a directing standpoint, choosing the order in advance allowed me to ensure that Coleman's performance builds every time we see him in this location.

In fact, much of the film involved modulating the performance to make sure that it was only "big" when we wanted it to be. Knowing where a performance is going and keeping that in mind at all times is often the best way to know where it should be at any other point in the film.

That said, this is the beginning of the end, so this is where we made sure the performance was more energetic than what we'd seen before. We unleashed the Alan.

Coleman Burleson (Alan Berman) reaches the height of his passion as he wraps up his speech to the House of Representatives.

And it works. We finally get to see Coleman break out of his perfectly tempered political calm—a little. And a little is all we need because we've built the performance accordingly.

As the scene progresses, Coleman's passion seeps out more and more—until the film matches his performance cinematically. The score creeps in underneath his impassioned monologue as he forces his audience (and the film audience) to pay attention—to take him as seriously as he is taking himself. It all seems a bit drastic for a comedy, but, as I've said from the beginning, this is a satire, not a farce. The comedy is only heightened by the seriousness of the presentation.

And so, as Coleman raises his voice a bit, the music fades in below it, and the reaction shots hint that maybe people are finally listening, scene 109 bleeds into scene 110—the final scene of the film.

Side Note: In this case, the beginning of the end comes in the penultimate scene. Even though it's the point where the audience is probably ready for things to wrap up, the end actually comes quickly once it begins—more quickly than the audience would probably expect, and that's a good thing.

We've all come out of movies complaining that we thought it was going to end two or three times before it actually did. Audiences rarely complain that something was resolved too quickly—as long as it's done in a satisfying manner.

Final Scene: Make It Count—Scene 110

Scene 110 is the final scene of *A Convenient Truth*. It's a moment that I've been excited about since it popped into my head in the early stages of drafting the script. It ties up the entire film in a way that audiences don't predict, but it simultaneously seems inevitable when it happens.

I won't spoil the exact end (in case there is one person in the universe who somehow made it through an entire book about a film's scenes that still hasn't seen it), but I will say that there is a finality to it. It's a hard stop. It goes big, so the audience can go home.

And here is another point worth emphasizing:

Go big for your final scene.

There were plenty of moments in the making of this little indie film (many of which I've described in this book), where the "correct" approach was: face the limitations head on, scrap the fantasy version of the scene, and use creativity to find the workable compromise version.

This "workable compromise" is the bread and butter of the indie filmmaker. Indeed, it may be the most important trick up the sleeves of filmmakers at all budget levels. But...

The final scene of your film is not the time for compromise.

This is the moment that you're leaving the audience with.

The entire film, whether the audience knows it or not, is always barreling toward your final scene. As a filmmaker, it's imperative that you don't make them regret waiting around for it.

In *A Convenient Truth*, we acknowledged this part of the structure directly. As Coleman continues the speech that we've heard parts of throughout the film, he says:

> You've all been very nice to sit here and listen to me preach to you about what I believe the future can be, what I have achieved in California so far, and what we believe this program can develop into. I owe it to you all now to show you this proposal in action.

And he does owe it to his audience—just as much as I owe it to the audience of the film.

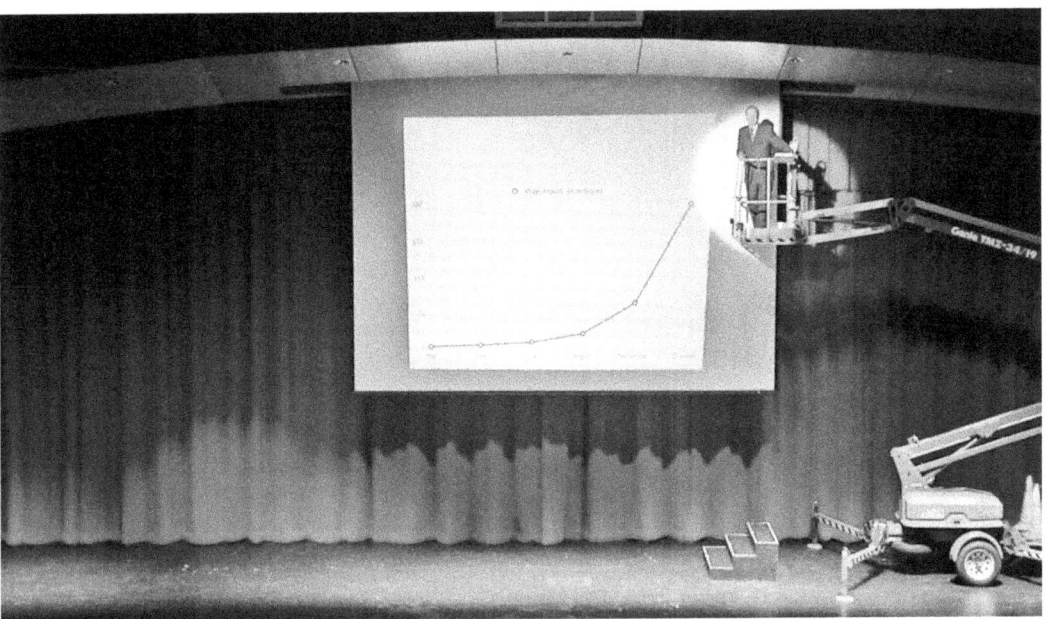

Coleman Burleson (Alan Berman) stands atop a Genie lift to demonstrate something on the graph.

Top: **Medium shot of Coleman Burleson (Alan Berman) on the lift.** *Bottom:* **The rising screen reveals cyclists backstage.**

This language of "owing" the audience is tricky because, as an artist, I initially bristle at the idea of having some sort of debt to the viewers of my art. You may feel this way too. Get over it. I did.

The reality of the situation is that an audience enters into a tacit agreement with the filmmaker—an unspoken contract: I will give you my attention for a precious chunk of time, and you will in some way entertain or move me. This won't always be possible, but it is important for the filmmaker to try.

Final Scene: Make It Count—Scene 110 195

    This is something that I couldn't fully grasp until I went through the entire process of making a feature from start to finish, and it instantly made me recall (and fully understand) something from my first week of film school. A brief anecdote:

    I was at NYU's Cantor Film Center, and the theater was filled with about 150 freshman film students. Some senior film students had been hand-picked to present as part of our orientation. And one of them, very wisely, asked for a show of hands. "Raise your

Top: Coleman Burleson (Alan Berman) on the lift as lights begin to go out. *Bottom:* Coleman Burleson (Alan Berman) in the last shot of the film, just before the last light goes out.

hand if you're here because you're an artist and you've got demons that you feel you really need to work out in your films," he said. A smattering of hands raised up through the room. "Great," he proceeded, "you can get that out of your system and then make films that the rest of us will actually enjoy."

I was not one of the people who had raised my hand, but a part of me was resistant to this thought. First, what he said was funny, and I kind of agreed with it. (One can only see so many films about teen suicide that end with "Fin.")

But there was another part of me that wondered who he thought he was. What if some of these people want to make something that is just for them? An audience of one could be legitimate, couldn't it? At the very least, there shouldn't have been so much certainty in his voice as he callously dismissed the dreams of so many young idealists around the room.

Some part of me still struggles with this audience dilemma. But, at least when it comes to film, the dilemma doesn't exist for me anymore—for one reason: because an artist chooses his or her medium.

If you really are that tortured artist whose sole purpose is to explore yourself and create something that makes you (and only you) feel something deeper, then take up painting—and never show another soul. Choreograph little dances for yourself and perform them in the mirror. Record a song and have it only ever play out of your earbuds directly into your own earholes. (You get the idea.)

But, film is about people. It takes collaboration to create it. And it takes an audience to complete its creation. The audience co-authors the film as they watch it by filling in gaps and reading subtext. And they continue to co-author the film after they leave the theater and (hopefully) talk about it with their friends.

As a filmmaker, I now know that it's best to accept this (even revel in it)—and maybe to stack the deck in my favor by leaving the audience with a final scene that they won't forget.

Part Three
Post Post-Production

So You've Made a Feature Film

That's so supposed to be the hard part. And it was. You turned words on a page into around 90 minutes of coherent moving images. You were understaffed, never had the right amount of money, and there were brief moments when you couldn't see how it would all come together. But there it is your editing software's timeline—the rough cut strung out from beginning to end.

For the first time, you've put together something that resembles a full-length movie. You've got your core creative team together for the moment of truth: an intimate viewing party for the rough cut that your collective grit made possible. Except the moment of truth is one of the worst moments of your life.

Your Rough Cut Will Make You Want to Cry

This is not an exaggeration meant to brace you for your shortcomings as a filmmaker. It's a genuine acknowledgment of a devastating part of the creative process. I don't personally know one filmmaker who doesn't report feeling this way after the viewing of their rough cut. Nor have I ever read or heard an interview with a filmmaker talking about how thrilled he or she was to see the rough cut come together.

The rough cut will be a smack in the face. It's hard proof that the idealized version of the film that you thought you'd made doesn't exist. It never will exist. Even though you know this intellectually ahead of time, it will take some time for you to comprehend it emotionally. You've spent months (more likely years) of your life creating something different than what you imagined. Try to avoid getting notes or making any drastic changes immediately. Have everyone take notes immediately after the viewing while the film is still fresh in their minds, but give yourself a few days before diving in.

After you've processed the initial shock, you should be able to move past the version of the film that you had in your head and realize that you're dealing with a new task: making the best possible film out of what you have in front of you. You are free to cast aside the hundreds of ideas that you had that you now know have nothing to do with the reality of this project. Maybe you can use those for another project. Right now, they are very decidedly irrelevant.

There's one more thing to focus on, too: there are some parts of the film that are better than what you had imagined. Through the wonder of collaboration, some actors made scenes better than you expected they'd be. Thanks to serendipity, you now get credit for a bit of improv. A clever music choice makes a few decent scenes into one really effective sequence.

Once you've reached a point where you're capable of this type of pro-active thinking, you're ready to start shaping that rough cut into something that you won't be ashamed to show a slightly wider circle of people.

I say "a slightly wider circle" because the right mix is crucial. You'll want to get feedback from people who are far away from any part of the creation of the film and will give helpful honest critiques. At the same time, the film (and your ego) is probably not yet ready for complete strangers to tell you why your movie is a piece of shit. There will be a time for this, and you'll have to be prepared to deal with it, but you want to feel secure that the best version of your film is being judged by such audiences. The magic middle ground for the process is to have a friends and family test screening. For more on this, read the section on "How to Know When You're Done Editing."

After our friends and family test screening at NYU, we went back to work and held a second test screening at a commercial theater in Pennsylvania. By the time the first outsiders see any version of the film, you should be ready to do all of the work necessary to finalize the film. You shouldn't hold test screenings and then let years pass with continued tweaking. A screening should signal that your film will be more broadly available to been seen (in some venue) soon. We held our second test screening in Pennsylvania because part of the film was shot there, and we even got some local press to write up the story of an indie shooting in P.A. and coming back to test the film. If done right, this can be the beginning of momentum for the film's run because people will hear that a screening occurred and expect that they might have their own chance to see it in the near future. Similarly, this is the point where you'll want to make sure that your film definitely has a professional online presence. Of course, hopefully you've been managing that presence since before you even shot a frame, but if not, you really need one now. You want to make sure that anyone who is motivated enough to seek out your film has an easy time finding more about it. This is also when you'll want to create an IMDb entry for the film, for the same reasons. You should have most, if not all, of the credits prepared at this point, and you can always make additions to the film's page once it's set up.

Your Film Is Ready to Be Seen. Now How Do You Get People to Watch It?

Once you're sure that you're not going to make any more changes to your film (really sure, this time), you're ready to begin submitting it to festivals. You can apply directly to most film festivals via their individual websites, but you'll more likely apply via one of the existing festival portals. The portals essentially allow you to store certain information that will be used for all festivals to avoid having to repeat the processes each time and also act as a good way to track your submissions in one place. When we were submitting *A Convenient Truth* to festivals, we did it via Withoutabox, which was pretty much the only game in town. It's an Amazon company and also links directly to IMDb (another Amazon company.) Since then, I've also seen a lot of positive response to Film Freeway, which presents itself as an alternative submission platform to Withoutabox that doesn't share some of its antiquated limitations. I have no personal experience with Film Freeway, but you should definitely research the pros and cons of both portals before choosing one, in addition to any others that may have popped up.

There will be temptation to begin submitting versions of your film when it's almost or "pretty much" complete, and some festivals even encourage this thinking by accepting early cuts of films, but this isn't a good idea. We submitted a non-color corrected fine cut of *A Convenient Truth* to the Sundance Film Festival out of submission deadline-induced excitement, but it was a waste of money. (Though the deadline itself was a great motivator.)

You don't want to give any festival reviewer, and especially reviewers from elite festivals like Sundance, any reason to dislike the film. Nor do you want to rely on their imaginations to know what the film will look like once it's color corrected or to understand that it will be even better once the sound design is complete. It's not their job to imagine what the film can be. It's yours.

If there's currently any part of your film that you're not confident in and that you still think you might be able to make better, don't submit it to festivals. You'll know when it's really ready.

If it is really ready, it's time to start researching—and another spreadsheet. You'll want to break your prospective film festival submissions into tiers, with elite festivals at the top, mid-range festivals next, and smaller, low priority festivals at the bottom. The reason for this is that the top-tier festivals often require premiere status for your film to even be eligible for programming. That is, if you've already shown your film publicly, these festivals have no interest in playing second fiddle. You'll need to be able to offer your World Premiere status in most cases to be screened at one of the major festivals. Which festivals makes up the top tier is a bit fluid and should be part of your research, but the types of festivals that I mean here are ones like Venice, Cannes, Sundance, Toronto, and Berlin.

The second tier of festivals will be much larger, and it will include festivals that you'll be very happy to play, but one that you wouldn't want to play at the expense of your eligibility for the elite tier. A bit of planning can ensure that you apply in the right order and avoid this. A good festival in this tier that is specially designed for debut feature filmmakers is the Slamdance Film Festival, which accepts films from first-time directors with budgets under $1 million.

The final tier of festivals that you'll want to research includes smaller festivals that have some specific reason that you'd like your film to be a part of. It may be that the festival is local, and it will be a great way for your network to finally see the film you've been talking about. If your film fits neatly into a particular genre, you may want to get programmed at a festival with a relevant theme and niche audience. If this is your first film or you're a filmmaker that belongs to a minority group, you may want to apply to festivals that give you special consideration. These festivals won't do too much for the publicity of your film, so you should have some other explicit reason for participating. The exception to this is that an argument can be made for the cumulative benefit that can occur if you can show that your film played in dozens of festivals and even picked up some awards along the way—though I've never gone this route or had that experience.

Once your spreadsheet is populated with tiers of festivals, you'll want to fill in the columns with the various submission deadlines and aim to submit to the early submission deadline of one of the festivals in your elite tier. You can then work backward from that date through the other festivals in that tier and follow along accordingly through the lower tiers. You may wind up applying to film festivals in your third tier a full year after you begin your festival submissions, and that's okay. The festival circuit is your film's first foray into the world, and you should both enjoy it and make it work for you.

Budget for your festival submissions ahead of time. Apart from the potential expenses that will arise from actually traveling to participate in the festivals that you're lucky enough to be accepted into, the submission fees alone will add up.

We submitted *A Convenient Truth* to about 30 festivals and spent just under $1,500 in festival submission fees. This is with good planning to ensure paying the least expensive "early bird" deadline fees for the majority of the festivals and even a few submission waivers that we received because of past work in festivals or requested submissions.

In the interest of transparency and being as helpful as I can be, I will forsake any instinct to guard my ego by skirting around the reality of our film's festival run. We didn't get into any elite festivals. We were lucky enough to be accepted into New Filmmakers New York's WinterFest, which checked two specialty boxes: it was a local fest for us, and it gave special consideration to emerging filmmakers.

This was a big moment, and we did well to use it as the next major step for the film. A lot of time will pass between wrapping up production and your festival premiere, so it's a great opportunity to reconnect with people that you may not have seen for a while—though ideally you've been keeping them in the loop along the way. Did it have any utility beyond the celebration that it was? No. But that was certainly worthwhile on its own.

A few months later, *A Convenient Truth* screened at the Garden State Film Festival, which is another local festival that is relatively big in New Jersey. We were again thrilled to be a part of it, but it was another one-off event. That is, it wasn't a festival that acted as a stepping-stone for the progress of the film. We were surrounded, as is the case at most festivals, by other filmmakers who were in the same boat as us. There was no direct conduit from the festival screen to the film market.

At this point, every filmmaker has a decision. You can chase accolades from every small festival that will accept you, hoping that a distributor will magically descend upon you, and spending as much as another year moving from room to room filled with other hopeful filmmakers (which has its own benefits), or you can make a move toward independent distribution.

INDEPENDENT DISTRIBUTION

Every filmmaker wants to see his or her film play on the big screen. It's very tempting to want a theatrical run for your film for vanity alone, but I can honestly say that was not my main motivation. Since, as I mentioned, no distributor was interested in purchasing the film and setting up small theatrical distribution, I made peace with the fact that *A Convenient Truth* was never going to be in theaters. It would never have a red carpet premiere with even a small platform release in New York and L.A.

Then, at a seminar on independent distribution at the Garden State Film Festival, one of the panelists mentioned a process called four-walling. Four-walling is basically when a filmmaker rents out a theater, pays the costs up-front, and then receives all of the money from the ticket sales. This mitigates the risk for the theater and has a higher potential upside for the filmmaker.

What exactly is that potential upside? Here's the math: the cost of four-walling a theater in New York, in this case the Quad Cinema on 13th St., was $11,000, including $1,000 that went directly to what was essentially an in-house publicist for the run.

Since our film's running time is less than 90 minutes, we were able to fit in five screenings per day (1:30, 3:30, 5:30, 7:30, 9:30) for seven days. We screened in a theater with 146 seats and tickets were $13 each. So, assuming you're irresponsibly optimistic, and you're sure you're going to sell out all screenings, your maximum potential sales are:

146 seats × $13 × 5 screenings × 7 days = $66,430

That's a big number. After you subtract your $11,000 rental fee, you've made $55,430 in one week. It's also *completely ridiculous*. I mention this because it's the type of math that you (or someone on your team) might be apt to do in support of your pre-existing desire to screen in a theater. Don't four-wall your film because you expect to make real money doing it.

First of all, very few people are going to attend your weekday daytime screenings, regardless of the film. You can't really count on many people attending any screenings other than those that take place after regular work hours. Second, you can't necessarily assume that anyone will even attend the screenings after work hours without putting in serious work and additional funds.

You might be defiant and want to go back to the math again, assuming only the nighttime screenings perform well. I appreciate your confidence.

146 seats × $13 × 2 screenings × 7 days = $26,572

Now, when you subtract your $11,000 rental fee, you've still made a profit of $15,572. This is still a very respectable week. Step back, though. Are you really confident you can fill a theater to capacity twice a night for seven days? You probably shouldn't be.

In order for people to come to the see your film at the theater, they have to be interested in it, and they have to know about it. Hopefully you've taken care of the first part by making a film that is interesting to a large enough subset of the population. Getting people to know about the film is a separate issue. The good news is that there are people whose job it is to help you with these things. It's literally all they do. The bad news is that I soon learned that the major publicity firms in New York won't even consider taking your film on unless you can sign on as their client for at least a month. They'll need at least 4–6 weeks of lead-time to do their jobs properly, and the price tag for that month is about $10,000.

Now, you're down to $5,572 for the week, assuming that the expensive publicist can help you sell out your two nightly screenings.

Of course, you'll also have other publicity and marketing costs that will pop up: posters, flyers, etc. And you'll need a print for the theater to actually exhibit. If you're screening film, that will have its own cost for the print, but you'll more likely be creating a DCP (Digital Cinema Package). Luckily, one of our producers had the skills and software (an add-on to Apple Compressor application called Wraptor that currently cost $1,099) to create a DCP for us, but DCPs are notoriously finicky, and if you're not particularly technical, you should count on a post-production house charging you at least $2,000 to create your DCP, which is essentially the film encoded into a specific file system on a hard drive.

I hope by now you're seeing that those margins are getting worrisome. If you're still optimistic, you might get to this point and say, "Well, so we'll only make a few thousand dollars" or "We'll break even, but the press, experience, and cachet of a theatrical release will still be worth it."

Or, you might know that you won't sell enough tickets to make back your money, but you're happy to use the four-wall as a loss leader that will stimulate sales of the film in its future life online. This is probably the only realistic perspective to have going into a four-wall situation, but if it's the reason you're going ahead with it, you need to have a detailed plan for *exactly* how this week of theatrical screenings will turn into future revenue.

One of the most appealing perks of the theatrical release was that certain important journalistic institutions like the *New York Times* and the *Village Voice* made it their business to review every film that has a week-long theatrical release in New York City, and we were excited about that opportunity. (At least that's what we were told—more on that later.)

I haven't put an immense amount of time into pondering the role of the modern movie critic in our constantly changing entertainment environment, but I did step back and appreciate one simple thing: critics take the time to sit down, watch your entire film, and write about it. Whether or not a critic's review is glowing, he or she has provided you with a valuable service.

The potential for highly visible reviews was enough to convince us that loss leader model was viable, and the path was now clear.

$11,000 stood between us and a week-long run in New York City, a public relations expert who came as part of the deal, reviews from established publications, and—most importantly—people seeing *A Convenient Truth*.

Being a filmmaker who had just completed my first feature film, I didn't have $11,000 burning a hole in my pocket, but I did have something of value: a completed feature film. We turned to Kickstarter to begin making the film work for us. We pre-sold tickets to the theatrical run (since ticket sales would go to us anyway in the four-wall situation), digital downloads of the film, special edition Blu-ray discs, and offered several other rewards.

If you're interested, you can see the details of the archived crowdfunding campaign here: https://www.kickstarter.com/projects/265792882/a-convenient-truth-movie-theatrical-run.

ELEVEN KICKSTARTER CAMPAIGN LESSONS

People have written entire books about the secrets of crowdfunding, but I'll impart the ten lessons that I learned from our campaign here because I've had friends and even acquaintances reach out to me for advice that they've ultimately found helpful. It's easy to find someone who has attempted a Kickstarter campaign, but it turns out it's significantly tougher to chat with someone who has successfully funded a campaign to raise a formidable amount. "Formidable amount" is obviously relative, especially with stars literally raising millions of dollars for their films, but I think $11,000 qualifies for most indie filmmakers. This is especially true by the time filmmakers have gotten anywhere near the completion or distribution phases of the film and have already spent more than they ever anticipated. Here's what I learned:

1. Keep the video short—shorter than you think it should be.

This is unfortunately true for all content, but even more so for content that is meant to be shared. Having a video at the top of your Kickstarter page is pretty much a necessary part of a successful campaign, but if it's more than even a couple of minutes long people won't watch it all. It's better to keep the main video short enough for it to end, get viewers curious, and encourage them to scroll down the page to learn more through the text on the page. If you can get them scrolling, they'll also see the rewards tiers and hopefully like what you're offering. Don't forget that the main video isn't the only video content allowed. In our case, I had a very brief video of me introducing the film to audiences at the top of the page, but we embedded the film's trailer lower down. Obviously, the trailer is much more relevant—both in terms of knowing anything about my filmmaking ability and learning about the film itself. However, it would have been a mistake to simply put the trailer at the top of the page. Kickstarter backers want to see the person that they're supporting. They want to hear directly what the funds will be used for from the person who will be using them. There's a reason that any company whose main business is sales still incurs the costs related to sending salespeople out in the field. People are more likely to give money when a face is involved.

2. Only make the campaign duration 30 days.

If you have what feels like a large fundraising goal, there will be temptation to run the campaign for the maximum allowable duration, which is currently 60 days. It's logical. More time to raise the money won't hurt. Except it does. A longer campaign period makes it impossible for potential backers to feel any urgency, and that is the bread and butter of the Kickstarter ecosystem. Potential funders need to understand that you can't accomplish the goal of your project if they don't help make it happen, and it needs to happen now.

3. "Leak" the launch to a handful of people.

You should confirm that several people close to you will back the project within its first 24 hours. There will be certain people who will definitely want to support you in any way that they can, and they can do so by pledging to the campaign early. Call it mob mentality, but others will be more likely to support the project after they've seen that others have deemed it worthy. Don't believe it? Start clapping or laughing in a crowd, and others will follow. The same is true with crowdfunding. Ideally, you want to get to about 1/3 of your goal within a day or so the campaign's launch.

4. Hold back one person to make a large pledge about two weeks into the campaign.

You'll need a big bump to get through the lull right around the 15th day. If you've done #3, the beginning of the campaign was already pretty successful. Plus, the excitement of a new campaign will have inherent momentum. Similarly, the rush of meeting what's left of a goal before the campaign deadline is built into the very core of Kickstarter's all-or-nothing philosophy. If the goal isn't met before a rapidly approaching deadline, the project doesn't get any of the funds that have been pledged. The desire to prevent that from happening will get people to donate as the campaign's end nears. You should spend the normally slow middle of the campaign making sure that the remaining funds to be raised at the end of the campaign will seem like they can be realistically received within the last days of the campaign. Ensuring that at least one large pledge comes in at this time is a good way to do it.

5. Directly call or e-mail individuals.

Mass e-mails are not going to get you there. Although you'll probably lean toward individualized e-mails, calls are worth the extra effort. The more personalized your outreach, the better the outcome. If you're an introverted artist, you're probably cringing while reading this, and I understand, but that doesn't make it any less true. You don't have to sell your project—merely let people know about it. They'll support you if they're so inclined, and try not to have any hard feelings if they can't or won't. The most important note here is to not think that your job is done because you write a "Dear All," e-mail to the hundreds of people in your address book.

6. Make sure there is an enticing reward at $25.

Twenty-five dollars is the sweet spot for most backers. Loved ones and strangers alike will be comfortable parting with this amount, so you want to make sure you offer something extremely appealing at the $25 reward level. In our case, we actually had two rewards at the $15 level, so that was our most-pledged reward level (41 backers), but this is because the nature of the campaign dictated it to be so. Since the campaign was specifically for the theatrical run of the film, $15 got people who could make it to New York an advanced purchase ticket to one of the screenings or, for those who weren't in the area, it got them a digital download of the film. We thought that charging $25 for either of those rewards would have been a bit of a stretch. That said, we made the $25 reward a combination of both of those rewards, so supporters "saved" $5 with the larger pledge amount. And, again, the value of the rewards was not in any way inflated. $25 for a movie ticket in New York City, and a digital copy of a film is actually a pretty good deal. The $25 reward tier was out second-most popular with 17 backers.

7. Have one really large award tier.

Receiving a high volume of smaller donations is sort of the idea behind a successful Kickstarter campaign, but don't neglect to offer one large reward level. One pledge at the highest level can give you a huge boost, and it's exciting for people following the project to see a significant jump in the pledged amount in a short period of time. We got two $1,000 backers, which was our highest reward level. One of these backers was family, but the other was an extremely generous friend. I had no expectation that he'd pledge that amount, and I was very touched by his support. Had the $500 reward level been the highest available, I imagine he would have pledged to that level, and I would have been equally impressed by his generosity, but we also would have raised $500 fewer.

8. Get other people involved.

Just as you didn't make your film alone, you should make sure that your creative team is reaching out to individuals every day. Crowdfunding is about networks, and you should engage your network to both directly support the project financially and share the campaign to their networks.

9. Do at least two things for your campaign every day.

Consistency is key. Basically, every free hour that you have while the campaign is on should be used to reach out, but that's also a generic mandate. Be more specific with planning, and give yourself two specific tasks for each day. If you can't think of and do two things each day that will help you raise more money, you're not working hard enough, and you probably won't reach your fundraising goal.

10. Throwing a launch party.

If you have the means (and I realize that's a big "if" because the whole point of a campaign is that you're in need of funds), you should consider having an in-person get together—some might call in a party—on the opening night of your campaign. It's fun to make an event out of the launch, and you can even have computers set up in the space for people to pledge right then and there. If you do this correctly, that night is a great way to reach that crucial goal for the first 24 hours that I mentioned in #3.

11. Don't set a goal for more or less than you need.

It's important to do the research before you launch your campaign to come up with the Goldilocks level for your fundraising. The fundraising goal should be a number that is based upon very specific calculations. It shouldn't be more than you need because you can imagine a lot of extra things that might be nice to do, and it shouldn't be less than you need because the full amount just sounds like it's too much to conceivably raise.

You should calculate the cost of producing whatever it is your campaign is aiming to create, and then make sure to add enough to cover the production and delivery of the rewards that you're offering. Once you have that total, add another 10 percent, and you will arrive at your Kickstarter goal. The additional 10 percent is to cover the 5 percent that Kickstarter takes off the top for their services and another 3–5 percent for credit card processing fees. If you neglect to add these considerations into the total, you may find yourself with a successfully funded Kickstarter campaign and still not having enough money to both satisfy the obligations that you made to your backers and creating whatever it is you're Kickstarting in the first place. I mention this because you don't want to ruin the goodwill that you've received by not upholding your end of the bargain. And, again, if you're running a Kickstarter campaign, the chances are you don't have a lot of extra funds around to casually cover a 10 percent oversight, un-researched reward costs, or even the expense of lots of postage.

Our campaign was successful, and we were able to raise enough money to cover the costs of the four-wall and the delivery of any physical rewards. We were able to have a theatrical release of *A Convenient Truth*!

The Four-Wall Experience

So was the decision to four-wall a good one for us? Yes and no. Mostly no, but partially because we did some things wrong.

Four Things We Did Right

1. We made a big deal of our theatrical premiere. After years of work on the project, we had a definitive moment of celebration. Our collective hard work had turned an idea into a film on a New York City marquee. Strangers could walk up to the box office and purchase tickets to view what we'd created. It was a good feeling, and we were smart enough to truly appreciate it as it was happening.
2. I also personally made the night of the premiere extra special by adding a unique title card to the end of the screening that asked my girlfriend if she would marry me. That's right, the premiere of the film doubled as my engagement proposal, and we were able to share both with about 70 of our closest family and friends in one moment.
3. Since the film premiered in New York and many of the cast and crew were locals, we were able to have a different person (or group of people) take part in a post-film question and answer session after each night's 7:30 p.m. screening. This gave outsiders an extra incentive to come to the theater to view the film, and it also tapped into the personal networks of each post-film speaker. That is, we sold more tickets because friends of the Q&A speakers especially wanted to attend those screenings. I'd definitely recommend a similar program if you're going to have a theatrical run.
4. Finally, we did get some reviews from film critics because of the week-long run in a New York City theater. In fact, we were reviewed by *The Village Voice*, *The Hollywood Reporter*, *Trust Movies*, and *The Movie Network* in advance of our theatrical run. We happily rushed out to have a "review poster" made with all of the positive quotes about our film, and passers-by could see it as they walked by the theater during the day. So I'll count getting reviews as a win, but they didn't significantly affect ticket sales in any way.

Five Things We Did Wrong

1. Related to point four above, there's one potentially precious review that we conspicuously did not receive—arguably the most important review on the east coast—the *New York Times*. Even though we were promised by the publicist that we'd be reviewed by one of the critics at the *New York Times*, it didn't happen. This was in February 2015, and we were told that the paper no longer had the capacity to review all films with a week-long theatrical release. As far as I can tell, we were literally the first film ever for this to be true. What luck! On May 22, 2015, *Variety* officially broke the story about this policy change (Lang, "New York Times Changes Film Review Policy"), and it became official that some films were being deemed unworthy of a being reviewed based on undisclosed criteria. We were obviously upset by the omission, and you can read more about this on *The Candler Blog* (Poritsky, "The 56 Films that Opened in New York This Year Without a Review in The New York Times") if you're interested. Whether the new policy makes sense or not, the important takeaway is that one of the main incentives for four-walling (at least in New York) no longer exists.

2. We didn't have the money to properly publicize our theatrical release. If you don't have the funds to really get people into the theater to see the film, you really shouldn't take on the expense of renting the theater in the first place. We hoped we could get by. Play the movie and the people will come. They didn't.
3. We didn't solicit IMDb reviews, tweets, Facebook shares, etc., from the audiences that we did have to help promote the film beyond its one-week life on the big screen.
4. Similarly, we didn't gather e-mail addresses from our audiences in order to directly market to them in the future. It stands to reason that someone who was motivated to come see the film in the movie theater is a good candidate to be someone who might want to purchase a copy of the film when it becomes available. Of course, that's assuming they liked the film when they saw it, but it can't hurt to take down an e-mail address for your mailing list while you have an interested audience.
5. We planned to independently release the film for purchase online on the last day of the film's theatrical run. We weren't sold on the "day-and-date" release that has become popular with some filmmakers, but we also didn't want a lot of time to pass between the "buzz" of the premiere and when the film would be made available to interested viewers. This was not a terrible decision on its own, but we did make the mistake of expecting there to be some undefined momentum from the theatrical run that the digital platform would automatically capitalize upon. Either no such momentum existed, or we failed to turn it into digital sales, which is a huge business failure. A clear strategy that links the theatrical release of your film to its next revenue streams is a must.

We ultimately made about $1,000 in ticket sales for the entire week's run. This is partially because a significant number of the audience members that we did have had pre-purchased their tickets via the Kickstarter campaign, but we still would not have been profitable if all of the tickets were traditionally purchased. If fact, the entire theatrical run was only anything other than catastrophic because it was paid for via Kickstarter. If the entire rental fee had been paid for as a more standard investment in potential tickets sales, it would have resulted in about a $10,000 loss. That's a big price to pay if all you're getting is some good feelings from a premiere party and a few (possibly helpful) reviews.

I've included some painful details here in the interest of transparency, so that it might help you as you consider four-walling for your own film. There are certainly some situations in which it could be the way to go, but only if you've considered all of the things that I've mentioned here and have a good answer for each one.

Would I personally do it again? No.

And I'm a filmmaker who loves going out to the movie theater and hopes that's always a thing, but it seems the focus for independent filmmakers should largely be reaching audiences via digital platforms.

With that in mind, there's a whole world of digital release options out there...

Digital Distribution of Your Independent Film

If the premiere of your film is its launch, digital distribution is its flight. It can be extremely tempting to feel like getting your film to its premiere is the end of something. You've done your part as a filmmaker and (to employ an overused but apt analogy) you've given birth to your film. It's officially out there in the world. Except your work doesn't end after you have a baby, of course. You now have to raise that thing.

This is an important moment to really ingest. It wasn't too long ago that a filmmaker's job was largely done after he or she brought it into the world. A large distributor would swoop in and take care of your film in some sort of long-term au-pair arrangement, and you no longer had to do any of the major worrying.

Of course, when that was true, it was significantly more difficult to make a film in the first place. Less product in the market meant hungrier distributors competing for content. The barrier to entry was much higher, but if you broke through that barrier, the path to distribution was clearer.

For better and for worse (but mostly for better, I think), it is now much easier to make a feature film. It is also much easier to make your film accessible to masses of people now that the availability of films isn't restricted by a limited number of theatrical screens. This means that the market is flooded with great content, and the big issue of the day is no longer content distribution but rather content discovery.

There are tons of digital distribution platforms, and there will be even more by the time you're reading this book that haven't yet been created. However, I'm going to go through the pros and cons that I considered during my decisions for the life of *A Convenient Truth*, and I'll mention only platforms that I'm fairly confident will be around for years to come.

iTunes

Our first inclination for digital distribution was the platform that was the de facto service for digital distribution of films at the time. iTunes revolutionized digital distribution for the music industry and carried that into the movie industry. (The major difference being that they simultaneously pioneered the hardware for listening to digital music with the iPod, whereas an iPhone is still a less than ideal device for viewing films.) iTunes still has a strong portion of the distribution market today, but it was close to the only game in town for a while there.

iTunes has a huge user base, and it's a platform from which people are comfortable making purchases. Apple makes the process seamless and intuitive, as only Apple can do.

Apple splits media purchases with filmmakers 70/30, meaning they take 30 percent of any revenue that comes from the sale or rental of your film. We were very willing to give over 30 percent of our sales for the ability to immediately be in the pockets of so many users with a certain comfort level with digital content. However, we didn't go with iTunes. Why? It was a purely financial decision.

Apple does not allow filmmakers to directly sell their films via their service. The platform is built upon the use of aggregators, which are basically middlemen that filmmakers must use as a conduit in order to make their content available on iTunes. Essentially, this is Apple deciding that allowing filmmakers to submit films directly for review would be an overly cumbersome process that would take too many resources on Apple's part. Since technical settings for movies are complicated by video codecs, file containers, resolutions, etc., there are many ways for filmmakers to improperly submit the necessary deliverables for the platform. (I personally believe most current filmmakers are capable enough to submit video files with the correct specifications if those specifications are communicated clearly, but Apple does not share that belief.)

This process adds a gatekeeper back into the distribution process, making it closer to a traditional distribution platform and doesn't fully embrace the freedom that digital distribution should represent for filmmakers.

The list of Apple-approved aggregators can be found here: https://itunespartner.apple.com/en/movies/partnersearch.

Upon researching iTunes submissions through aggregators, we found that most of them charged about $1,500 for their services, and that would often also include getting the film onto several other platforms. In some cases, there would be an additional cost for each additional platform on which you wanted to make the film available. In others, there was a lower upfront cost (closer to $1,000) but the deal would also include some sort of limited revenue sharing. In those cases, you're now giving around 15 percent of the revenue to the aggregator in addition to the 30 percent that Apple is taking. In scenarios like this, you're now looking at making about 55 percent of sales. With a standard purchase price of $9.99 for an HD film, it's going to take quite a few sales at $5.50/sale before you're even out of your initial aggregator-created hole.

There is one possible exception that does exist that allows filmmakers to submit directly from an Apple-approved encoding house (rather than a full aggregator) by essentially going through the process of becoming an approved distributor.

However, this is a false alternative. In order for the privilege of Apple dealing with you directly, you have to apply to iTunes Connect. Here's some selected text from their website about this process:

> Use this application to tell us about yourself and the content you are interested in distributing.
>
> This application is intended only for people who either own or control a catalog of content for digital distribution. Authorized representatives are also permitted.
>
> Content Requirements:
> - 5 feature-length movies or documentaries that were released theatrically (or) 100 feature-length movies or documentaries that were either released theatrically or direct-to-video.
> - Digital distribution rights for all content you intend to sell on the iTunes Store.
> - All associated music and talent rights cleared for digital distribution.
> - All movies in a territory-appropriate language (or) dubbed or subtitled in a territory-appropriate language.
> - Note: iTunes does not accept NC-17 or X-rated movies (or any unrated movies that could have received these ratings). iTunes also does not accept how-to videos, user-generated content, or other types of video that are not normally considered feature movies or documentaries. Exercise and fitness videos are

currently grouped with TV content and concert films are grouped with music content (a different contract is required for each type of content).

You read that first bullet point correctly. Have you had five feature films released theatrically? If you had, you wouldn't be reading this book. One hundred feature films released direct-to-video is about equally ludicrous.

The other requirement that held us back slightly (but was much less of a consideration) was that iTunes requires a closed caption file for every film on its platform. This is another added cost that we didn't feel like spending at the time. More importantly, I'd never had to caption any of my short films before, so I didn't know where to start. (I didn't realize how easy and inexpensive this process is, but more on that later.)

Since Apple didn't seem like the right fit at the time, we researched other options, and we settled on the VHX platform.

VHX

After considering our options, we decided to digitally distribute our film via VHX for several reasons, and they all centered around a philosophy of allowing filmmakers to distribute directly to their audience. VHX allowed for almost no barrier to entry. Anyone could create a website for a film, upload it, and sell directly for a total cost of zero dollars. That's right, no up-front costs. For filmmakers who have just spent more than their life savings making a film, this is a huge deal. (Note: we got onto VHX when it was still in its early stages, and there is now a one-time upload fee of $99 for any video longer than an hour—so basically any feature film.)

VHX presents itself as a hip, new distribution platform based out of Brooklyn that "gets it." When I posted a question on a forum, a staff member answered it within minutes. I'd get periodic personalized e-mail in my inbox from an actual person on the marketing team about my film. Their mission is to be an open distribution platform that works for the super famous and the little guy alike. Rather than bringing VHX sales to a separate website, the platform even allows for the creation and hosting of a dedicated film site as part of the package. In short, I liked everything about their approach to digital distribution.

Reading all of this, one might imagine that the drawback for such boutique service would be a less favorable revenue split for the filmmaker—better services and no up-front fees means they have to make their money by taking a larger portion of the sales revenue—but that is not the case. In fact, VHX takes just 50 cents + 10 percent of each purchase.

But wait, there's more! The platform offers real-time metrics to allow filmmakers to really see how their marketing efforts directly translate into sales. (Unlike iTunes, which delivers delayed purchase reports, which has no business in modern digital sales and keeps you in the dark about how your marketing is translating into purchases.) VHX also allows filmmakers to very easily send screeners and free copies of the film out. Screeners would be helpful if you already have the film on the platform but still need to submit temporary versions of it to festivals, critics, or others who might need to view it. Free copies, however, are an extremely valuable service. As I mentioned, we Kickstarted our four-wall of the film, and it was hugely helpful to be able to use the free copy feature to fulfill the 54 digital download rewards that were part of that campaign. Similarly, professionalism dictates that any cast and crew members who helped make the film should be given a copy of the completed film. Being able to distribute these copies to the 64 people listed in the credits with the touch of a button was incredibly useful. That service alone would have been worth paying for.

I've made the case above for VHX because it explains the logic that went into choosing it as our distribution platform, and it really does work for some filmmakers, but it didn't work for us.

For starters, VHX is not a known platform (and was even less well-known when we released *A Convenient Truth*). If you have to take time to explain what VHX is in the first place, you're already starting one step further away from the ultimate goal of getting someone to rent or buy a copy of your film.

Further, a few of VHX's selling points are no longer as relevant. It still exists as its own brand, but Vimeo, another video platform, purchased it in 2016. The site now reads, "VHX, a Vimeo Company." Though I have nothing against Vimeo, this purchase does take away some of the appeal of dealing with a small startup outfit. Also, as I mentioned, there is now an up-front cost for setting up feature film distribution. They still allow filmmakers to issue free copies, but they now limit this feature to 100 per month and charge $1 per digital copy after that. Granted, you won't likely need to give out more than 100 copies per month, but the changes are all symptoms of a company that needs more revenue than it's currently pulling in.

Now, it's true that any distribution platform is only as good as the marketing driving potential audiences to it, but after more than a year of the film being available for purchase, I can say that the lack of awareness of the VHX brand has felt like an extra hurdle to overcome. Even a relatively high percentage of the free copies that we sent out have still never been opened (you can track this on the excellent site dashboard as well). There are dozens of eager cast and crew members who have still never opened their copies of the film simply because the platform is foreign to them. It's not fair, as the platform is really well-developed, but it is reality.

The film is still available on VHX for transactional interactions (rentals and purchases), but in May 2016 a new player entered into the streaming game.

Amazon Video Direct

Amazon Prime's video service has been around for a while, but in May 2016 the platform was opened up to independent content producers—without any middlemen. Filmmakers can sign up for an Amazon Video Direct membership using their existing Amazon.com accounts and immediately start adding titles to their library.

Titles can be either standalone movies or episodic shows, and a separate subscription based model is also available, which is a way for non–Prime members to subscribe specifically to the content that a filmmaker offers. So filmmakers get to choose how their content would best be consumed and make it available accordingly. In addition to streaming options with Prime, Amazon Video Direct also allows for simultaneous transactional services, meaning non–Prime subscribers can purchase or rent traditional digital downloads of your film as well, if you choose to allow that option. Finally, there's also an option to allow users to stream the film for free with the only revenue coming from advertisements before the content is viewed (filmmakers get 55 percent of whatever the ads generate)—though this typically appropriate for shorter content and doesn't seem to be intended for feature films.

The platform's instructions make the movie file specifications relatively clear for filmmakers, and it will automatically create several versions of your film (including an SD version) from the single file that you upload.

For rentals and purchases of your film, Amazon splits revenues 50/50, which is less favorable for the filmmaker than both iTunes and VHX (and most other platforms), but there are no upfront fees to make up. This split is not too worrisome though because—since all of these platforms are non-exclusive—you can always direct customers to the platform that gives you the highest percentage if all things are equal. If they're not equal, then that means that the Amazon platform itself is partially responsible for the customer's purchase, so the split seems worthwhile.

Transactional details aside, the vast majority of the Amazon-based views of your film will be through their streaming service. Tens of millions of people have Amazon Prime memberships and therefore easy access to your film. You should not take that for granted.

As of this writing, Amazon Video Direct is only available in four countries: the U.S.A., the U.K., Germany, and Japan. The revenue generated from streaming in these countries was a bit scary to learn.

In the United States, Amazon pays royalties of 15 cents per hour streamed of your content. In the other three countries, Amazon pays the equivalent of 6 cents per hour. For *A Convenient Truth*, which is just under 1.5 hours in length, that means that I will receive about 22 cents every time the film is viewed in its entirety on the streaming service. The royalties are prorated by the minute and added together, so credit is given for every minute streamed, but this is clearly not a get-rich-quick scheme.

Similarly, the rental pricing is $2.99 for HD and $1.99 for SD, earning me $1.50 or $1, respectively with the 50/50 split. The purchase prices are $9.99 and $7.99. After all of the work, time, and expense that went into creating a feature film, the ultimate product that I have for sale can net $5 (on Amazon) or $7 (on VHX) at maximum for any single purchase. It's clear that this is a difficult business model, but not all decisions are based entirely upon financial considerations. At the end of the day, a filmmaker wants his or her film to be seen, and Amazon Video Direct seems to offer a significant channel for making that happen.

A Convenient Truth has been available on Amazon for less than a month, and my dashboard currently tells me that 8,027 minutes have been streamed so far—without one dollar spent on advertising. I've also gotten one random SD rental. That rental is not important because of the single dollar that it generated for me, but it is important because it represents the film's newly attained ability to reach interested audiences, which it couldn't (or didn't) for the 21 months that it was available for digital download or rental via VHX.

The platform is very new, and it's not without its quirks. First, since the great upside is that filmmakers deal directly with their content library, there are also downsides to this. You'll want to upload your highest quality file for conversion, which Amazon terms your "mezzanine file." In the case of *A Convenient Truth*, our mezzanine file was a QuickTime MOV encoded with Apple's ProRes codec. Knowing the codec is not important, but what's relevant is that the file weighs in at 124GB. That's a huge file size, and for many internet service providers upload speeds are still significantly slower than download speeds. Uploading our film took over 30 hours, and there was always the looming possibility that the operation could somehow be interrupted and would have to be started over. This is also the reason why you'll definitely want to make sure the file specifications match the listed settings exactly before beginning an upload.

Much like iTunes, Amazon Video Direct requires a closed caption file for all of the content that it distributes. I mentioned that part of my original decision for not going with iTunes was the cost of and my lack of familiarity with the subtitling process, but going through it for Amazon Video Direct showed me exactly how silly this was. Amazon supplies a list of companies that provide subtitling services in their support section. I went with Rev (www.rev.com) because they only charge one dollar per minute of your film's running time. For *A Convenient Truth*, that meant that the cost was only $82, and the process could not have been simpler. I converted the huge ProRes file into a proxy mpeg with a resolution of only 426 × 240 pixels, since a high-quality file is not necessary for the process. (The closed caption file is separate from the film file, so it can be linked to any file that has the same timing information at a later time.) Using the h.264 codec, the 124GB file was now only 196MB in size, which made the upload time very short. My caption file (.srt extension) was ready for download 24 hours later. As with any service, errors will be made, so I double-checked the file by loading it into VLC media player and playing it along with the film. Then, when there was something I wanted to change (a typo or the timing of a caption), I opened up the caption file in a software called Aegisub and made the changes myself. Caption files are essentially plain text, so they're extremely small and easy to manipulate. With two pieces of free software and a head start from an $82 service, I was able to have a completed and corrected closed caption file for my film in a day and a half.

With the caption file prepared, all of the necessary files were now ready to be uploaded and reviewed by someone on Amazon's end. This is the strangest part of the entire process. The system's default is for there to be no e-mail communication from Amazon in any way. There's no automated message when your film has been received. There's no quick note when it's being reviewed. Instead, once you've uploaded a file to the "Your Videos" page within your account, four half-filled green dots appear next to the title—one for each of the corresponding streaming sites: Amazon.co.jp (Japan), Amazon.co.uk, Amazon.com, and Amazon.de (Germany). If something is wrong with one of the videos or promotional images that you've submitted, an error message will pop up on your dashboard but, again, you will not be notified via e-mail. This means you can waste a lot of time waiting for your film to be ready if you don't log into your account often to check on the status. You'll know your film is ready for streaming if those half-filled green dots turn into solid green dots when you check in. I'm not joking. That's really the system. Filmmakers don't even get an e-mail to alert them when their films are now able to be sold or streamed on the platform—something you'd expect Amazon would have an interest in their content providers knowing.

With these growing pains noted, Amazon is still a great resource for filmmakers. It has the funds, infrastructure, and history to make it a safe assumption that the platform will only become even more prevalent with time—consider how far Kindle books have come since the service was first launched. Though, again, similar to the music analogy with Apple and the iPod, Amazon also created the hardware (Kindle tablet) that helped the transition to digital along. I also feel pretty secure that streaming services will come to additional countries in the future, which means whole new audiences for your films without any added cost.

Finally, I want to add one more special advantage to the Amazon platform that it might be easy to overlook. Namely, it is currently one of the best ways for audiences to view your content on their television sets. Many smart TVs, DVD players or Blu-ray players with built-in Wi-Fi capabilities, and even video game consoles have the ability to install the Amazon video app (or come with it pre-installed), allowing users to simply login to their Amazon accounts and access a whole world of digital content in their living rooms instantly. One of the big pitfalls of having the film available on VHX was that it lent itself toward viewing the film on a computer screen, which is obviously less than ideal. VHX does have a dedicated App Store app that allows users to view their libraries on their iPhones or iPads, but this is yet another step that you're asking a customer to take in order to view your film. As I mentioned, the task is already hard enough.

Apple offers its AppleTV as a dedicated device to serve this exact purpose, but it hasn't become anywhere near as ubiquitous as the iPod or iPhone. Feedback from people who viewed the film via Amazon Video Direct in its first month of availability offered anecdotal evidence that people are extremely happy to finally have a simple way to view it on their big screens. They're also more likely to encourage friends to view the film because of their comfort level in saying something like "watch this on Amazon" or "here's the Amazon link." It's the exact opposite of beginning a conversation by having to explain to someone what "VHX is."

YouTube

YouTube is, of course, the video platform known by everyone. Whereas iTunes, VHX, and Amazon have begun from a place of professionalism and worked to include independent filmmakers under that umbrella, YouTube is the original amateur video platform, which has recently made a move toward professional content. I say "professional" in the traditional sense of monetization, not to make any determinations about quality. High-quality content has existed alongside cat videos on YouTube pretty much since its inception. And, yes, there may even be some high-quality cat videos out there. I'm not here to judge.

The point is, through advertising revenue before and during content and now a foray into the subscription model with "YouTube Red," which is a premium service that removes the ads for users, content providers can make serious money through both direct sales and streaming on the YouTube platform. I don't have any personal experience with *A Convenient Truth* on YouTube, so I can't elaborate any further, but I did want to mention it as a platform that filmmakers should consider.

What About Netflix?

Of course, Netflix is the gold standard of digital content platforms. As of November 2016, the company profile on their website boasts, "Netflix is the world's leading Internet television network with over 86 million members in over 190 countries enjoying more than 125 million hours of TV shows and movies per day…" ("Overview," Netflix). Any filmmaker would be justifiably excited to have his or her film offered on the platform.

However, getting your film onto Netflix is closer to the traditional distribution system than any of the other digital distribution platforms. Filmmakers aren't in control of their films in the same ways that they are with the other platforms that I've described here, and they're reliant on an aggregator or some other middleman to land their film a Netflix deal. Additionally, Netflix deals do not pay filmmakers based on the number of times that their films are actually streamed. Instead, the deals are structured as one-time payments in exchange for a license to offer the film on their service for a set period of time. This type of arrangement can actually be preferable if the payment is sizeable enough and the budget for your film was reasonably low, but it could also be deadly if you accept an extremely low licensing fee in exchange for the excitement of making your film available on Netflix. Sure it will make you feel good, and it will make the film essentially as easily available as any film can be with today's technology, but there is a negative to that fact as well. That is, you've just made your film available to over 86 million potential viewers. Hooray! But wait, that's also 86 million people who will never pay any money to see your film. This generally falls into the "a good problem to have" category, but it is something to consider—especially if you might be undercutting other potential sales revenue for your film and you have investors to pay back.

I don't have any personal experience with the platform except as an end-user, and I like it a lot, but I would caution first-time filmmakers about putting too much emphasis on the platform. Your film can be a success in so many ways, and none of them are contingent upon whether or not you can get it onto a specific distribution platform.

Physical Media

I'm not sure how much longer physical media will be relevant, but I want to mention it briefly here, as it is another way to make your film available. One of the rewards for our Kickstarter campaign was a signed, limited edition Blu-ray copy of the film. We went with Blu-rays because I didn't think it made sense to put so much time and effort into a high-definition film only to have it sold on a standard-definition DVD disc. However, if I did it again, I would likely create DVDs as well, for two reasons. First, after the theatrical release, I had many people come up to me to ask where they could get a DVD of the film, most of whom were disappointed when I told them we only had Blu-rays. The leap to streaming content happened so quickly that it seems many people still have DVD players in their homes but a lot jumped straight to platforms like Netflix before ever bothering to buy a Blu-ray player. Second, as I mentioned in the Amazon Video Direct section, the first digital rental of the film came in the SD format. In short, I can't tell people how to watch the film, so I should do my best to have it ready for viewing in any format that someone might actually be interested in watching (within reason ... I'm not about to port it over to VHS for the holdouts).

The production of the Blu-ray discs was handled through Discmakers (www.discmakers.com), which is a company that I'd recommend. The site lets you download templates for all of the resources that you'll need to put your disc and packaging into production, and it makes it quite easy to come out with professional-quality products. If you're not design savvy, you should be able to find someone who knows Photoshop (or a similar program) to help you relatively easily. You can also preview exactly how things will look with the site's handy visualization tools.

Our run of 100 Blu-ray discs cost about $600 and, like any form of production, the cost per unit is reduced as the number of units ordered rises. For reference, blank Blu-ray media cost about one dollar per disc at the time of the printing, so we were pretty pleased with the overall expense, which allowed for a good profit margin while still selling the disc for a price that consumers could reasonably expect. This also meant that we were able to offer Blu-rays at the $50 reward tier within our Kickstarter campaign, which also included a digital copy of the film delivered via VHX. I understand that most people pledging to a Kickstarter campaign are primarily doing it because they want to support whatever is being crowdfunded, but that doesn't mean you shouldn't try to make the rewards somewhat commensurate with the actual prices of things out in the world. (I'm sure your T-shirt is made of the softest cotton and expertly designed, but $100? Really?)

Any Blu-rays that were not spoken for through the Kickstarter campaign were made available for purchase through PayPal on the film's website. I used PayPal because I already had a PayPal Business account and because their fees were roughly equal to the other options out there, but you should research the many service providers that exist when you're getting ready to sell items and choose the one that both fits your need to accept credit cards in person and best integrates into your website's hosting platform.

Plan for Self-Distribution from Day One

I feel confident that planning to self-distribute from the onset is the right approach to independent film because there is no downside. (When I become a parent, I'm going to buy my kids Christmas presents on the off chance that Santa doesn't take care of that for me. If one Christmas morning I wake up and Santa has descended upon the house, I'm certain my kids won't be mad about all the extra presents laying around.)

If I had been planning to self-distribute from day one, there are a few things I would have done better:

Have a dedicated behind-the-scenes photographer and videographer on set at all times.

We hired a set photographer, Roger Smith, for one week of our shoot, and his photos have been very helpful, but having even more media would have meant more content to share with our potential fans early on. I wish we had a lot more photos to play with, but I especially wish we had been posting short clips from the set each day in order to get people interested in the film before it was even complete. Once photography was over, it would have been great to post new videos to social media to keep the momentum going and raise awareness about the film in the deadly days of editing when it is so easy for everyone to forget about the project.

Gather potential fans early.

This means creating a website, Facebook page, Twitter account, Instagram account, etc., and using them to let people know about the film during pre-production. Don't only use Facebook. Facebook doesn't give you access to the e-mail addresses of people who are interested in your film. You've done the hard work to get their attention, so you should have the ability to reach that audience directly via e-mail. I wish I had used MailChimp or some similar service to gather e-mail addresses for a film newsletter from the start. You can still do that. Do it.

I'm not saying that you should create busy work for yourself and have to write up a monthly newsletter to send to these people. They won't read it anyway. But you should be growing an e-mail list that allows you to easily reach people who have told you that they're interested in your film.

This is not some abstract exercise of gathering followers. Your audience becomes your market. These people are a partial answer to the question, "How do I find audiences who might be interested in watching my film?" once it's complete. And you will be asking yourself that question a lot. Thinking even further into the future, the work that you're doing now to gather fans is work that will make this whole process that much easier the second time around. Some of the audience members will specifically be interested in your film because of its subject matter, but after they've seen the film, they may become fans of you as a filmmaker. You'll be more personally profitable as a filmmaker if you can reach out directly to interested audiences for your next completed film, and you'll certainly be more marketable to potential investors when you start your next project if you can show that you have a huge number of people waiting to pay money to see what you create. In this way, the movie business is like most other businesses. Acquiring new customers is difficult and expensive, so if you can show that a lot of potential customers come with you wherever you go, you'll set yourself up as an intriguing asset to others looking to make money (or have a clear path to making money for yourself).

The point about your next project is worth stressing here because it is almost impossible to consider while making your first feature film. Your current project is taking up every free moment of thought, and you just want to get this first film completed. It's an understandable (and almost necessary) single-mindedness, but it comes at a price. Second feature films are notoriously difficult to accomplish, and a staggering number of filmmakers never get beyond their first one. This is so true, in fact, that the Sundance Institute even announced a special program called the "FilmTwo Initiative and Fellowship" in 2016, describing the challenge of creating a second feature film as "often the greatest barrier to a sustainable career as a filmmaker" ("Sundance Institute Announces "). In case you're not lucky enough to be accepted into and supported by such a program, creating a relationship with the fans who will become the built-in audience for your second film is a good plan.

What's Next?

Regardless of anything else that has occurred over the making of your film, once it's done, it's done. It exists out in the world forever. This is the beauty of the medium, but it can also be a struggle for the filmmaker. By the time you've taken the project from script to screen, you will undoubtedly be sick of it, but that's precisely the time when you'll have to talk about and promote the film more than ever. There's no way around it. You'll be tied to that film for the rest of your life, and you'll have to market it as much as possible. You'll be driven to get it seen and, in turn, it will generate revenue for you indefinitely without any additional creative work. This can often be one of the most frustrating phases of the project. It's all hustle and filled with phrase like "marketing and promotion," "public relations," and "return on investment." If you were the main creative force behind the film, chances are that these phrases do not excite you, and you'd much rather move on to your next creative endeavor. And if protracted film projects are good for one thing, it's time for generating hundreds of other project ideas along the way that you'd love to pursue once the current project is over. However, abandoning your film after it's complete but before pushing it through the difficult release stage is one of the worst things you can do. The film project isn't really complete until you've worked hard to make sure that you get as many people to watch it as you can. You owe that to all of the people who helped make the film a reality and, yes, you owe it to yourself. Further, you shouldn't consider your main work finished until the film is available on a platform that makes it easily viewable for potential audiences in the future. I only feel like I can mostly move on from *A Convenient Truth* now that I can point to Amazon Video when someone asks where he or she can see the film.

But the creative drive is real and should not be ignored. My advice is to have it both ways. You'll have to do what is necessary to promote the completed film, but it's also important to simultaneously look toward the future.

The most basic reason to contemplate your next move is because you may find yourself in the enviable position of having someone ask you, "So what's your next project?" If you're lucky enough to garner interest as a filmmaker with your film, you'll definitely want to have a good answer prepared for this question. In many cases, the ideal situation would be for your first film to help you attain funding for your second film, and it's on you to know what you'd like that second film to be. Working on a pitch for situations like this is good practice.

The more important reason for thinking about your continued work is about personal survival. Creativity needs to be exercised, and that means daydreaming about the next thing you'd love to do is actually important. It took me several months of postpartum-esque depression before I made this realization. Yes, it's important for me to be responsible about my obligations to the film's life after its release, but it's also necessary to take care of my own mental and emotional state after such a big moment in my life ended. Recognize this and embrace it, rather than thinking about it as psychological hokum.

Once I understood that creative outlets are a real need of mine, I pursued them voraciously. I put my writing hat back on and started a new feature screenplay, but I also wanted to add much shorter-term channels of fulfillment to my plate. After years on a single project, nothing seemed more appealing to me than short form works that would allow me to collaborate with other talented people. Shooting a short over a weekend, editing it in a couple of weeks, and releasing a project online immediately sounded like a dream.

I quickly shot and edited a promo video for a band, edited several short video campaigns for non-profits, helped a sketch comedy group put some of their stuff onto video, edited lyric videos for a local musician, shot and edited a concert, etc. Trust me, everyone wants a video. So there was no shortage of opportunities once I made myself available. It's been great to snap back into these types of productions, and it means that I'm sitting down in front of either Final Draft or Avid every single night (many days both). In short, creative days are pleasurable days. I'm more satisfied with the work, and I think others around me are happier with this version of me as well.

In some ways, I feel like if I'm not a little overwhelmed with projects I'm probably taking it too easy. Of course, I make sure to not take on more than I can reasonably accomplish for clients, but many of the additional projects are my own curiosities—again, catching up on pursuing all of those ideas that I wished I could create while I was too busy with *A Convenient Truth*. The flip side of this is that I also need to remember to respect my own time. As I said, everyone wants a video.

It's good to be helpful to others in need of videos, especially when you've just finished your feature and are looking for projects to keep you in practice, but after the initial rush of actually producing things quickly has worn off, you should step back and take stock. To be crass about it, it's important to ask what you're getting out of each project before taking it on. It doesn't always have to be about money for your work. It could be a chance to collaborate with great people or exposure, but, as they say, exposure doesn't pay the bills. Additionally, spending a lot of time on short form video that never gets seen by anyone can be frustrating.

Most importantly, each outside project that you take on is subtracting time from the hours that you have available for your personal creative endeavors, which we've just established are legitimately important to your well-being.

A Note About Post-Film Recordkeeping

Professionalism doesn't end when the film is complete. No matter how small your budget, you likely took money from others in order to finish it. Even though in many cases some of the people who gave you funds to get the film made may not truly expect a return on their investment, this should not be your expectation. Do not let yourself off of the hook—even if you're in a situation in which your investors might.

I'm not an entertainment lawyer or an accountant, but hopefully at the point when you agreed to take money from investors you simultaneously worked out a system for how those investors will be see their returns once the film begins generating revenue. Sometimes these agreements can be extremely complicated with certain investors insisting upon being in "first position" and getting their money back before anyone else. Other times, everyone agrees to recoup their money on the same schedule, but you should still sort out how regularly everyone will receive these payments. Will these payments be flat amounts once a certain revenue threshold is reached? Will the payments be made based on the percentage of the overall production budget that was invested? Are collaborators who weren't compensated their full rates receiving a percentage of the revenues as they come in? Or after the entire budget is recouped?

This topic is far too broad to be discussed here and experts should be consulted to properly sort out the arrangements, but I did want to point out that it's on you (unless you've hired a dedicated accountant) to keep an accurate recording of any revenue generated by the film. This is especially easy to ignore because of the incremental nature of the revenue that the film will likely be earning. That is, you might get a few dollars from a digital purchase, or even a few cents from a streaming service royalty, so it could seem silly to record every little bit of revenue. However, if you don't, you're essentially stealing. If the amounts that you're dealing with are very small, it may be that you make payments quarterly, or even yearly, but the accounting should always be current, in case anyone with an interest in the film asks for the information, which they are entitled to do. Staying on top of this each month will make this accounting an annoying, ongoing task, but it will be much easier than trying to cull together the various sources quickly for months or years at a time. If you're planning on doing that, you're likely not doing it all, which is not acceptable.

The flip side to this revenue recordkeeping is tracking the continued expenses. Even though the film is complete and the majority of the expenses related to the project are behind you, there will still be ongoing costs. At minimum, you'll have the pay to host the film's website for the foreseeable future, but ideally you'll also be spending money on advertising and marketing in order to continue promotion for the film's extended life. This means that your budget spreadsheet is never finished. It also means that the revenue that you're generating is weighed against these new expenses, as well as those that you previously incurred to make the film.

It's definitely not something that most filmmakers signed up for when they were dreaming of making their film, but it is necessary, and once you have a system in place for keeping track of your film's post-completion revenue and expenses, it won't be as arduous as it sounds.

Podcasts to Keep You Going

Most filmmakers will already have their own practices for keeping up-to-date with industry news and discussions of the craft, so I don't think I need to tell people to read *Variety*, *Hollywood Reporter*, or whatever other sources they likely already enjoy. However, I do think it might be helpful to list out some podcasts that I've found useful for various reasons, as it's still a relatively new medium.

Podcasts About Craft

The *Scriptnotes* podcast is co-hosted by screenwriters John August and Craig Mazin. The two veterans take the time every week to come up with about an hour of interesting content related to the craft of screenwriting and the film industry more generally, for no real reason other than to share their knowledge with aspiring screenwriters. I've listened since their first episode and even attended a live event in New York. At this point, the podcast has a large, well-deserved listenership.

The Q&A with Jeff Goldsmith puts out consistently engrossing long-form interviews with filmmakers that usually begin with their "breaking-in" stories, follows through with brief highlights of their career, and then focuses in-depth on the process of creating a specific new film that the artist is promoting at the time. This has been an invaluable resource for hearing about the unique and shared struggles that screenwriters experience, and I've found that listening to the conversations has been helpful in trying to get through my own writing dilemmas. I've been listening to Jeff Goldsmith since he was the editor of *Creative Screenwriting Magazine* and hosted a similar podcast under that banner. He's currently the publisher of *Backstory Magazine*.

Film critic Elvis Mitchell hosts *KCRW'S The Treatment*, and he's an extremely knowledgeable and an expert interviewer. The podcast comes from a weekly radio program, so the format is much more strictly regimented, which means both regular content and shorter episodes. It's a dense 30 minutes that delves into the writing of a single film, and it will leave you wanting more.

Podcast for Industry News

KCRW's The Business is a related podcast hosted by Kim Masters, the current editor-at-large for the *Hollywood Reporter*. This is the quickest way to get caught up on all of the industry news that you'll want to know about in 30 minutes or less. I've found myself in conversations about the industry multiple times in which I only knew about what was being discussed because I listened to this podcast on the subway ride up to the meeting or party.

Podcasts for Critical Reviews

The */Filmcast* is the official podcast of slashfilm.com, and it covers multiple bases. It usually starts with some film news, continues with a segment about what the hosts have been watching recently, and then dedicates 45 minutes to an hour to a review of a single film. All of these segments are worth listening to, but it's especially useful to creators to get three to four distinct opinions about current film. Since the discussion is longer than most you might have access to, the format really lets filmmakers understand the nuance behind why some viewers might like a film while others don't.

Filmspotting is an extremely long-running podcast with hosts that have varied over the years. It features many segments including film news, reviews, and their trademark Top 5 lists at the end of each episode. After hundreds of episodes, the Top 5 lists are necessarily often extremely specific, and they're a great way to help listeners discover interesting films that they may not otherwise have comes across. I often look forward to listening to an episode specifically because the Top 5 list is one that intrigues me, and I know I'm going to have a few new films to add to my watch list. Writers Alison Wilmore and Matt Singer host *Filmspotting: SVU*, which is a sister podcast with the added specification that all of the films that they discuss are available on some streaming platform. (SVU stands for "streaming video unit" in addition to being a meta acknowledgment of their spin-off status, à la *Law & Order: SVU*.) It's an easy way to help narrow down what you might want to watch from your Netflix, Hulu, Amazon, and similar options.

How Did This Get Made? focuses on movies that are terrible in one way or another. They might be huge hits that are creatively challenged, flops that had huge budgets, or just small films that are largely incomprehensible. The important thing to remember when listening is that the filmmakers for each of these films genuinely set out to make a great film when they started, and a lot can be learned by tracing where it all went wrong. Plus, the hosts, Paul Scheer, June Diane-Raphael, and Jason Mantzoukas, are hilarious.

Podcasts for Fun and Idea Stimulation

Podcasts about film are important to filmmakers for obvious reasons, but it's also good practice to make sure you remember that there is a world outside of films. Remember? That's the stuff that the films you're making are about. It's really easy to jump from one podcast about the latest trends in the industry to another, but I've found it continuously nourishing to listen to content that has nothing to do with film at all.

Radiolab by NPR is probably the podcast most likely to consistently blow your mind. The topics are far-ranging and, as far as I can tell, are only selected based on if the reporting around them can result in superb storytelling. I never know what the episode is going to be about before I start listening, but by the end I've always heard one to four stories that I think will probably be elements of movies in the near future.

Science VS is a similar, newer podcast that fills the same role. A podcast that encourages the listener to more deeply engage with the nature of the real world through science is one that will always be useful to writers and filmmakers who are aiming to explore interesting questions and then communicate a deep understanding to their audiences.

Finally, *99% Invisible* is a similar podcast that revels in good, short storytelling but through the filter of topics related to design. Since these episodes often relate directly to visual material (signage, architecture, etc.), filmmakers are likely to have an easy time engaging with the subject matter—even though it is also extremely varied.

These are probably more than enough to keep you busy listening, so I haven't even included all of the podcasts that I would recommend, but I do think that most people will not regret giving any of these a try and many will find them sincerely helpful in their own work. If science, technology, or design don't particularly interest you, then these specific podcasts might not be for you, but the general concept stands—make sure you're nurturing your interests outside of filmmaking.

DON'T QUIT (OR APOLOGIZE FOR) YOUR DAY JOB

I want to wrap up by acknowledging a macro point about the creation of my first feature film that hasn't made its way into the discussion thus far but is crucially important: I had a day job for the entirety of *A Convenient Truth*'s creation. I wrote the screenplay after work—two to four hours at a time, every night. The film was shot while taking vacation days and over a few weekends. It was edited in any free time that I could find in my schedule that also worked for the editor.

Further, I didn't make this film in spite of having a day job. Rather, the film only exists *because* I had a day job. Films, even small independent films, are expensive, and although we did get outside investment for part of the budget, we would not have had the funds to complete the film if I didn't have a regular income.

Many artists can earn a living through freelancing, which is great. However, especially for artists who attend college to learn their craft, it is sometimes not possible to earn enough money to support themselves through freelancing upon graduation. I personally had significant student loans that came due six months after I put on the cap and gown, which is unfortunately an increasingly common occurrence, and I wanted to continue living in New York City. Even the hypothetical idea of trying to pay New York rents and student loans on a freelancer's income is enough to give me anxiety, so I chose to look for a salaried position instead.

It's important to note that I'm not saying a full-time position is the way to go or that it's better than freelancing in any general way. I'm saying that it was the right decision for me. I realized years ago in a psychology class that Maslow's Hierarchy of Needs applies to my creative life. The theory states that certain needs must be taken care of before others can be fulfilled. The hierarchy begins with basic physiological needs and then moves onto safety needs, which includes financial security. Luxuries like creativity can only be satisfied if I'm not worried about the needs that come first in the hierarchy. In short, I would be unable to write a screenplay or work on a film, if I were worried about where to get my next meal. Some people are able to be creative without steady income because financial insecurity affects them differently than it does me, but the important thing is that I know how the hierarchy is relevant to my psychology.

Once I had decided to go the day job route, there was one more important consideration: it had to be a job that I didn't take home with me. I got a job at a front desk, and it had a built-in dividing line. If I wasn't sitting at that desk, I wasn't working. If someone sent me an e-mail at 5:01 p.m., I wasn't going to answer it until the next day. I wasn't going to be consumed by anything work-related in the hours that needed to be dedicated to my screenwriting or filmmaking. We might not always be able to choose whether or not we need to work 40 hours a week, but we can make the decision to apply for jobs that will not take over our lives and eliminate any free time for creative pursuits.

A few years ago, I was at a networking event and someone asked me what I did. I sheepishly replied that I was a writer/director, but I had a day job. "Don't apologize for having a day job," the man replied quickly. "Almost everyone here does something else." In today's economy, that's more and more true, and it's not something to be embarrassed about. There's no right way to go about pursuing a career in the film industry, and it's taken time for me to own the fact that my accomplishment of finishing a feature film is not less than that of others because it was low-budget, or because no important distributor came knocking on my door once it was complete, or because no one paid me to make it. Regardless of the obstacles of the process, I'm proud of *A Convenient Truth*—proud of both the end result and the hard work that its existence represents.

It's true that the list of filmmakers who can boast a completed feature film has expanded significantly in the past decade, but the number of filmmakers who've started a feature film and never finished it is even larger. That number is dwarfed by the number of people who'd "like to make a film someday."

I put in the work to bring a feature film into the world, and that accomplishment is a reward that I truly hold dear. I hope that this book will help you soon know the feeling.

References

Lang, Brent. "*New York Times* Changes Film Review Policy, Can't Guarantee Coverage (Updated)." *Variety.* 2015. Accessed November 27, 2016. http://variety.com/2015/film/news/new-york-times-changes-film-review-policy-cant-guarantee-coverage-1201502465/.

"No. California Wind Farm Won't Be Prosecuted for Eagle Deaths." *Digital Journal,* 2014. Accessed November 27, 2016. http://www.digitaljournal.com/news/environment/no-california-wind-farm-won-t-be-prosecuted-for-eagle-deaths/article/387932.

"Overview." Netflix. Accessed November 27, 2016. https://ir.netflix.com/.

Poritsky, Jonathan. "The 56 Films That Opened in New York This Year Without a Review in the *New York Times*." The Candler Blog. Accessed November 27, 2016. http://www.candlerblog.com/2015/05/22/times-unreviewed/.

"Sundance Institute Announces New 'FilmTwo' Initiative to Support Second-Time Feature Filmmakers." Sundance Institute. May 17, 2016. Accessed November 27, 2016. http://www.sundance.org/blogs/news/2016-filmtwo-second-time-filmmakers-nbc-universal.

Index

auditions 9–14

budget 8, 18–20, 133–135

camera movement 43–44, 74, 83
captions 214
casting 8–14, 150–151
color correction 95–97

distribution 8, 201, 209–220

editing 35–37, 53, 57, 62–63, 68, 86–89, 108–111, 167–169, 188–190

festivals 199–201
four-walling 201–203, 206–208
framing 32, 51, 74, 82–83, 141

improvisation 9, 41–42, 105
insert shots 61–63, 106

Kickstarter 203–206
Kuleshov effect 174

locations 26, 32, 71–73, 89–91, 126, 144–146, 186

montage 58–59, 125–127

rough cut 198–199

schedule 15–18, 182–183
sequences 47, 55, 65, 97–99, 116–118, 132, 138–144, 155–167
stock footage 24–26

test screenings 110–112, 199
transitions 30, 73–76, 91–93, 130–132, 133, 182

www.ingramcontent.com/pod-product-compliance
Ingram Content Group UK Ltd.
Pitfield, Milton Keynes, MK11 3LW, UK
UKHW050531150426
5217IPUK00026B/1884